DOWN, DOWN, DEEPER *and* DOWN

How Carlisle United failed to maintain the status quo

Howard Falshaw and John Irving Clarke

Grosvenor House
Publishing Limited

This book is published by
Grosvenor House Publishing Ltd
Link House
140 The Broadway, Tolworth, Surrey, KT6 7HT.
www.grosvenorhousepublishing.co.uk

A CIP record for this book
is available from the British Library

Paperback ISBN 978-1-83615-382-5
eBook ISBN 978-1-83615-383-2

DEDICATION

This book is dedicated to Julie Clarke and Lisa Falshaw for letting the boys be boys and play out so often.

CONTENTS

ACKNOWLEDGEMENTS

Thank you to photographer Ben Holmes for permission to use the cover photograph; to Jon Colman of The News and Star and the Carlisle united website for borrowed quotations; to Julie Scott at Grosvenor House Publishing Ltd. for her help, advice and support in bringing this book to publication; to Peter Scholes for kindly writing the foreword to this book; to the owners, staff and players of Carlisle United without whom we'd have nothing to write about; and finally to the thousands of Blues fans who share our obsession and reassure us that we're not completely mad.

FOREWORD

They say good things come to those who wait. *They* also say it'll all end in tears. They say an awful lot – much of it contradictory, much of it hard to believe and much of it, downright nonsense. We don't even know who *they* are, but what we do know is that even *they* would be stuck for words to describe the last two seasons down at Brunton Park. Thankfully, a couple of fellow Blues have tried to make some sense of it all by documenting the few highs and many lows of the soap opera that is Carlisle United Football Club.

As a fellow fan and amateur scribe, Howard and John asked me to pen a few words to introduce this new book - a torturous timeline of torment, capturing the mood of our continued capitulation and descent into the non-league league we never ever thought we would clap eyes on again.

Who would have thought that after the celebrations and euphoria of a Wembley win, we would be planning trips to Truro and Braintree less than two years later. It was unfathomable. Unthinkable. Unimaginable! And yet, despite the club's new owners and new found wealth, that is exactly where we were heading.

So how did we find ourselves in this mess? It wasn't meant to be like this. Our new American owners arrived with fanfare and fanzones, ready to lead us up to the promised land. Instead, we find ourselves in the land (and the league) that time forgot.

Sad? Yes. Unexpected? Yes. Frustrating beyond belief? Yes. Typically, Carlisle United? Oh, yes!

The sun set on our new dawn quicker than a blackout in the Blitz. Carlisle United never do things the easy way and, if this is the start of a new era, it seems we have to take a few steps back before we leap forward again and OWN THE NO... I mean, scramble back into the Football League again by hook and by crook.

It would seem that, before we climb to the top, we must sink to rock bottom first. In years to come, Howard, John, you and I, will laugh about last season. A hazy, distant memory as we lift trophy after trophy and really do OWN THE NO...no, stop it. I shouldn't hope and dream. This is Carlisle United after all. The path is never an easy one to take following the Cumbrians.

Having just endured the worst season in our club's history, you might just want to shut the curtains, turn off the lights and rock back and forth in the corner of the room, doing your best to forget what you had just witnessed. However, if you want to relive the nightmare over and over again, I suggest you continue reading and enjoy this jolly jaunt to 'celebrate' the lows and lows of the 2024/25 season. Go on, treat yourself.

Over to you Howard and John...

Peter Scholes

PREFACE

I blame John Irving Clarke for this book! To explain.

In November 2023 I published my first book, "From Despair to Delirium" (From Delirium to Despair was considered as a title for this book). It was an account of the two seasons that culminated in Carlisle's promotion to League 1 in May of the same year, and was based on Facebook posts I'd been writing after every game. I continued writing the posts as the club embarked on life in League 1, hoping they might lead to another book.

By this time, I'd made the acquaintance of Mr. Clarke. Like me, he is a retired English teacher; like me, he lives in Wakefield; like me, he is both cursed and privileged to be a supporter of Carlisle United. We became increasingly frequent companions on trips to Brunton Park and other northern grounds in Leagues 1 and 2.

By the time we reached February and March of 2024, I was struggling to find new ways to write about yet another dispiriting defeat in a dismal campaign. I also realised that such a tale of woe was not great material for another book. I decided to save my words and money for a new season, a new campaign under our new owners would surely see a return to winning ways.

How invested in the new season I would be remained open to question. My son Adam and his best mate Ben, who constituted 50% of The Wakefield Blues, were both university bound, and I wasn't sure how many games John would be able to commit to. I didn't want to be a Billy No Mates season ticket holder. Fortunately, John, unprompted, got in touch to say he was up for season-ticket size commitment and so two senior citizens rapidly agreed to spend a modest proportion of their annual pension on regular trips from Wakefield to Carlisle.

Of course, those season tickets were purchased in the belief that we would witness a successful campaign, ending in promotion, and underwritten by the largesse of the Piataks' ownership. With so many other northern clubs in League 2, we also believed that our season tickets would help us get tickets at small away grounds, as part of the triumphal march back to League 1.

It was then that I came up with an idea to put a different perspective on my regular Carlisle posts. As John and I would be sharing a car to many games, standing together in The Paddock or sitting in adjacent seats at away grounds, and watching exactly the same events unfold, why didn't we both bring our own perspective to bear on those events? When I put the notion to John, he hesitated briefly to consider his other writing commitments before declaring himself 'in'. And thus, this book was born.

It isn't an entirely equal partnership. John's other literary commitments meant that he wasn't able to write about every game, so when there's only one account of a match then it's mine. When there are two, John's follows mine. All our accounts were composed without prior knowledge of what the other was writing. Nothing has been revised with the benefit of hindsight.

In the process of proof-reading and editing the manuscript, it's interesting to see for how long we both remained naively optimistic. And even when that optimism wore off, it took a lot longer for either of us to fully acknowledge just how bad the situation really was! It's noticeable that although we sometimes reached the same conclusion, we often took a different route to get there.

By the time you read this Carlisle United will have embarked on life in The National League. Remarkably, given successive, dispiriting relegations, the mood around the club remains positive, with Mark Hughes' decision to stay at Brunton Park providing some welcome stability. It's still hard to credit that almost seven and a half thousand United supporters were at Brunton Park for the final game of the season, despite relegation being confirmed a week earlier. Not only that, but they also gave the players and staff a resounding send-off after the final whistle.

We hope you enjoy our reflections on a difficult season. It's fair to say that writing about the games was sometimes a more enjoyable experience than actually watching them!

Howard Falshaw

Introduction
The season of Light,
the season of Despair

It would be a time to take stock and consolidate, to evaluate the recent experience of a victorious Wembley play-off final followed by an immediate relegation. A time to regroup and then begin a fresh assault with a new economic standing powering Carlisle United's 2024 – 2025 season. New players would be recruited and new facilities would be in place from which to watch these players. It would be a time to dance.

Optimism though, would need to be tempered and assumptions about an automatic promotion held in check. As they unfold, seasons tempt and seasons tease. Heroes emerge and villains skulk towards the shadows; Fortune smiles or curses, victories are held aloft while grievous injuries are nobly borne (or not.) It is the great unknown where there are no promises and no guarantees, but this is where the narrative arc of the book would lie. That is, the book which Howard proposed, the one charting a journey through a season and the one to which he invited me to contribute.

I was delighted to accept, as deep down, I knew this could be the time, the best of times or…

John Irving Clarke

CASTLE
SPORTS GROUP

Dear Fans and Supporters of Carlisle United,

We hope this letter finds you in great spirits as we look to the next season and the bright future of the club. Our commitment to transparency and open dialogue remains unwavering and we will continue to keep the lines of communication open.

We are embarking on a transformative journey and want you to be a part. As a cornerstone of the community, the club not only embodies competitive spirit and resilience but also serves as a beacon of economic and social development in Cumbria.

Since November 2023, there have been significant renovations to Brunton Park. These enhancements are designed to improve the experience for fans and provide state-of-the-art facilities for players. Moreover, in our commitment to excellence and community development, we are poised to invest an additional £4 million into building a new training facility. This ambitious project aims to elevate the potential of "The Blues" and nurture local talent, ensuring investment impact extends well beyond the pitch.

Central to our plans, we are now investing over £4.5 million to bring premier-level hospitality facilities to Brunton Park. For the upcoming season, we are introducing several exciting developments:

- Four new hospitality rooms in the East Stand
- Eight new executive hospitality boxes in the East Stand, with four already sold on long-term deals.
- Purchase and deployment of new pitch-side LED perimeter advertising boards.
- An expanded West Side fan zone, including a large screen TV for pre- and post-match viewing and community gatherings like Euro 2024
- Warwick End development to include a new fan zone, toilets, concessions, and improved disabled viewing area.
- Refurbishment of the Neil Centre to create new Academy facilities and offices, bringing sports and community areas up to standard.
- Purchase of a new minibus for the Academy
- Redevelopment of the West Stand first-team internal football area to include a new first-team locker room, improved staff changing facilities, and a new officials/referee room.
- Stadium and training pitch improvements
- A significantly increased football player budget to ensure we can be successful on the pitch.
- Acquisition of six new player residences to provide improved housing.

We invite you all to join us on this journey by supporting Carlisle United in a manner that best suits your passion for football and commitment to the club and community development. Should you wish to discuss this further, please feel free to contact us directly at commercial@carlisleunited.co.uk.

As we move forward with these exciting initiatives, we call on all fans to rally behind the team. Purchasing season tickets, securing an executive hospitality box, or becoming a regional partner or sponsor are just a few ways you can make a difference. Together, we can achieve great heights and ensure a bright future for Carlisle United. Thank you for considering this opportunity to support "The Blues."

Sincerely,

The Piatak Family

For all official communications follow @CastleSportsGrp on X

xvii

Chapter 1
PRE-SEASON

Thursday 2 May. The retained and released list.

Well, the retained and released list is pretty predictable and unremarkable. Most tellingly, only six of the players who were in the match day squad at Wembley, less than a year ago, remain at the club. Roll on the summer signings.

Wednesday 15 May.
Castle Sports Group statement.

Earlier today the Castle Sports Group, which is the company set up by the Piatak family, the new Carlisle United owners, released a statement on "X" (formerly known as Twitter) which reveals the full extent of the financial league we are now operating in. I've included the full text below.

There are three key issues. Firstly, £4 million is being invested in a new training facility. Secondly, £4.5 million is being invested in improvements to Brunton Park. Thirdly, there will be a significantly enhanced playing budget.

Wow! We are really moving into different territory now. For years the club has been saddled with a debt amounting to about a quarter of that amount. Now that debt has been cleared, and the club is investing four times as much in what happens off the pitch. When you add the planned financial commitment to what happens on the pitch, it's not difficult to see why the fan base remains intact, and hopes are high for the future, despite our dismal season and relegation.

The tone of the statement from Castle Sports Group is also very encouraging. It's very open, inclusive and honest.

Just get the summer recruitment right!

Tuesday 18 June.

The big question now is whether I purchase a season ticket for the 2024-25 campaign. I'm confident it will be a good campaign, but Adam will be away at university, as will his best mate Ben, and I'm not sure that the fourth member of the Wakefield Blues, John Clarke, will be able to commit to so many journeys north, so it might mean a number of solo trips. However, with next season's League Two having a distinctly northern bias, meaning a lot of away games are within range, the option of having priority for tickets at pokey away grounds is very tempting. I'll keep you posted!

Monday 24 June.

It feels as if today marks the start of the new season in more than one way. It does in a very real sense, as today saw the players report to Brunton Park for the start of pre-season training.

Probably more importantly, for me, today also saw the purchase of my season ticket for 2024-25. To be honest, the idea of a season ticket had been slipping off the radar recently. With Adam and Ben, half of The Wakefield Blues, heading to university in the autumn, I didn't really fancy being billy-no-mates for many of the games and journeys. And then, John Clarke, the fourth member of the Wakefield Blues, said, out of the blue, that he was up for a season ticket. I needed no further encouragement! We have both shelled out today and now await the publication of the fixture list with increased anticipation. I'm fervently hoping that we're away to one of the southern clubs on the opening day of the season, as we'll still be on holiday in Kefalonia.

League Two has a massive northern bias next season, which means that a lot of away games are within range from Wakefield. Walsall is definitely do-able, and there are only six or seven clubs further south, which means there's the potential to attend over eighty per cent of the games. Having a season ticket will provide a distinct advantage when it comes to getting tickets for away matches. Though with well over three thousand sold already, a season ticket will be no guarantee of a ticket for magnificent, high-capacity grounds like those of Harrogate, Barrow and Salford!

In an interesting sideline, I've been asked if I'd be willing to loan some of my Chris Balderstone memorabilia for a Carlisle United exhibition that will be taking place at Tullie House Museum and Art Gallery in Carlisle later this year, to mark the 50th anniversary of United's season in Division 1. I'm more than happy to provide an original Number 9 Carlisle shirt as worn by Chris Balderstone.

Wednesday 26 June.

The announcement of the new season's fixtures; the launch of the new kits; a new signing; It's been a busy day at Brunton Park today!

I'll start with the fixture list. We'll be on holiday in Kefalonia on the opening day of the season, so I'm delighted that we're away to Gillingham on that day, an away trip that was never on the radar. And we return in time for a home tie against Stoke City in the Carabao Cup, followed by a 'local' derby against Barrow for our first League home game. I've known worse starts to a season. Not only that, most of the long away trips to the south come in the first quarter of the season. That means that as we embark on our inevitable march to the League Two title, we'll be in a position to attend most, if not all, of the games in the run-in!

As for the new kits, I love them both. It was predictable that the home kit would be a homage to the shirt for our season in the sun. Given the necessity to adorn every available space with a sponsor's logo, I don't think that the club could have done a much better job, though I wish they'd gone the whole hog and adopted the white shorts and red socks of the Division One season. It was a great move to invite Les O'Neill, Ray Train, Bobby Owen and Tom Clarke, all legends of the Division One team, to be involved in the promotion of the new kits. My sources tell me that Bobby Owen was absolutely made up to be part of the launch. I'm also impressed by the away kit. It's original, but in a less brash way than last season's fruit salad shirt.

Finally, I received a really nice phone call yesterday from one of the organisers of the Carlisle United exhibition that will opens at Tullie House next month. They're very keen to have my Chris Balderstone memorabilia as part of the exhibition, particularly his Carlisle shirt, as they currently don't have any shirts from earlier than the eighties. The upshot is that I may be taking a trip to Carlisle next week to take my souvenirs, having been promised a sneak preview of the exhibits.

Monday 1 July.

I'm writing far too frequently at the moment, considering this is meant to be the close season!

What an interesting and enjoyable day Adam and I have had. We've spent much of it travelling to Carlisle and back, which could be described as our own bit of pre-season training. The reason for our trip was to deliver some items of memorabilia for "Backing the Blues – 120 Years of Carlisle United", the exhibition which opens in the city later this month, as reported in my previous post.

What an Alladin's Cave we walked into when we arrived at Carlisle Art College. To trot out an old cliché, it had to be seen to be believed. I had a vague idea of what we might find, but Adam was absolutely gobsmacked. The collection filled two prefab classrooms, so obviously a lot of material won't make it into the final exhibition. There were the predictable piles of matchday programmes dating back many seasons. There were two coat-hanger racks jam-packed with old Carlisle shirts, all carefully dated and catalogued. But there were so many other, unexpected things, alongside old newspaper cuttings and match tickets. There were old signed footballs; tiles from the boardroom floor dating back to the Michael Knighton era; a message from (Sir) Bobby Robson to Chris Balderstone, written on the notepaper of a Suffolk hotel, saying how highly he rated his excellence in two sports and how much he regretted never having signed him for Ipswich Town; old trophies; iconic photographs of key moments in the club's history. I could go on all night.

Nonetheless, the reaction when I unveiled the genuine (not replica) shirt from the 1969-70 season, as worn by Chris Balderstone (him again) was something to behold. The curators had apparently recently declared a moratorium on any new donations as the opening of the exhibition approaches but had decided that this shirt was too important to exclude, as it pre-dates any other shirt they have by over a decade.

What was most impressive was the dedication and enthusiasm of the volunteers who are collecting, cataloguing and curating the material for the exhibition. It's a massive task, requiring untold hours, and their pride and pleasure in showing us everything was manifest.

The exhibition runs until November, when the plan is to establish a permanent club archive, including the mass of material that won't make it into the exhibition. I'll be more than happy to donate a significant amount of my memorabilia to that archive. Apparently the Piataks, our new owners, are fully supportive of plans to create a permanent Carlisle United Museum somewhere on the Brunton Park site.

With perfect timing, just as we turned off the M6 at Junction 43 to drive into Carlisle, the club announced the signing of striker Charlie Wyke on a two-year contract. Wyke had a previous stint at Brunton Park, scoring at a rate of just under a goal every two games, before Bradford City triggered the release clause in his contract. Following success at Valley Parade, he also had successful spells at Sunderland and Wigan Athletic, before spending the second half of last season on loan at Rotherham. He'd been widely rumoured to be about to re-sign for Bradford, and to secure his signing, with his experience in higher divisions, is something of a statement signing for Carlisle. Adam informs me that the response of Bradford fans on social media has been somewhat vitriolic!

Today has been a lovely reminder of why there's something special about supporting Carlisle United, meeting other people who probably surpass my passion for and devotion to the club. And to cap it all, we've been invited to the official preview and formal opening of the exhibition.

Tuesday 2 July.

I'm going to go way off piste with this post, though there is a very tenuous Carlisle United link at the very end!

A couple of "incidents" in recent days have taken me unexpectedly back to my days as a boarding pupil at Pocklington School in the Seventies, a school described by Adrian Edmondson of "The Young Ones" fame, as "a very minor public school halfway between York and Hull – or, as the joke went, halfway between York and Hell." Edmondson is the key link here – we attended Pocklington School at the same time, Ade being in the

year above me. This fact gave me enormous credibility
with pupils I taught in the early to mid-Eighties, when
"The Young Ones" was redefining TV comedy. Not
only did I attend the same school, I trod the boards with
him in a school production of Bertholt Brecht's "The
Caucasian Chalk Circle".

I was recently given Edmondson's autobiography
"Beserker" as a Fathers' Day gift. I'm currently reading
it, and he writes about his time at Pocklington at
considerable length. It's a scathing indictment, and
while my memories might not be quite as negative as
his, I can vouch for everything he describes. He doesn't
mention any teachers by name, but I can recognise
almost all those he refers to, and none of them emerge
well.

The second incident occurred when I was scrolling
through my "People you may know" thread on
Facebook. The name of a certain David Crowe cropped
up, stating that he also attended Pocklington School. I
distinctly remember being in A-Level History and
English Literature groups with a David Crowe. I click
on his "info" and the dates correspond. In a remarkable
moment of serendipity, I notice that he now lives in
Kendal, just a few miles from where I grew up, and the
place where my brother lives. A friend request followed,
since when we've updated each other on the last forty-
eight years. It seems our trajectories have followed
remarkably similar paths. We both became teachers
(History in David's case, English in mine), both taught
for many years in West Yorkshire, and both reached the
heady heights of middle management (Head of Year in
David's case, Head of Department in mine). And here
comes the Carlisle connection. When David got his

Head of Year post at a school in Brampton, just outside Carlisle, he and his family settled in Kendal. Not only that, but he also taught Paul Simpson's sons when Simmo was in his first spell as United manager.

It's a small world.

Thursday 18 July. "Backing The Blues – 120 Years of Carlisle United". Tullie House Museum and Art Gallery.

Yesterday was rather a special day in my fifty-seven years as a Carlisle supporter. Adam and I had the pleasure and privilege of being guests at the preview/opening of the above exhibition. The reason for our invitation, as referred to in a previous post, was that we'd loaned a genuine Carlisle United shirt to the exhibition, as worn by club legend Chris Balderstone in the 1969-70 season. I make no apologies if I'm repeating myself here. Chris Balderstone was playing First Division football for Carlisle in April 1975. Just over a year later he was walking out at Headingley cricket ground to make his Test Match debut for England against the might of the West Indies, one of the greatest cricket teams of all time. Just spend a moment to take that in. The same person performed at the highest level in two professional sports, just over a year apart. If anyone ever deserved the accolade, Chris Balderstone deserves to be described as a bloody sporting legend. The scorecard for his Test Match debut, painstakingly completed by my dad, also forms part of the exhibition.

But back to last night. For an hour and a half, I had the privilege of being in the company of Carlisle legends. Within five minutes of entering the exhibition I had spotted George McVitie, who played in the first game I ever attended at Brunton Park, before returning to the club in the mid to late seventies for a second impressive spell. I had the pleasure of a conversation with him, in which I explained why we had been invited (the shirt). He told me that when he was an apprentice at Carlisle, he was given two washing machines and two scrubbing brushes. One of his responsibilities was to wash the playing kits before passing them on to the wife of Dick Young, then the Carlisle coach, for ironing. He also claimed to have made a significant contribution to Billy Rafferty's famous hat-trick against Cardiff City in 1976, which transformed a 3-1 deficit into a 4-3 victory in the final six minutes of the game. His contribution? He'd been substituted well before the legendary hat-trick! To be fair, he had scored Carlisle's first goal himself.

Imagine my disbelief when Billy Rafferty himself walked into the room just a few minutes later! By this time Adam was dismissively describing me as a "fan girl" as I admiringly pointed out the latest club legend to enter the room. I was just about to approach Rafferty when the evening's formalities began. At the time he was stood with two other club icons: Mick Wadsworth who led the club to the Third Division title and a first Wembley appearance in 1975; John Halpin, who gave the club untold years of service as player, coach and Football in the Community Officer.

I also had a chat with Les O'Neill, a stalwart of the First Division team, who scored three goals in our first two games in the topflight, helping us to top the table after just three games. I recently eulogised him in my list of Carlisle's Top Ten Midfielders and was more than flattered that he knew who I was.

The exhibition itself is excellent. It's probably of limited interest to those outside the Carlisle United diaspora, but there was such a range of exhibits, including the boots with which Jimmy Glass scored his immortal goal, a season ticket from the early twentieth century, and a wedding dress with the train in Carlisle's away colours of the time, the red, green, gold and white of then sponsors Eddie Stobart.

After the formalities of the evening were completed, I also got the opportunity to talk to the club's CEO, Nigel Clibbens. He's a Wakefield boy born and bred, and attended Outwood Grange School, though some time before Lisa started working there. I took great pleasure in telling him how the Chris Balderstone shirt came into my hands, given that Nigel also started his football career, albeit in administration, at Huddersfield Town before moving on to Carlisle United, just like Balderstone.

Finally, I also got to speak to Jon Colman, the Carlisle United correspondent for The News and Star. We've communicated before, and he wrote an excellent piece about the publication of my book last November.

Sunday 21 July – close-season update.

With the start of the new season just under three weeks away, ground improvements continue apace. I saw the new, permanent giant screen in the fan zone on a recent trip to Carlisle, but the developments inside the ground are yet to be completed or revealed. Meantime, the rebuilding of the squad continues. It's pointless to comment on individual players until I've seen them play, but it's worth looking at the apparent strategy behind the new signings.

There has been major, and much needed, strengthening of the defence. Two new centre-backs and a new full-back on each flank. One of the new centre-backs is Aaron Hayden, who enjoyed an excellent season at Brunton Park before being tempted away by a long contract and vastly increased wages at Wrexham. Having helped them to two successive promotions he has now returned to his old stamping ground.

Likewise, Charlie Wyke, who I credit with being the principal reason for Adam finally coming out as a Carlisle supporter, following a thumbs up at the end of a game at Grimsby some years ago. He has a proven goalscoring record in Leagues One and Two, and his return is made even sweeter by the annoyance of Bradford City fans, who were convinced that he was returning to them, not us. A strike force of Charlie Wyke, Luke Armstrong and a consistently fit George Kelly has the potential to terrorise League Two defences in the season ahead. It's also an attack that we could only have dreamed of twelve months ago.

The one area in which I think we need to make a new signing is the link between midfield and attack. Someone who is going to supply goals for the forward line as well as score a few themselves. Someone who can fill the sort of role that Omari Patrick and Jordan Gibson filled.

All the new arrivals have led to a couple of departures. Jack Armer has signed for Burton Albion. I'm disappointed to see him go, because I thought he was excellent in the promotion season, working the left flank with Jon Mellish. But to be honest, he struggled a bit with the step up to League One. Alfie McCalmont has signed for Gold Coast Mariners in the Australian A-League. This continues a growing trend of players who haven't quite cut the mustard at Brunton Park moving Down Under – Zak Clough and Ryan Edmondson. I doubt that the A-League represents a step up from League One or Two, however attractive the lifestyle might be.

It's encouraging that the close-season headlines have been about expenditure off the pitch rather than on the squad. We've learned about the millions being spent on improvements to Brunton Park, and further millions earmarked for the development of the new training ground. I've no doubt there has been significant investment in the playing squad, whether in the form of transfer fees or salaries offered. But the club, wisely, hasn't been trumpeting that.

As far as pre-season action is concerned, we've won two games and drawn two, the most recent being against St Mirren who will be competing in the Europa Conference League this season.

I'm not sure what our first game of the season will be. The Carabao cup tie at home to Stoke City just two days after we return from holiday is a possibility, but the Cumbrian derby against Barrow, just four days later and broadcast live on Sky TV is a definite date.

Monday 29 July – nothing happened today!

Literally nothing – no new signings, no pre-season friendly, not even any new posts on the club's recently relaunched website. We're in that strange limbo where pre-season is well under way, a number of new signings have been announced, four or five pre-season friendlies have been completed, but we're still almost a fortnight from the beginning of the new season, waiting for the final pieces of the jigsaw to be slotted into place.

That's not to say that plenty hasn't happened in the eight days since my last post. I think I've finally come back down to earth after the excitement of meeting some of my United heroes at the launch of the Tullie House exhibition. Perhaps most significantly, last Thursday saw the funeral of Andrew Jenkins, most recently Chairman Emeritus, a former Chairman and owner of the club, and a club Director for over sixty years. If anyone deserves the accolade of "Mr Carlisle United" then Andrew Jenkins is that person. The East Stand was renamed in his honour just a year ago. It was touching to watch the richly deserved send-off he received from players and coaches, club staff and supporters as the funeral cortege circled the exterior of Brunton Park. His final, and perhaps most significant, contribution to the club was to oversee the smooth transition of ownership to our new American owners, taking the club into financial territory it has only dreamed of previously. R.I.P. Andrew Jenkins.

Off the field developments continue apace. As well as the revamp of the club website, CUTV has been launched and I'm already a subscriber. It's not quite as grand as it sounds, but it does give access to a fair amount of video material that isn't freely available on the club website or YouTube, such as extensive footage of the Tullie House exhibition. Images of the newly refurbished home changing room have been released and I have to admit that it looks very impressive. I assume that, in keeping with primitive football psychology, the away changing room is still a shithole!

On a more personal level, two senior citizens in the Wakefield area have now received their season tickets for the forthcoming season and are probably far more excited about that fact than befits their age. The Falshaw family may be on foreign soil when the new season begins, but we'll be making up for that immediately we return. Less than forty-eight hours after we return to British soil, a full complement of the Wakefield Blues will be heading to Brunton Park for the Carabao Cup first round tie against Stoke City. In an indication that the ground improvements are going down to the wire, the Andrew Jenkins Stand and the Warwick Road End will still be closed for that game. Just four days later a reconfigured version of the Wakefield Blues will be returning to Brunton Park for the first home league game of the new season, the "local derby" against Barrow. I trust that it will be access all areas by that time.

I'll conclude with a couple of opinions rather than the information updates that have constituted most of this post. On Saturday we lost for the first time in pre-season, at National League Rochdale. That prompted some doom and gloom on social media. I care not a jot. We had a decent pre-season a year ago and look at the nightmare season that followed. My second opinion regards new signings. A striker on loan from a Premier League club is heavily rumoured, but my priority is an attacking midfielder, someone who can supply the excellent strike force we have assembled and also drive forward as a supplementary attacker. Another Owen Moxon in other words.

Chapter 2
THE WHEELS COME OFF

Saturday 10 August. Gillingham v Carlisle United. Priestfield Stadium. EFL League 2.

So, the 2024-25 season begins not with the anticipated bang, but with a resounding whimper. There's no other way to describe a 4-1 defeat on the opening day. I seek comfort in the fact that in the 1973-74 season Carlisle's first away game was a 6-1 defeat at Luton, and we got promoted to Division 1 at the end of that season.

But before I begin the post-mortem into Saturday's debacle, an update is required. Since my last post, a fortnight ago, Carlisle have concluded their pre-season with an encouraging 2-1 win over Stockport. We have also signed a Premier League striker on loan, Dan Adu-Adjei from Bournemouth. He scored on debut in the Stockport friendly and started Saturday's game at Gillingham. On a less positive note, our midfield has been decimated by injuries, and new left back Cameron Harper is also injured, leading to the last-minute signing of Ben Williams, most recently of Cheltenham Town, on a short-term contract until January. He also went straight into Saturday's starting eleven.

It's hard to credit the transformation in the club since this time last year, both on and off the pitch. Only two of Saturday's starting line-up were at the club at the beginning of last season. Two of the subs were starting just their second season at Brunton Park, and substitute goalkeeper Gabe Breeze was only awarded his first full-time contract a year ago. The new owners have wasted no time in investing over £4 million in ground improvements: a giant video screen now permanently installed in the fan zone; LED advertising boards installed around the ground; new hospitality boxes; a new directors' box; the launch of CUTV; the relaunch of the club website; £4 million earmarked for the new training ground; significant investment in the playing squad (best reserve judgement on that for now!). As Harold McMillan famously said, "We've never had it so good."

But ultimately, the club will be judged by results on the pitch, which is why Saturday's result was a timely reminder that money doesn't automatically guarantee success. I must admit that this game was viewed from afar, as we were on holiday in Skala, Kefalonia. Adam managed to find a way to stream the game, but I was more focused on the pool, the beach, cocktails and Greek cuisine! I did find time to meet up with the owner of Ionian mini market in Skala, who is also a United supporter, for reasons far too complicated to explain here.

After Gillingham's early opener Adam kept reassuring me that United were very much on top, but the scoreline remained 1-0 at half-time, despite the match stats very much favouring Carlisle. A dreadful defensive error gifted Gillingham their second goal, before Jon Mellish pulled one back and offered hope. Having watched the brief highlights, the remaining two Gillingham goals could both be put down to defensive frailty, with Harry Lewis in goal perhaps shouldering a share of the blame.

The personnel may have changed, but the weaknesses appear to be in the same areas – something Paul Simpson needs to address as a matter of urgency.

Tomorrow a full complement of the Wakefield Blues heads north for the Carabao cup-tie against Stoke, our own season-opener and a welcome antidote to the post-holiday blues.

Tuesday 13 August. Carlisle United v Stoke City. Brunton Park. EFL (Carabao) Cup Round One.

The Wakefield Blues are back on the road again!

Around the end of February, I made the decision that there was no point squandering any more money travelling to watch the depressing death throes of a desperately disappointing campaign. The money would be better spent following a successful 2024-25 campaign. It was therefore something of an article of faith that we attended the first home of the new season, even if it was a game we were unlikely to win, playing a team two divisions above us, not long departed from the Premier League. So yesterday evening found Adam, Ben, John and me following the familiar route north.

Having checked the weather forecast for Carlisle and found a 2% likelihood of rain I decided not to bother with a waterproof. I was a little disconcerted as we drove through a significant amount of rain on the journey, but fortunately it stayed dry for the duration of the match, though there was plenty more rain on the journey home.

It was announced yesterday that Carlisle United had been ranked second of the ninety-two League clubs for fan engagement and had received a gold award for that accolade. A lot of the credit for this achievement should go to Simon Clarkson, the club's Supporter Liaison Officer, I've had the pleasure of meeting Simon a couple of times recently in connection with the Carlisle United exhibition at Tullie House and am very impressed by his commitment and dedication. Simon was also responsible for preparing the successful bid for National Lottery funding that helped finance the Tullie House exhibition.

Some of the reasons for the fan engagement award were evident once we arrived at the ground. As well as the established food and drink outlets in the fan zone, a now permanent giant screen is in place, providing an excellent area and atmosphere for fans to congregate before entering the ground. Not only that, the new directors/owners were there, mingling with the fans. One of them spotted Adam's Jacksonville Jaguars hoodie (the Piataks are major sponsors of the Jaguars) and we had a very enjoyable five minutes chatting with them about American Football, the upgrades to Brunton Park, and life in New York.

On entering the ground, further improvements were evident. Although the Andrew Jenkins Stand was closed, apart from the away section, the new hospitality boxes were clearly evident, and the media section has now been moved across the ground to the West Stand. The new LED advertising boards were in place and in operation, and the playing surface looked as impeccable as ever.

The 2-0 scoreline is probably a fair reflection of the game. Stoke were a decent team, with some slick passing and movement, and hit the woodwork twice in addition to their two goals. Carlisle had their moments in the first half, and it was good to go into half-time on equal terms. Unfortunately, the team displayed a familiar trait, conceding early in the second half, but had further chances before Stoke settled the game with their second goal.

With so many new or returning faces, it's worth spending a little bit of time on individual performances. Goalkeeper Harry Lewis has received more than his fair share of criticism since joining United from Bradford in January, some of it unduly vitriolic, but yesterday was one of his best games in a Carlisle shirt. He couldn't be blamed for either of the goals, and on at least three occasions his agility kept us in the game. It's time to give the guy a break. Jack Ellis did a decent job at left wing back, playing on the opposite side to his usual position. Jon Mellish was the Jon Mellish we know and love. 100% committed as ever, he made some surging runs out of defence, but was also guilty of some woeful final passes and rash challenges.

The rest of the defence was composed of new faces, or, in the case of Aaron Hayden, a returning face. Archie Davies at right wing-back had a bit of a torrid time defensively in the first half but looked good going forward in the second half. That leaves new central defenders Hayden and Terrel Thomas. All I'll say is that it was good to have central defenders who were not only good in the air, but looked comfortable on the ball, able to carry the ball forward themselves if there wasn't a pass available.

In midfield Harrison Neal was his usual reliable self, constantly harrying opposition players, snapping into tackles and making himself available for passes from teammates. If he's got any faults, it's that he's not the most creative of players, and his shooting leaves something to be desired. Ben Barclay did a competent job as the midfield anchor, but I agree with the fans who say that if he's the best we've got to offer in that position, then we have a bit of a problem. We need Callum Guy, Taylor Charters and Dylan McGeogh back from injury as soon as possible, and hopefully a new creative midfielder signing.

Josh Vela impressed me as the forward apex of midfield. He made some incisive attacking runs and pressurized the defence. He received short shrift from the referee, who was quick to punish him for alleged fouls, and slow to punish the opposition when Vela was on the receiving end. To be fair to the referee, any official who can manage a competitive game without issuing a single card deserves considerable credit.

Up front, Charlie Wyke and Damiel Adu-Adjei offered relatively little. They were up against Championship defenders, and received pretty poor service from midfield and defence, so I don't want to be too harsh on them.

Midfield remains the area of major concern. There were too many occasions when Stoke were able to cut incisively through midfield or bypass it completely, and there was a failure to provide decent service to the strikers. When Luke Armstrong came on as a substitute, he looked more like the player I've seen be so effective for Harrogate against Carlisle. That's probably because he was receiving the ball to feet or chest, rather than competing with big defenders for hopeful aerial balls lumped forward from defence. I remain confident that he will come good, when the team find a way to play to his strengths. Harrogate managed to do it, so why can't we?

The first acid test of the season comes on Saturday when we host Barrow in the Cumbrian 'local derby'. Anything less than a victory will have the cynics calling for Paul Simpson's head. I'm confident that we'll do it, and it will be good to see the whole of Brunton Park open again, following the improvements to the Andrew Jenkins Stand and the Warwick Road End. A slightly reconfigured version of the Wakefield Blues will be there.

Saturday 17 August. Carlisle United v Barrow. Brunton Park. EFL League 2.

Good days have been in precious short supply over recent months for supporters of Carlisle United, but this was undoubtedly a good one for a variety of reasons.

It was an extended and amended version of the Wakefield Blues that convened at Brunton Park. John and his wife Julie were already in Carlisle, visiting John's sister, so the arrangement was to meet in The Paddock prior to kick-off. Ben had an athletics meet, so his place on the back seat was taken by Sam, another of Adam's mates, who now and again puts aside his affiliation to Leeds United and joins us for a Carlisle game. John's place in the front seat was taken by my good friend from our days in Wetherby, Jason Westerman. Jason used to join me for the odd Carlisle game, the most recent being a League Cup second round second leg tie against Spurs, a mere twenty-seven years ago. That was also the final time I had the privilege of meeting Chris Balderstone in person. Jason was also with me to witness a remarkable 5-2 win over Hull City at Boothferry Park, a game we were losing 2-0 after just fifteen minutes.

A 12.30 kick-off (thank you Sky Sports) meant an early start from Wakefield, but the delays that John and Julie had experienced on their journey to Carlisle a day earlier failed to materialise and we were turning off the M6 by quarter to eleven. It took us another twenty minutes to travel the remaining mile to the car park, but we were still in good time. As we walked down Warwick Road to the ground, I pointed out to Jason that fifty years ago I was making exactly the same walk to watch United play their first ever home game in Division 1. There was no encounter with the club's owners in the fan zone this time, but we did have time for a quick pint before entering the ground to ensure we had a crush barrier to lean on. It was sufficient time for Jason to be suitably impressed by the giant video screen and the general buzz in the fan zone.

The ground was relatively empty when we assumed our place in The Paddock, but this was a 'local' derby against Barrow, and the ground rapidly filled as kick-off approached. The official attendance was 9,813 (885 away fans), not bad for a club who had experienced a dismal relegation campaign last season and had started the new one with two defeats. The pre-match formalities included an impressive minute's applause for late Chairman Andrew Jenkins, and a further round of applause from the Andrew Jenkins Stand as the Piataks took their place in one of the new hospitality boxes. The pre-arranged meeting with John and Julie didn't happen until half-time, despite me keeping an eagle eye out for them.

The first half was very reassuring. Carlisle continued some of the good habits they had displayed on Tuesday night, but against inferior opposition they had more impact. United dominated possession in the early stages and fashioned some good moves, though without any end product, Barrow offering little threat at the other end. They displayed some neat cross-field passing, but no real penetration.

In the 35th minute Bournemouth loanee Daniel Adu-Adjei chased a ball down the left. As the defender fell to the ground, Barrow appealed for a free-kick, though it was obvious from the highlights that he either tripped over his own feet or took a dive. Undeterred, Adu-Adjei left him in his wake, cut in from the left and confidently curled the ball inside the far post from a narrow angle. It's always difficult to know what you're getting with loan signings, but the early signs are that we may have got a good one here. He gave the Barrow defence a torrid time and probably deserved the man of the match accolade he was awarded. The only concern at half-time was that we should have maybe been a further goal ahead.

Central defender Terrel Thomas was replaced by Sam Lavell at half-time, having suffered a twinge in the first half, but the transition was seamless, so much so that I didn't realise until the 60th minute that the change had taken place! Barrow had more possession in the second half, but the Carlisle defence and midfield largely managed to confine them to unthreatening areas. But as long as the score remained 1-0 there was always that fear that one defensive lapse, or a moment of attacking inspiration could wipe out that lead.

As the fourth official indicated a surprising six minutes of added time, the score remained 1-0. A minute later defender Aaron Hayden took a viciously hit pass full in the face. The ball rebounded into touch and Hayden collapsed to the turf. As the crowd gasped and groaned at the force of the impact, Hayden simply got back to his feet and trotted back into position. I suspect it may become an iconic moment of the season.

But the drama wasn't over yet. In the 95th minute Josh Vela was harshly penalised for a tackle on the Barrow left. The free kick was launched into the area, and after a couple of half-clearances was forced home. The Barrow bench leapt from the dugout, arms aloft and jumping into each other's arms until they realised the assistant referee on the far side had raised his flag for offside. Apparently even Tom Piatak Snr. joined in the mockery of the Barrow contingent, though I think it merely consisted of a sarcastic bye-bye wave, rather than the wanker gestures that were in evidence around us!

A few moments later the final whistle went, and we could celebrate our season being belatedly under way. It was a suitable riposte to the doom-mongers who were already calling for Paul Simpson's departure. I'm not going to indulge in another player-by-player analysis of the performance, but I will make a few salient points. Jon Mellish had one of his less impressive performances in a distinguished Carlisle career, and Charlie Wyke again had disappointingly little impact up front. It's testament to the rest of the team that they still managed to get across the line.

I was quite critical of the midfield after Tuesday's game, so credit where credit's due. Ben Barclay looked more comfortable in the holding role, Harrison Neal was tenacious in the tackle and always available. I'm going to stick my neck out and say that Josh Vela may prove to be our player of the season. As the attacking apex of the midfield, he put in some good runs and passes in support of the strikers and also had a couple of decent passes. But I was most impressed by his willingness to also race back and put pressure on Barrow players when they were in possession. He was equally adept in both attacking and defensive duties.

For the second game in a row, I was quite impressed by the officiating. I suspect that the referee on Tuesday wouldn't have brandished any of the yellow cards awarded in this game, with the possible exception of Ben Barclay's foul. But the assistant on the far side was particularly impressive. He must have flagged Barrow offside at least eight times in the second half, despite the abuse he was receiving from the away fans directly behind him. Most of the offsides were blatant, but he still had the guts to raise his flag when the decision was more marginal, most notably in the case of Barrow's cancelled equaliser.

There was still time to call in at The Blues Store and buy a copy of Peter Scholes new book on United, "The Place I Belong", to which I am a modest contributor. It'll have to wait a couple of weeks, but I look forward to reading it.

It felt slightly strange starting the journey home when most games were just about to kick off. But it was nice to be home by teatime, secure in the knowledge of a well-earned three points.

Saturday 24th August. MK Dons v Carlisle United. Stadium MK. EFL League 2.

Oh dear. This is not quite how the new season was meant to begin. I know we're only three games into the League 2 season, but two of those games have seen dispiriting defeats away from home by a three-goal margin. A goal difference of minus 5 after just three games is far from encouraging.

I can't pretend to be able to offer any detailed analysis of this performance. On Saturday afternoon, with Adam at Leeds Festival and Ellie on holiday in Turkey, the remaining members of the Falshaw family opted to sample the pleasures of Hebden Bridge. There we enjoyed excellent food outlets, lots of independent shops (for books, clothes, pottery, antiques, jewellery etc.) and barely a brand name in sight. I was reduced to regular checks of my phone for score updates. Having watched the brief highlights, it's alarming how easily our defence was cut open, each of the MK Dons' scorers being left with a pretty simple tap-in.

What I can offer is my considered opinion on what ails Carlisle United at the moment. Before I start my analysis, I should state clearly that I am not one of the many doom-mongers already calling for Paul Simpson's immediate departure. He returned to a club on its knees and engineered an incredible escape from relegation. He then maintained that momentum into the following season, leading the club to a remarkable promotion. It's easy now to look back and say that promotion in 2023 was a triumph of overachievement. It was incredible at the time, and I wouldn't swap it for anything. Simpson had taken a group of players who were abject failures under Chris Beech and Keith Millen and transformed them. A nod here to Millen's recruitment in the January 2022 transfer window. It might be his only achievement in his short time at Brunton Park, but he brought in players who were central to initial survival and eventual promotion – Kris Dennis, Jamie Devitt, Omari Patrick,

Joel Senior, Dynel Simeu. Quite a contrast to the woeful recruitment for the League 1 campaign in the summer of 2023. But even though last season was dismal, Simpson deserves time to turn round this disappointing start. Let's not forget the years of mediocrity that preceded Simpson's return, with frequent changes of manager having little effect.

I also have full confidence in our new owners. The enthusiasm with which they spoke to us before the Stoke game a fortnight ago about the changes they are introducing at the club was clear evidence that they are not the type of chancers who have gained control of too many football clubs in recent years, at every level. They know that Paul Simpson has a clear vision for the future of the club, both on and off the pitch, having the club in his heart, and that has no doubt played a major part in making the shaping of their development plans easier. There's no guarantee that you would get that with a new manager.

None of this is to say that Paul Simpson should not worry about the current dismal trajectory. Just as the winning momentum of the 2022 escape from relegation was carried over into the following season, there is an equal danger that the losing mentality of last season is perpetuated in the current campaign.

A few questions need asking.

What were the circumstances behind Paul Gerrard's departure? It was obvious to anyone in The Paddock possessed of a functioning pair of ears and eyes that his influence extended way beyond his title of goalkeeping coach. Did he want a more significant role in the coaching set-up than either Simpson or the club were prepared to give him?

What exactly are the jobs in the current coaching team? Gavin Skelton and Billy Barr are joint assistant mangers, but what precisely are their respective roles and responsibilities?

Why are the club failing to get the best out of some excellent recruits in the January 2024 transfer window? Luke Armstrong was consistently superb against Carlisle in a Harrogate shirt, and I was delighted when we signed him. Why have the coaching staff not worked out a tactical plan that plays to his strengths? Harrison Neal is an excellent holding midfielder, tigerish in the tackle and always available for a pass. He's a "water carrier" par excellence but needs a creative midfield partner to build on his tireless industry. Josh Vela has impressed me with both his attacking enterprise and his willingness to put in a defensive shift. So why do we have a team that consistently proves to be less than the sum of its parts?

Why do we have so many players on the injured list? Two of our most recent signings have yet to feature in the regular season, and did someone not do due diligence on Georgie Kelly's fitness before he was signed? I hope he proves to be a success for us, but the signs are not promising.

I don't pretend to have answers to any of these questions. I have no knowledge of the inner workings of a football club. But they remain questions that need answering.

Saturday 31 August. Carlisle United v Tranmere Rovers. Brunton Park. EFL League 2.

I think this could be quite a long post! I've already spent three days processing the events of Saturday and their ramifications. It'll probably take as long to commit them to print, now that I've finally put finger to keyboard. But let's not get ahead of ourselves.

Saturday dawned bright and sunny. Given the vagaries of English (and particularly Cumbrian) weather, fleeces and waterproofs were loaded into the boot, but thankfully neither were required. As we started our journey, I commented to John that this is as good as it gets on a Saturday morning – heading North for a Carlisle game, the Test Match Special team in the background, with their inimitable, inconsequential and slightly surreal burbling to keep us entertained.

I'd arranged to meet Peter Scholes, the author of "The Place I Belong", the latest addition to the canon of books about Carlisle United, in the fan zone before the game. I spotted him as we turned off Warwick Road towards the West Stand, and we agreed to rendezvous in a few minutes once he'd dealt with immediate business. That left time to bump into Simon Clarkson, the club's Supporter Liaison Officer and moving force behind the Tullie House exhibition and introduce him to John. As 2.30 approached, with no sign of Peter, I decided my back and knee took priority and we headed into The Paddock to ensure I had a crush barrier to lean on during the afternoon's entertainment.

I felt reasonably confident about the game. Carlisle have had a pretty good record against Tranmere over recent seasons, and I felt this was the moment when the new season could start to generate some momentum. The game was given some additional edge by the return, in Tranmere colours, of two prominent players in the 2022-23 promotion campaign, Kris Dennis and Omari Patrick. Dennis became the first Carlisle striker in 17 years to score over 20 League goals in a season, and Patrick scored the equaliser at Wembley that led to ultimate triumph in the play-off final. I was impressed by, and part of, the generous ovation each of them received from the fans in The Paddock as they left the pitch after the warm-up. Equally impressive was the minute's applause prior to kick-off to mark the death of Sven Goran Erikson.

A further digression before I get onto the game itself. During the warmup, the Tranmere players' shorts looked remarkably similar to those of Carlisle's away kit from two seasons previous. Closer examination revealed that their kit manufacturers are Errea, Carlisle's suppliers two years ago, and that their away kit does use the same combination of maroon and orange, albeit in a different design.

There was the lurking worry that Dennis or Patrick might twist the knife on their return to Brunton Park. It took only six minutes for that fear to become reality as Patrick scored from inside the box as Carlisle failed to clear an attack down the Tranmere left. To be fair to him he respected his former club and fans by indulging in the most muted of celebrations. Fortunately, it took only two further minutes for Carlisle to restore parity, when Archie Davies scored his first goal for United, following a deft touch from Adu Adjei.

Carlisle were having the better of the first half, in terms of both possession and goal attempts, without creating real clear chances. That failure to convert dominance into goals was punished in the 37th minute when Patrick twisted the knife even further. Following a short corner on the Tranmere right, he exchanged a quick one-two with a teammate before curling a superb shot into the far left-hand corner. To be honest it was an outstanding goal, one that we were perfectly positioned to "enjoy".

The rest of the half brought no further goals, but the interval did bring an opportunity to message Peter and re-arrange our meet-up for after the final whistle.

The second half became increasingly depressing. Carlisle's play in possession became progressively more ragged, and on too many occasions the ball was lumped aimlessly forward. A change of formation, with Jon Mellish moving from defence into midfield, failed to have the necessary effect. He made a handful of stirring runs, but his final delivery was poor. The longer the game went on, the less likely the team looked to score. None of the substitutes performed badly after being introduced, but none of them had sufficient impact.

As the players were leaving the pitch, Jon Mellish became involved in a brief altercation with a fan not far from us, before being steered away by one of the coaching staff. To be honest, if you want to have a pop at someone then Mells is the last person that should be. He may not be the most polished player, but his effort and commitment to the club over nearly two hundred games, is there for all to see. Paul Simpson was booed by a significant number of supporters, and for the first time I felt that he might be losing the fans. During a post-match interview, he expressed the view that a couple of comments from the crowd had "crossed the line." It's rumoured that one of those comments was along the lines of "I hope your cancer comes back." If that is the case, I hope the club are able to identify the culprit and ban them for life, from the human race as well as Brunton Park.

Having left the stadium, John and I finally managed to hook up with Peter in the fan zone. It was quickly agreed that, given the mediocre fare we'd just witnessed on the hallowed turf, the conversation should be about writing and books rather than football. A highly enjoyable fifteen minutes followed, concluding that we'd meet up again soon for a proper chat and a beer. We were blissfully unaware of what was unfolding a few yards away at the time, in the depths of the West Stand.

As we indulged in post-match analysis on the journey home, the conclusion was that we have assembled a good squad of players for League Two, but that they are not performing collectively as a team. The coaching staff are failing, for whatever reason, to make the most of the resources at their disposal. The two loan signings from Bournemouth look very impressive.

I had just parked the car on our arrival back in Crofton when Adam checked his phone and blurted out, "He's gone." That was indeed the case. Paul Simpson, along with Assistant Managers Gavin Skelton and Billy Barr, plus Head of Performance Jake Simpson, had left the club with immediate effect. There's a lot to unpack here, so please bear with me!

Firstly, I'm immensely sad that Paul Simpson is no longer a part of Carlisle United Football Club. Like Alan Ashman he led the club to three promotions, the difference for me being that I witnessed all three of Simmo's successes, whereas I was too young to enjoy Ashman's first two triumphs. And I would rank the escape from relegation in 2022 an equal achievement to any of the promotions. He inherited a club and a team that was on the ropes. In weeks he transformed a disparate, demotivated and dispirited group of players into winners. Those last fifteen games, many of which I attended, are among my best memories as a Carlisle supporter.

Was it the right time to dispose of his services? No individual is bigger than the club, and while I expected him to be given a little longer, the owners have acted decisively to try and prevent a disappointing start to the season becoming a bad one. With the right appointments this can still be a good season. Possibly Simpson adhered a little too rigidly to a 3-5-2 formation, and while he was willing to juggle personnel, wasn't sufficiently willing to change tactics and formation. I do think it was the right decision to remove the entire senior coaching staff. It makes it much easier for the new incumbent to set out their own stall.

Tom Piatak Snr has announced that the club are looking to appoint a Sporting Director and a Head Coach, with a clear delineation of responsibilities. That seems to make sense to me. The days when an Arsene Wenger or Alex Ferguson could oversee and mastermind every aspect of a club's development are long gone, at whatever level. There are those who believe that Paul Simpson was spreading himself too thinly, spending too much time on the wider development of the club, at the expense of on-the-pitch affairs. If that is the case, perhaps his subordinates should have been more proactive in stepping up and taking responsibility.

I understand any United supporters who shudder at the phrase "Sporting Director" and who suffer nightmares about David Holdsworth. But I think the role can be an important one – it all depends on who is appointed. I'm not going to indulge in idle speculation about who might fill either role. I suspect the appointment of the Sporting Director will come first and that will have a significant impact on the shortlist for Head Coach. All I will say is an emphatic "no" to a return for Keith (it's never my fault) Curle, and that if former Barrow Manager Pete Wilde is appointed, I'll be returning my season ticket.

Perhaps it is not so odd for a former English teacher to have a quote from Shakespeare running around in his head. After leaving Brunton Park's recently upgraded Fan Zone on Saturday and walking through the turnstiles to take up my position in the Paddock, it was a delight yet again to look upon the perfect condition of the Brunton Park pitch. Looking up I also noted the swallows which darted about, flashing against the blue sky, and flirting with the roof of the main grandstand. It was a line from Macbeth which ran through my head,

> *"This castle hath a pleasant seat, the air*
> *Nimbly and sweetly recommends itself…"*

Of course, the unwitting Duncan cannot be fully aware of the full range of hospitality offered by the Macbeths as he turns up for an overnighter – that's Jacobean Drama for you. Likewise, beyond win, lose or draw, the terrace fan cannot know in advance the full extent of the ramifications of the encounter he is about to witness.

For this fixture, the Wakefield Blues contingent were confident but at the same time they were fully aware of the immutable law of the returning former player which states that any such player should score against his former club. As such, the returning Omari Patrick offered a threat. As a Carlisle player, he often blew hot and cold, but this would be an opportunity for him to turn up the burners to full blast. And if that wasn't enough, Tranmere also had Kristian Dennis among their number, surely another source of returning goal scorer threat.

But we were nothing if not positive and we knew that a win for Carlisle would settle things down a little bit, and we could ignore what was mostly superstition and overlook any misgivings about consequences still hanging in the stars.

Little did we know – that's football for you.

It is worth mentioning that both Patrick and Dennis received a warm reception from the Paddock regulars as they completed their warmup. It was a class act, but that's how it should be.

The game got off to a cracking start when Tranmere scored after six minutes. Some guy called Omari Patrick bowing to inevitability and scuffing a shot in off the base of the post. But within a minute, Carlisle equalised after Jordan Jones, who was producing some good touches on his debut, bent his foot around the ball to deliver a dangerous cross into the box which was touched on by Daniel Adu-Adjei and finished by Archie Davies.

An equaliser, game on and time for Carlisle to let slip the dogs of war. Except that it wasn't quite like that, it was more a case of huff and puff, but Carlisle did dominate. Ben Williams was getting forward from left back for a header and a shot from his right foot, neither of which resulted in the necessary goal. Three other chances went wide of the post when the keeper stood rooted. If this game was going to settle things down a little bit, then these chances ought to have been converted.

It was Tranmere who eventually settled the match as early as the thirty seventh minute when that man Patrick again completed a well-worked corner routine by shaping an exquisite shot around the flailing Harry Lewis into the corner of the Carlisle goal.

For Tranmere, their hard work on the training ground had been validated and their self-belief was bolstered. Carlisle now faced a resolute back line and a midfield which was packed, intent on denying any space at all and in this Tranmere were largely successful. Dominic Sadi, on loan to Carlisle from Bournemouth, showed a lovely first touch and composure on the ball, but the Carlisle forwards failed to take advantage of his promptings. Luke Armstrong came off the bench and got his head to a powerful Davies cross but without the required result.

Tranmere, on the break, remained dangerous and a further goal for them would certainly seal the game and that looked odds on when Patrick picked up a ball on the edge of his own box and ran almost the length of the pitch to the opposite box where he slipped a pass to a supporting colleague who then bore down at an angle on the Carlisle goal. But, as the pundits say, Lewis in the Carlisle goal made himself look big and produced a vital save.

Why did this save not receive the acclaim it deserved? Maybe it was because play continued, or maybe it was because it didn't suit the narrative adopted by the ignorant. During his infrequent involvements in the remainder of the game, Lewis's efforts were followed by sarcastic cheers. Disappointment was rising and frustration was rife, but this response from the crowd was disgraceful. Whither the class act now? The usual defence for such actions is to say that spectators pay money at the gate and are entitled to express a response in whatever way they choose. Okay, jeer your own players if you like, but don't claim to be a "supporter."

The jeering was a forerunner of the booing and verbal abuse which followed the blowing of the final whistle. A lot of this was aimed at Paul Simpson, and if this was designed to remove Simpson from his post, then the boo boys got their way.

By the time we had driven back to Wakefield and settled down with a cup of tea, the news came through via a message from Carlisle United that Paul Simpson, Manager, Gavin Skelton, Coach, and Jake Simpson, Performance Manager had all stepped down from their posts. The platitudes about thanking them for their services were also added.

So, a few observations from an eventful day:

The four teams that Carlisle have played so far this season are in the top half of the table.

Barrow, beaten by Carlisle in the second game of the season, are now third in the league.

A resolute Tranmere side conceded their first goal of the season in today's game.

Carlisle were unexpectedly promoted two seasons ago. Arguably better sides were left behind them. Stockport and Mansfield come to mind.

Carlisle began the following season with a weaker squad than the one which won them promotion.

Carlisle are in the process of assembling a new squad. The number of new arrivals in the dressing room has now reached into double figures. Not to allow some time for gelling is a nonsense.

A good man has now gone.

Time and the hour runs through the roughest day.

Chapter 3
STILL WE SEARCH FOR SUCCESS

Tuesday 3 September. Carlisle United v Nottingham Forest U21s. Brunton Park. Bristol Street Motors Trophy group stage.

This post will be as brief as the last one was long, as befits this Premier Leage corrupted competition.

We went into the game with the interim management team of Mark Birch, Stephen Rudd and Jamie Devitt in charge. That's basically the youth coaching team. Jamie Devitt only returned to the club two weeks ago as part of the youth set-up, and almost instantly found himself playing an important role in first-team affairs. The starting lineup was much changed from Saturday, with only about three players surviving, but including a couple of significant returns from injury.

I watched the game intermittently on Sky Sports Plus. It was good to see the team playing significantly on the front foot for much of the game. It was depressing to see the defence cut open predictably easily for the two goals, the second of which came deep into time added on. Why can't we close out games anymore?

A couple of decent debuts from youth team players, but ultimately a meaningless defeat in a meaningless competition. Roll on Saturday at Valley Parade, where close to 2,000 Blues will be in attendance, despite recent travails.

Saturday 7 September. Bradford City v Carlisle United. Valley Parade. EFL League 2.

This afternoon started so well. It was one of the shortest trips of the season for The Wakefield Blues, just over forty minutes to Bradford. We parked within ten minutes' walk of Valley Parade and had decent seats almost an hour before kick-off. John was absent, having inexplicably decided that Denver, Colorado was a more attractive destination than Bradford on a grey autumnal afternoon. More fool him!

Valley Parade is by some distance the best ground in League Two (excepting Brunton Park of course) and played host to a crowd of 18,041 for this game. That included 1, 756 United fans, not bad for a team that suffered a dismal relegation last season, is currently struggling in the nether regions of League 2, and dismissed its manager and coaching staff just a week ago. As kick-off approached and more and more fans took their seats, the volume and atmosphere built accordingly. It was a timely reminder of what is so great about supporting Carlisle United and particularly following them on the road.

The feelgood factor lasted for all of two minutes, time enough for Charlie Wyke to squander a decent opportunity. Then disaster struck. Keeper Harry Lewis rolled the ball out to Jon Mellish who was under no pressure. He dithered momentarily, then slipped, gifting possession to Bradford. A cross and an easy finish later and we were already a goal down. To rub salt in the wound the goal was scored by former Carlisle player Andy Cooke. Harry Lewis has his fair share of critics among the Carlisle support, but to blame him for this goal, as some did online, is plain ridiculous. You'll find no greater advocate of Mells than myself, but this was his mistake, and I'm sure he would admit as much.

Despite such a woeful start, there was plenty to be encouraged by in the remainder of the first half. Terell Thomas looked composed in defence, and fluid movement and passing saw some good opportunities created, the best being a curling shot from Jordan Jones that was tipped over the bar. The vocal support remained constant throughout.

We should have been level early in the second half when Wyke hammered an absolute sitter against the post. Fortunately, we only had to wait another five minutes for the equaliser, though to describe the goal as fortuitous would be an understatement. Following a short corner, the ball was played into the Bradford area, where it looped up off Harrison Neal's foot. It appeared to be dropping comfortably into the hands of the Bradford keeper, until he inexplicably fumbled it into his own net.

Joy unconfined, but only for a few minutes. A bad Terrel Thomas slip let Bradford in, and it took a superb double save from Lewis to keep the scores equal. Lewis was booed throughout by the Bradford fans, no doubt resentful that he jilted them for a better (and bigger?) club. To produce such saves in front of the home end was the best possible riposte. He could not be held responsible for the winner a few minutes later when Andy Cooke was left criminally unmarked to head home. For the second week in a row a former player had condemned us to defeat with a brace of goals. Why wasn't Charlie Wyke the one returning to Valley Parade to haunt his former club? He had the chances!

Despite some earnest endeavour, a second equaliser was never forthcoming. Defensive frailty, poor final balls, and midfield inertia were again to the fore. So, what is wrong at the moment? I'll attempt to be a little more constructive than the moronic "supporter" who shouted, as the players came over to acknowledge the fans, "You're fucking shite, the lot of you." If he has a brain, perhaps he should use it to explore alternative forms of entertainment on a Saturday afternoon.

The points that follow are in no particular order.

I don't think this is a bad squad, as some fans seem to think. If I look at individual players, I think that most of the current starters are an upgrade on what we had a year ago. The problem seems to be a lack of cohesion and tactical flexibility, perhaps not surprising when you consider that Jon Mellish was the only player in the starting eleven who was even at Brunton Park a year ago. So here are a few memos for the new Sporting Director and Head Coach, whoever they may turn out to be.

Take the captaincy away from Charlie Wyke and give it to someone who has the confidence to be an organiser and a leader, preferably a midfielder or defender, though our current defenders seem far too quiet, lacking the arrogance to harangue and cajole their colleagues. They may be good defenders, but the team needs more than that from someone.

Watch videos of Luke Armstrong in a Harrogate shirt and learn how Simon Weaver got the best out of him. I'm happy to admit that his performances have largely been underwhelming since becoming our record signing, but I got tired of United's inability to handle him when he played against us. He's not a conventional target man, which is the role he was forced into last season, but he's a very good footballer who isn't being used to maximum effect. It doesn't matter how much you pay for a player; you still need to work to improve him and play to his strengths.

Teach the team how to press properly. Whatever you might think of Chris Beech and his lack of a Plan B, his high press approach was extremely effective. Countless times opposition defenders had to resort to hoofing the ball long because they had no option, usually surrendering possession. There was a telling moment in Saturday's game when Josh Vela moved forward to pressurise a Bradford defender. Because no-one moved to cover the space he had vacated, it was easy for the defender to find a pass and initiate another attack. Vela's gesture of frustration was a telling indication of why the team is currently struggling.

To conclude, a handful of comments on individual players, none of them meant to be damning.

Charlie Wyke – I'm still, just about, one of the fans who thinks that once he bags his first goal, others will follow. But I'm not sure how much longer I'm prepared to wait for that first goal, given a couple of the chances he missed in this game. And I think he could do without the added burden of being captain.

Jon Mellish – is he good enough to play as a central defender in a back four? He's at his most effective as the left of three centre backs, with a Paul Huntington type to direct and cajole him. I can't see any of our other current central defenders doing that job. I also think he misses the presence of Jack Armer at left wing back, with whom he had an excellent understanding. In the short and medium term, might he be more effectively deployed in midfield, with his surging runs and ability to be in the right place at the right time to score important goals?

Harrison Neal – I'm a great admirer of his tenacity and doggedness, but is he a starting player when we have a full squad available? I worry that he lacks pace and creativity. This may sound harsh, but I felt that Dylan McGeoch showed more composure and vision in a late cameo on Saturday than Neal had offered in the previous 75 minutes. And that's before I mention the currently unavailable Callum Guy, Ethan Robson and Taylor Charters.

Harry Lewis – give the guy a break!

The best way to keep track of the fortunes of Carlisle United is to be there in person at the match. I know, insight doesn't come much more profound than that, does it? If you're in Carlisle and the match is at Brunton Park, then nip down Warwick Road, pay your money and then cheer or groan to your heart's content.

Matters become more complicated If you don't live in Carlisle, if you're exiled in some far-flung spot such as Yorkshire for instance. Then you must travel the requisite distance or else find some way of keeping tabs on the game through various broadcasting media. But be warned, agony can lie in such arrangements. As a latest score is announced you can torture yourself with thoughts such as, can the boys pull this one round? Can they get a goal back? Or more unusually, can they hang on to this lead?

I have to admit that there have been occasions when I've endured the Saturday afternoon torment of not being at the match by switching off all forms of communication, waiting until the final whistle must have blown, before switching back on again and bracing myself for the message of doom: hit me with it!

I'm sharing these thoughts as Carlisle prepare to face Bradford City tomorrow at Valley Parade, a mere twenty miles from my home address, but I will not be there. Instead, I shall be 4,548 miles away in Denver, Colorado. It is my intention to be frequenting the coffee bars and bookshops, sampling the local craft beers, and plotting some forays into the Rockies. I know, it's a tough life, eh?

The toughest part will be keeping track of Carlisle United's historic season under new ownership, and, as of last Saturday, a new caretaker managership. There is also this trail of profundities to maintain. What are the prospects for tomorrow's game at Bradford?

Carlisle versus Bradford has taken on quite a resonance of late, probably on account of the League two playoffs the season before last when Carlisle overcame a 1-0 deficit from the first leg with a 3-1 win in the second, a game which went into extra time in front of a packed Brunton Park crowd. Emotions ran high, Wembley beckoned, and the pitch was duly invaded. Mark Hughes, the Bradford manager lost his job shortly after that, not a fate which would befall Super Paul Simpson, his opposite number at Carlisle.

As Willie Nelson once memorably sang, "Funny How Time Slips Away."

But I digress as I attempt to convey the difficulty of focussing on the upcoming game. Social media comment has to be handled with some very lengthy tongs. The emotive outpourings can be filed under "unreliable" or to use a term which I have frequently heard over here, they are horseshit. Instead, I offer you some salient points from the impeccable viewpoint of the Mile High City.

If last week's Tranmere game offered the opportunity to settle things down for a while, the same applies to the match at Bradford only more so. Even Caretaker Managers need a win for starters. A draw might buy some time, but a defeat is unlikely to be acceptable in any form. The mad braying will continue.

The clamour for more attractive football needs to be handled with care. Away from home this season, Carlisle have conceded three goals at Gillingham and four goals at Milton Keynes. These look like bad defeats but the scorelines disguise the fact that Carlisle were in contention in both games until silly mistakes occurred or defensive weaknesses became evident. Rather than beginning the revolution marching behind the banner of more attractive football, the new management team should make it a priority to cut out silly mistakes. (Let's also take some time out here to say that heavy defeats might also have been sustained against Stoke in the Carabao Cup and in the Tranmere game had it not been for the vital saves made by Harry Lewis. The goals at M.K. Dons were not his fault and neither were the two against Tranmere. If you've been joining in the mindless jeering of one of your own players, then give your head a shake. The evidence on the pitch is that Harry Lewis is turning up for work, he's doing his bit. Give him a break.)

Carlisle's memorable i.e. only win this season against Barrow came about as Harrison Neal and Josh Vela put in a real shift in midfield. Barrow, third in the league as I write this, were not allowed to play, and when fans construct their dream attacking midfield line up, they should remember that someone has to do the tracking and tackling, to contribute that invaluable ability to stick a foot in. Just saying.

I like Terrel Thomas and Aaron Hayden at the heart of Carlisle's defence. They have some pace; they look reasonably confident on the ball and they are prepared to get to the ball before their opponents when that opportunity arises. But like any central defensive pairing, they need protecting. This usually means a midfield holding player or some kind of shield and here I refer you back to my previous comments on Neal and Vela. But also, a sound defence depends upon the two full backs or wing backs, whatever you want to call them.

Who'd be a full back? Back in my picking sides in the schoolyard days (we are delving into ancient history now) no-one wanted to be a full back as they were the guys at the back doing the boring defensive stuff. They had no-one to emulate when even the lads told to go in goal could pretend to be Lev Yashin or Gordon Banks. (I told you this was ancient history.)

But times change. Playing full back became an attractive proposition. My mate at college was happy to move to left back from his midfield position and he won a place in the British Colleges side. When I asked him about his positional move, he was unequivocal about how at full back you receive the ball in more space, you can look up and pick a pass and the game is in front of you. Or, when the time is right, you can make a surging run with the ball. That was a few years ago but it still makes sense. Who wouldn't like to be a Paolo Maldini, Philip Lahm or Trent Alexander Arnold? Great, when you're going forward, but defensively?

It's one of the classic football mano a mano situations. The full back wants to dominate his winger, close him down quickly and give him an early taste of the cinder track. But the full back also has other considerations as he knows his coach will want him to keep the back line straight and to follow the defensive mantra of defending narrowly i.e. be on hand to cover behind the central pairing.

I mention all this because Carlisle have conceded goals when the channels between the back four have been too easily exposed. There were the three identical goals at M.K. Dons plus the joy that Tranmere found in reaching the by-line to anguished shouts from the Paddock of "Too easy, too easy." It points to the fact that a top priority for the new management team must be the performance of the full backs.

Cameron Harper was brought from Inverness Caledonian Thistle amid great expectations, so much so that previous left wing-back Jack Armer was allowed to leave. As luck would have it, Harper then sustained a pre-season injury and has not yet made an appearance. Ben Williams, previously released from Cheltenham, was picked up and given a six-month contract in what looked very much like a stop-gap effort. But let's not hang him out to dry. He has a very good left foot and plays some telling forward balls. He is very keen to get in defensive blocks and tackles, so much so, that he tends to buy every dummy going. Even so, in the time-honoured football phrase which damns with faint praise, he can do a job for us. Or it could be more than that. His spell as a Carlisle player may well be a short one, but I hope not. With sharp concentration on his positional play and keeping things tight when they need to be, he could turn out to be a great find. Go for it, Ben, and good luck.

Likewise, Archie Davies at right back, recently recruited from Ireland, is an exciting prospect going forwards; fast, skilful, and fearless in taking on obdurate defenders. He had an attacking run against Tranmere which won insufficient acclaim, probably because of other events which transpired after the game. But he also emerged from the game with a goal to his name which is as good a way as any to win popular support, so the signs are good. But we can't overlook the difficult first half he had against Stoke when he faced a very tricky winger, or indeed, last Saturday when Omari Patrick rolled into town with his party tricks. Defending, Archie! That's a full back's first job, it's time to roll up sleeves and see to it. He's a good player and he looks ambitious enough to accomplish this important development of his game.

So that is my take on the game from four and a half thousand miles away and fifteen hours before it is due to take place. Call it prescience if you like, but I'd like to congratulate the lads on a well-earned point and applaud the new management team on their emphasis on defensive positional play and the merits of keeping it tight. Confidence can only be gained from performances such as this.

Well done lads. Now it's onwards and upwards.

Saturday 14 September. Carlisle United v Fleetwood Town. Brunton Park. EFL League 2.

I should have known better. I set off on Saturday morning with hope in my heart, genuinely believing that this would be the day on which our season was finally kickstarted into action. That feeling was reinforced by an untroubled journey north, though without the company of John Clarke, otherwise occupied in Denver, The Rockies, or some other Stateside location. The plan was to meet with Peter Scholes in the fan zone for a pint and a slightly longer conversation than we managed after the last home game.

Alas, just like the anticipated result, it was not to be. We did meet briefly, enough time to shake hands and for Peter to explain that he had understandably more important matters in hand. His dad had celebrated his eightieth birthday the day before and in celebration was to be part of the pre-match formalities. He didn't emerge from the tunnel holding Jon Mellish's hand but was part of the line-up for photographs in the centre circle, along with the captains, the match officials and the mascots for the day. He appeared to be thoroughly enjoying himself. It was a lovely case of life imitating art, as an almost identical event happens in Peter's novel "One Last Waltz".

I did get into the ground in time to see John's nephew, currently part of the youth team, keep goal in the shoot-in that forms part of the pre-match warm-up. The starting line-up featured a couple of significant changes. Josh Vela and Harrison Neal, both much heralded signings in the January transfer window, dropped to the bench. They were replaced by Dylan McGeoch, actually fit for a change, and Jon Mellish, moved into midfield from his usual position as left centre back. As at Bradford a week ago, the formation was clearly 4-3-3.

The feelgood factor didn't last for long. A couple of early surging runs from Jon Mellish boded well, but in only the 11th minute Fleetwood's Danny Mayor took advantage of a loose touch by Cameron Harper and found it all too easy to drift through the defence and finish past Harry Lewis. It was a familiar story – gaps in midfield and poor defensive positioning. Mellish crashed a shot against the post just a minute later, but just seven minutes later things got even worse. The match report on the club website describes events thus. "On 19 minutes, Ryan Coughlan doubled the Cods' advantage with a top finish following an error in midfield between Dylan McGeoch and Harrison Biggins." I'd describe it slightly differently. Following an error in midfield, Fleetwood gained possession, and the ball was played down the right to an attacker in a clearly offside position. Despite appeals from players and screams from the crowd, the assistant referee inexplicably refused to raise his flag. The offside player was free to centre and leave his striker colleague with an easy task to double the lead. To rub salt in the wound, Aaron Hayden was shown a yellow card for his perfectly reasonable protests.

Against my better instincts I'm going to return to a familiar topic – the standard of officiating in Leagues One and Two. The linesman on our side of the pitch was dire. He spent most of the game waiting for the referee to make the decision before raising his flag to indicate which team had won a throw in. I suspect that the offside non-decision is one for which the club will eventually receive an apology from the EFL. As Paul Simpson said on more than one previous occasion, such apologies are meaningless – the points have already gone. I'm not sure about the referee. He issued eight yellow cards, four to each team, in what was a far from dirty game. I could suggest that the card count implies that he struggled to control a game that was never in danger of getting out of hand. Or perhaps I should praise him for sticking to the letter of the law and applying the rules of the game unrelentingly. He did show an encouraging willingness to play the advantage rule but then award a free kick if no advantage accrued.

At 2-0 down at home after barely twenty minutes we were staring down the barrel, with potential humiliation on the horizon. Fortunately, things didn't get quite that bad. In the 41st minute a weaving run from Jordan Jones concluded with him being upended in the Fleetwood penalty area. Charlie Wyke duly dispatched the spot kick to reduce the arrears. Am I the only United fan who was beginning to think that that was the only way Wyke would get off the mark in his second spell at the club?

Things improved further in the 51st minute when an exquisite pass from McGeoch set up Wyke for a well-worked equaliser. I was pretty impressed with McGeoch's performance in this game. His starts since he arrived just over a year ago have been all too infrequent, but he slipped easily into the role of midfield anchor, recently vacated by Harrison Neal. He showed the same tenacity in the tackle, and the same willingness to make himself available for passes from colleagues.

He also brought a couple of qualities that Neal appears to lack. He was talking constantly, cajoling and organising those around him, a quality that appears to have been sadly missing for some time. He also appears to know what to do with the ball when he has it, be that a short, safe pass, or the type of defence splitting longer ball that led to this goal. Neal, for all his work rate and earnest endeavour, has a tendency to look like a rabbit caught in headlights when he wins possession. McGeoch would have been my choice as man-of-the-match, despite Wyke's brace.

The momentum was very much with Carlisle, and Luke Armstrong came close to transforming a 2-0 deficit into a 3-2 advantage. Briefly we could dare to dream of just a second win of the season. But in the 67th minute the familiar failings were all too evident. Fleetwood cut through the Carlisle midfield as if it wasn't there, the right side of the defence appeared to be AWOL, and Mayor duly restored Fleetwood's lead.

Heads dropped at this point. There appears to be a worrying lack of mental resilience in the squad at the moment. Substitutions had little effect, set pieces were squandered and too many passes went astray. There was little real prospect of an equaliser.

The stats are not good: one win and five defeats from six league games; fifteen goals conceded by a porous defence at an average of more than two a game; only six goals scored at an average of one goal a game. The announcement of a Sporting Director and Head Coach appears to be imminent. I'm not going to indulge in idle speculation about who might be appointed and their respective strengths and weaknesses. The sooner the appointments are announced the better, so that they can start to restore some confidence and shape to a capable but clearly demoralised squad.

With the room still in darkness, I could not read the time on my watch, which lay on the bedside table. It felt as though it was late, our Mile-High City lifestyle of traipsing round museums and bookshops in the heat was taking its toll. It was the heavy curtains which darkened the room and beside me, Julie, my wife was still asleep so I decided to slip out of bed and take some bearings for the day.

The gap in the curtain revealed evidence of life in Saturday morning Denver. Six flights down at sidewalk level, a miniature jogger resolutely jogged, and two walkers were taking their chance with a pedestrian crossing. Cars were fewer than usual on a Saturday morning, but they milled around the lights: the illuminated white walking man symbol, the prohibitive red hand signal with the audible injunction to Wait! And the countdown for those daring to cross, you have these many seconds left to live. Above and all around, the giant blocks of concrete and glass were ready to throw their brutalist shadows, while in the distance over to the western skyline, wisps of cloud shimmied over the peaks of the Flat Iron Mountains. Everything presaged another day of temperatures climbing towards 30 degrees and beyond.

Following the ding from my phone came the reminder that four and a half thousand miles away with a seven-hour time difference, Carlisle United were beginning their pre-match warm up. I could picture it all, the running exercises, the stretching, the small-sided games

and then the applause for players and staff as they
retreated up the tunnel to the dressing room

What was less easy to picture was how the scene
would be ninety minutes plus time added on for injury
later. My confident predictions for the Bradford game
had been way off the mark largely because I allow heart
to rule head. The flame of optimism still flickers even if
it is not a blazing flare. Come on you Blues! It is not too
late for a New Manager Bounce, albeit temporary, to
take place, and of course, it's a home game. Fortress
Brunton Park. It was always a football truism that
teams don't like to play at Carlisle, though as the great
man sang, "Things Have Changed."

I checked the team line-ups for some kind of
indication of how things would be. Lewis in goal and
Davies and Harper at full-back, fair enough, while
central defensive duties would be shared by Lavelle and
Hayden. I guessed that Terrel Thomas was injured but I
had to accept that I didn't know for certain as there was
no direct line of communication from Brunton Park to
my current location.

Midfield presented a more interesting picture. I had
been singing the praises of Neal and Vela against
Barrow, still our only league win of the season, and the
line-up showed them both starting on the bench. This
could only be because better players had become
available for these slots, but again, I couldn't comment
as I needed to have more evidence before my eyes. I did
know that the previous season we had been crying out
for a midfield player with the composure to pick the
right pass as play progressed towards the opposite
penalty area, to instigate an intricate move, or heaven
forbid, to take someone on. Let's frighten some

defenders. (Note from my inner consciousness, you're looking for a Bridges or Beardsley, aren't you?)

I turned to the BBC Sport website before heading down for breakfast to learn that we had in fact already conceded a goal. It took Bradford six minutes to score against us and now it had taken Fleetwood a whole ten minutes. Was this meant to represent some kind of improvement? And then right before my eyes, the figures changed, and the deficit doubled. Insert your own swear word of choice here and then repeat it because after some intermittent connection, the link disappeared altogether. A blessing you might think, but no. I'd learned that we'd got back on level terms thanks to a Charlie Wyke double. He'd broken his duck and now surely the goal fest would begin. Furthermore, the stats had been good, the momentum must have been with us and victory within our grasp. Cue that old saying about hope being the killer.

Truth was, I didn't know what the hell was happening, and I didn't find out until technology reasserted itself and the final scores presented themselves. Oh, the agony of that swoop from joy to despair. Carlisle 2, I read, the joy of holding on for a point, Fleetwood 3. The despair of realising that they'd let that point slip. Another defeat at the Fortress. Pick the bones out of that.

It's not easy, in fact it's highly frustrating to attempt any kind of objective analysis with so little information to hand. A win today with results elsewhere going our way could have seen us climb seven places in the league. A draw would have sent out a message that we are well on the way to turning a corner. But we lost.

Highlights on YouTube later showed that we conceded three soft goals but Jordan Jones did win a *penalty after dribbling into the box and I refer you to my earlier point about Beardsley and Bridges, while Dylan McGeouch played a superb ball across a retreating defence for Wyke to score his second. The Carlisle United website report would later report that the Fleetwood winner came against the run of play but that, my friends, is clutching at straws, especially when you're miles away from home and becoming increasingly tetchy in the rising heat.*

Who's next? Swindon are next, the team that scored four goals without reply yesterday while Carlisle were toiling against Fleetwood. Well, bring them on. This is where our season starts. I'm blowing fiercely on that flickering flame of optimism even though social media speculation about the identity of our new manager has raised the name of Joey Barton.

God help us!

Saturday 21 September. Swindon Town v Carlisle United. The County Ground. EFL League 2.

At last, another win, and an away one at that. Respect to the 483 United fans who made the long journey to Swindon. But before I get onto the significance of today's result, there is the odd preliminary matter that needs addressing first.

Firstly, there's the relatively trivial matter of the appointment of a new Head Coach, one Mike Williamson. My first reaction was one of sympathy for the man, for having to share his surname with the worst Education Secretary in living memory. To be honest, I know little about him other than what I've read since his appointment. He apparently did a good job in non-league at Gateshead, and certainly transformed MK Dons' fortunes last season. He's relatively young and reportedly favours an attractive and attacking brand of football. He also has past associations with a handful of Carlisle players, most notably Jon Mellish and Luke Armstrong. I hope he's the man to bring out the considerable best from Luke Armstrong. Let's reflect on the significance of his appointment. Apparently, MK Dons did not want to lose him, but when United stated that they were willing to meet the release clause in his contract, and Williamson stated an interest in the Carlisle job, they had no choice. That makes a strong statement about Carlisle's increased bargaining power under the new ownership. It's a far cry from the era, not so many years ago, when we lost Charlie Wyke to a wealthier club like Bradford because they were the ones who could afford to meet a release clause.

Not only have we prised Williamson away from MK Dons, but he's also brought with him the three senior members of his coaching staff, who are obviously well-versed in his methods of working, and will know precisely what their individual roles will be. This highlights the wisdom of Tom Piatak in dismissing the entire senior coaching team in addition to Simmo. Williamson starts with a clean sheet, not having to inherit the baggage and senior staff of a previous regime. It must make it easier for him to hit the ground running. To take him and his senior coaching team also deals a satisfying blow to Franchise United.

The Wakefield Blues have also suffered major losses this week, though no release clauses were activated. John may have returned from the States, but yesterday

Ben departed for Cardiff University, and today Lisa and I took Adam to begin his three years studying Economics at Nottingham University. Wakefield Blues super sub Sam Hardy is already well settled in at Northumbria University. That gives me the perfect opportunity to recite the apocryphal story about Northumbria University. When polytechnics were upgraded to university status, the original plan was for Newcastle Polytechnic (where I once saw Dire Straits live as the support act to Talking Heads) to be rebranded as the Central University of Newcastle-upon-Tyne, until graphic designers started playing around with letterheads and initialisms. The upshot is that, until mid-December, only John and I will be making the regular trip to Brunton Park, as well as any accessible away games. I think it's fair to say that Adam will join us when we play Notts County away (and likewise for Walsall, Crewe and Port Vale?), but I'm not sure we'll be making the long trek to South Wales to join Ben when we play at Newport County.

And so to the game itself. I was pleased to see Williamson give Luke Armstrong his first start of the season, and equally pleased to read his fulsome praise of him in his post-match interview. I am unwavering in my belief that Armstrong was an excellent signing, and that we have yet to see the best of him at Brunton Park. I'm a big fan of Paul Simpson, but one of his significant failings was that having signed Armstrong, he failed to adjust the team's formation and style of play to bring out his strengths. I'm sure he'll be much more effective playing off, and slightly behind, a conventional target man like Charlie Wyke, a role he appeared to occupy in this game, rather than being the target man himself.

I'm not sure that a back three of Lavelle, Mellish and Barclay is a defence on which a belated promotion campaign can be built, but with recent signings Hayden and Thomas both injured, they certainly did the business yesterday. I liked the change of formation to 3-4-3, with Davies and Harper pushed forward as wide midfielders, rather than wing backs, though obviously they had to do their share of defensive duties. Both have plenty to offer going forward.

My engagement with the game itself was fairly limited. We were on the way home from Nottingham by the time it kicked off, and as I was driving my information was confined to updates on Radio Five Live's coverage. I was delighted when Mark Chapman announced that Carlisle had taken the lead through Sam Lavelle, but subsequently mystified as Lisa, who had the game pinned on her phone, kept informing me of the time added on at the end of the first half, which eventually amounted to a scarcely credible eleven minutes. It transpired that the delay was due to an injury to one of the assistant referees. It's a pity that it couldn't have happened to the muppet who ran the line on our side of the pitch at Brunton Park a week earlier. We were back home by the time Armstrong settled the result with the second goal.From most accounts it wasn't a pretty performance, but the result was all that mattered on this occasion. It was slightly reminiscent of Simmo's first game back in charge, when an early Omari Patrick goal at Leyton Orient was followed by a doughty defensive performance that secured a much-needed win and ignited that remarkable charge to safety. I can look forward to next week's game at home to Grimsby with a little more confidence.

At quarter to four on a September morning the heat of the previous day has not entirely dissipated and we stand in our shirt sleeves outside our Denver hotel with our various pieces of luggage waiting for the airport shuttle. We speak with lowered voices possibly out of deference to the dormant city or, more likely, in dread anticipation of the journey before us. A taxi shuttle to the airport, a four-hour flight to J.F.K. New York and then a six hour wait for our seven-hour onward flight to Manchester. We do not know at this stage that we will be delayed for an additional hour and a half at J.F.K. until a suitable plane becomes available. Our journey home will take us eighteen hours during which time we will regain the seven hours by which Denver trails behind the U.K. Some serious jet-lag beckons.

Getting any worthwhile sleep on the overnight flight from J.F.K. to Manchester is little more than optimistic hope. Over ten years now of travelling to see our son at his American address has allowed me to try several strategies to mitigate the effects of jet-lag. None of them work. Currently, I put my faith in the following plan: watch two films in succession and then in the darkened cabin read for a while before putting out the personal reading light and see if I can gain any precious shut-eye. There is no evidence for saying that this plan is better than any other and I know that my faith will be misplaced as another night of elusive sleep beckons. However, plenty of time will become available to chew over the fact that, all being well, as we land Carlisle United, under a newly appointed Coach, will be twenty-four hours away from playing their next fixture of the 2024/25 season and I will be in the same country. We are due to land in Manchester on the Friday morning and on the following day Carlisle are due to play Swindon away. Swindon! I might as well be half a continent and a full ocean away as there is no chance that I will be able to make if to Wiltshire and the County Ground. I have to content myself on the long sleepless journey by working through all of the connections between Carlisle United and Swindon. How often have their respective paths crossed and is there any point in digging through the entrails in this way?

Dredging into my earliest memories as a Carlisle supporter, I recall the figure of Stan Harland. Whereas Hugh McIlmoyle was the focus for my hero worship and Eric Welsh, an international footballer for Northern Ireland when George Best was unavailable, provided some speedy wing play glamour, Stan Harland was solid. A no nonsense half-back, you could put your faith in Stan, and whereas I was prone to idolise other players, I admired Stan Harland. The qualities I admired in him were probably those which persuaded Swindon to buy him from Carlisle and install him as captain. It was in this role that he led Swindon out at Wembley to beat Arsenal in the old League Cup in 1969.

A player making a move in the opposite direction seventeen years later was goalkeeper Scott Endersby. He made 52 appearances for the club including one during a vital game against Sheffield United at Brunton Park. Carlisle needed points to stay up while Sheffield had a sniff of promotion in their nostrils. The stakes were high. Unaffected by this, Endersby made a number of outstanding saves to ensure that Carlisle kept a clean sheet and an Ian Bishop goal secured a victory. It was all to no avail though as Carlisle ultimately were unable to avoid the drop. Even so, it is a game that remains in the memory for the tension, the battling rearguard action from Carlisle and those great saves. Whenever the discussion about Carlisle's greatest keepers arises, I am often surprised that the name of Scott Endersby does not crop up more often. I can only assume that it is because of those relatively few appearances and also the date. That 1987 relegation from the old Third Division marked the beginning of a terrible slump in Carlisle's fortunes, one that the fans are probably inclined to try and forget.

Another goalkeeper taken on loan from Swindon in 1999 made something of a name for himself. He made a mere three appearances for the club but in the last of those appearances he managed to score an injury-time winning goal to preserve Carlisle's league status. His name eludes me now but I know that our glass conservatory is named after him.

Moving on, John Gorman was a classy left-back. He made 229 appearances for Carlisle and was part of the famous "Season in the Sun" First Division team. Gorman, Balderstone, Bowles, Hatton and Tommy Craig. What riches! At various times, Carlisle have fielded some left-footed players who have been a joy to watch. John Gorman is included in that list on merit as a tenacious defender and a very creative attacker. Forgive me if I'm fantasising here, but I'm sure he was doing Cruyff turns before Cruyff. The Swindon connection is that after working as Glenn Hoddle's assistant manager, Gorman was manager of Swindon in his own right at Premier League level. To get a measure of the man, readers could do worse than get hold of a copy of John Gorman's autobiography, Gory Tales: The

Autobiography of John Gorman where his dignity and integrity emerges.

Of course, I'm sifting through all of these loose connections between Swindon and Carlisle and leaving the "biggie" until the end. The events of Saturday 19th February, 2022 had huge implications for Carlisle United which in some estimations very nearly heralded the demise of the club. On that fateful Saturday, Swindon were in town and they brought with them a former player, Harry McKirdy, a fast winger with shedloads of potential and an instinct for self-destruction which was similarly large. He had the knack of winding up his own fans and was always unable to ignore the slightest level of goading usually opting for some kind of immature response. When he scored in this fixture the temptation to "celebrate" in front of the home fans was just too great and he indulged himself with a complete lack of class. Much more worryingly, Swindon scored two more second half goals in quick succession and the eventual three-nil defeat was regarded as a case of getting off lightly for Carlisle. Not a result or a performance to be easily dismissed as it was only halfway through February, still plenty of football to be played as they say, but the general consensus among the fans with Carlisle rooted in the bottom two, was that the club was doomed. Survive the threat of relegation? Many fans couldn't even envisage winning another point that season. Not unless a miracle occurred.

We're talking Carlisle here though, a place not unknown to miracles. Cutting a long story short, four days later the Manager, Keith Millen was dismissed, as was David Holdsworth, the Director of Football. There was no time for speculation about the identity of the *new manager because within minutes a name was announced. Step forward Super Paul Simpson who had already performed a miracle by getting Carlisle promoted back into the Football League at the first attempt in 2005 and he would now perform a second (I told you I was cutting a long story short) by keeping Carlisle up after the Swindon debacle. Heroic status was duly placed upon Simpson but Harry McKirdy shouldn't be overlooked. An unexpected saviour, his anti-hero status should be blessed by Carlisle fans.*

But as you may have noticed, I digress. I was only picking out loose connections between Swindon and Carlisle, a gentle pastime as a fixture looms, and an aid to getting some valuable sleep on a fully booked plane making its way across the Atlantic. I don't read any significance into these past connections, as the cliché goes, it's eleven versus eleven as soon as you cross the white line and face up to the serious business of winning three points. I'd done my damnedest to find out as much information about the forthcoming game but it had been scant. Swindon had scored four goals without conceding any in their last game, that I knew. They also had an ex-Carlisle player in their ranks in Danny Butterworth who had made the move south just as the transfer window was closing. God knows, we are very familiar with the law of returning players. Surely not!

Against all of this, Carlisle finally had in their favour the possibility of a New Manager Bounce effect. Yes, appointed on Thursday, Mike Williamson had two days to galvanise his new squad of players and begin his own brand of miracle working. I was able to dig up an interview on YouTube which showed him to be a measured kind of chap, not given to hyperbole and very aware of the importance of developing an ethos amongst the players. I have to say, in a phrase I'm fond of but I haven't the foggiest what it actually means, I like the cut of his jib.

I've never felt more remote from a game, I've always maintained the notion that my hands in pocket, silent observational stance on the terrace is highly influential – the players know I'm watching – but not now. There's nothing I can do, it's over to you Mr Williamson and as one of his predecessors, Bill Shankly is alleged to have said, "May the best team win, so long as it's Carlisle."

Saturday 28 September. Carlisle United v Grimsby Town. Brunton Park. EFL League 2.

I was about to say that I'm lost for words after this game, but that would be a contradiction in terms, because it's precisely words that I'm going to have to rely on to make sense of this curate's egg of a performance.

With Adam and Ben departed to Nottingham and Cardiff University respectively, and John back on British soil but with a prior commitment to Dearne Arts Festival on Saturday, the Wakefield Blues were drastically depleted. It looked like I was going to be Billy-No-Mates for this one. Even a message to Peter Scholes drew a blank. He wouldn't be available for a pre-match meet-up because he had a prior commitment to a holiday in Tunisia. Fortunately, the generous loan of John's season ticket and a quick interchange of messages with Jason in Wetherby meant that I did finally have company for the trip, albeit the company of a Leeds United supporter.

The day dawned bright but cold, with rain forecast for Carlisle between two and three o'clock. I therefore travelled with a wealth of warm and waterproof clothing, determined to be prepared for anything the elements might throw at us. By the time we broke our journey at Scotch Corner it had warmed up considerably, and our journey over Stainmore and into the Eden Valley was bathed in bright sunshine. By the time we approached Penrith and joined the M6 the sky had clouded over and the promised rain arrived as we approached Carlisle though it was only light drizzle. Having parked, I decided that I could do with an extra layer for warmth, but that my leather jacket and United baseball cap would be sufficient protection from any light rain. We'd arrived in plenty of time, and it proved to be a good job we had. When we got to the ground we entered the fan zone for a pre-match pint, and within ten minutes of buying our drinks the light drizzle had become a steady downpour, sufficiently heavy for me to walk back to the car and undergo a complete change of outerwear. Ironically, by the time I'd walked to the ground for a second time and rejoined Jason, the rain had stopped, there was blue sky a-plenty and the sun was out again.

There was considerable anticipation ahead of the game, for Carlisle supporters at least, if not for Jason. With the exception of the 470 who made the long trip (most of them are long from Carlisle!) this would be the first time we would see the team play under the direction of the new coaching team. Would there be any changes in selection? Would there be a different formation? Would there be a significant alteration in the style of play? The answer to all three questions was yes.

Jon Mellish was dropped to the bench, the first time in about three years that he hadn't started a game when available. Dylan McGeoch was also absent, through injury. Josh Vela and Dominic Sadi were the replacements. The 3-4-3 formation at Swindon had become 4-4-2, on paper at least.

The final question, about the style of play, was the one that was answered with the most emphatic yes. The first half was the best forty-five minutes of football I have seen from a Carlisle team in quite a long time. The most obvious change in style was the emphasis on playing out from the back. I don't think that Sam Lavelle and Ben Barclay would be most supporters' first choice central-defensive partnership, but they looked well up to the job in those forty-five minutes. They looked composed on the ball, and not afraid to take time to find the right pass, rather than hoof the ball aimlessly forward. Lavelle in particular was a revelation. I've never been one of his greatest fans, as I have strong reservations about his positional play, but he was immense in the first half. He was dominant in the air, calm in possession, and scored the opening goal from a corner, with a superbly timed run and glancing header.

The full backs were excellent going forward, eager to take on and beat defenders. Vela and Biggins were tenacious in midfield, breaking up Grimsby possession and moving forward. Jordan Jones was excellent, running at defenders and usually beating them before supplying Armstrong and Wyke. Most importantly, United looked like a team that had rediscovered the art of passing to a teammate. The ball was largely played along the ground, which immediately plays to Luke Armstrong's strengths. And on the odd occasions when the ball went high or long, Charlie Wyke did his best job yet as target man, flicking headers on or controlling the ball before supplying a colleague, despite the inevitable holding and pushing. It was a patient, though quickly executed passing movement that left Dominic Sadi with an easy task to score Carlisle's second goal, his first in senior football.

Before I start to sound too euphoric, I should mention that Grimsby scored an equaliser between the two Carlisle goals. They also lost their goalkeeper who was injured in the process of the first goal being scored. It quickly became evident that the injury was serious, and it led to a significant delay. It was pleasing that as he was stretchered off there was generous applause from all sections of the ground. I didn't discover until the following day that his replacement was only sixteen years old and was making his EFL debut in unexpected circumstances. We really should have tested him more in the second half. The club website match report described the goal as coming from a defence-splitting pass. I'd qualify this by suggesting that the pass was aided by the familiar failings of gaps in midfield and poor defensive positioning. It didn't seem to matter too much at the time, because the lead was quickly restored and Carlisle were so dominant. Even my younger daughter Imogen, whose interest in football usually ranges between non-existent and 0%, and who was shopping with her mum in Leeds at the time, had checked the match stats at half-time and informed me when I got home that Carlisle had utterly dominated the first half, no matter which metric you applied – possession, passes completed, corners won, chances created , shots on target.

All of which makes it even more difficult to explain the decline that occurred in the second half. Grimsby switched from zonal marking to 1-to-1 marking and Carlisle failed to respond accordingly. The momentum of the first half disappeared, as the ball was given away far too easily in midfield and the controlled passing of the first half vanished. The full backs proved less effective in their defensive duties than they had in the first half and were much less effective going forward. Too many times, Grimsby players were able to get to the byline and deliver a cross or beat another defender and threaten from a different angle. Both the Grimsby equaliser and winner came from such moves. It should highlight to Mike Williamson where his priorities lie, in solidifying the defence and defensive midfield. It was slightly concerning that no substitutions were made until after the Grimsby equaliser, and that they seemed to be defensive changes, designed to secure a point rather than secure a winner. The change in the balance of the game was evident much earlier. And in the dying minutes, after Grimsby had scored their winning goal, the defence still seemed preoccupied with the coach's mantra of playing it out from the back, rather than getting the ball forward quickly because time was running out.

The officiating was predictably poor. As soon as the second minute the referee waved away appeals for a blatant foul on Charlie Wyke in the Grimsby penalty area. Who knows how the rest of the game might have developed if we'd taken the lead so early. And in the second half the assistant referee on our side failed to flag for an obvious offside right in front of us. It was sadly reminiscent of a similar failure in the last home game which led to a Fleetwood goal. On this occasion Harry Lewis pulled off an excellent save, but games can turn on such crucial moments.

The attendance was good, about 7,500, of which about 7,000 were home supporters, but we'll have to start picking up points soon if that level of support is to be maintained at the lower end of League 2. The boos at the final whistle were in marked contrast to the applause that greeted the first half performance.

As we drove home, we passed a farmstead just before Warcop on the A66, where four or five police vehicles were in attendance. It later transpired that an eight-year-old boy had suffered gunshot wounds to the face and head from which he later died. It put the events of the afternoon into sober perspective.

The worst of the jet-lag has kicked from the system and the body clock has recovered from the debilitating effects of jumping around global time zones. In addition, leaping out of bed and sweeping back the curtains reveals a bright blue morning. A perfect omen.

Okay, it's not a Colorado picture perfect blue sky, it's a Wakefield watery blue and that's the point. It's home, Clarke Towers, chez moi. It's Saturday morning and Carlisle United are also due to be at home and I will no longer have to speculate or pontificate from afar. My sketchy season so far of played six, watched two, can begin to be rectified and my comments on games will have greater authority bestowed upon them by virtue of actually having been there to see the game.

So, bring it on. Carlisle versus Grimsby as Carlisle continue to herald a new era of flowing, attractive football with Mike Williamson at the helm. One game in and he is already three points to the good thanks to a magnificent win at Swindon seven days earlier.

At this point, eagle-eyed readers may wish to point out that the win at Swindon may have been hard-earned and in some respects, it was fortuitous, but it may not have merited my use of the word magnificent. In which case, I refer you back to the verbs "leaping" and "sweeping" in my first paragraph, also hyperbolic, and I must confess that it is many years now since I leapt out of bed and swept back the curtains, if I ever did so at all. No, what we are about here is the presentation of a picture, one which conveys anticipation and unrestrained joy. We can use U2 on the soundtrack for it is indeed a Beautiful Day to travel the distance to Carlisle, to drink in the atmosphere in the Fan Zone and then to take up a place in the Paddock to watch the Blues begin the steady accumulation of points to take them to a much higher, rightful place in the league. A day when Grimsby will be the fall guys, I think, pitching up at Carlisle when the lads, released from recent uncertainty, will be ready to put on a show.

There is only one small flaw in this Koh-I-Noor of a plan and that is that I can't go to the game.

There it is in bold black and white. On a beautiful late-September day, ideal for both travelling and watching football, I am not available because twelve months ago, before there had been any thought of buying a 2024/25 season ticket, I manned a stall at the Dearne Community Arts Festival humbly selling a few books and engaging unwary passers-by in interactive poetry exercises. Yes, the p-word – poetry which is usually best not mentioned at all as it seems to be an instant deterrent, like Jehovah's Witnesses in the town centre asking you if you would like to talk about Jesus. But my proselytising must not have been in vain as I was offered a return visit twelve months hence, an offer I duly accepted, not thinking for a minute, "Oh no! That might be the day when Carlisle are due to play Grimsby!"

Eyebrows might be raised at this point, but I ought to point out that I missed Carlisle's most recent Wembley appearance, the play-off final against Stockport because I had a prior engagement at a poetry event. And those of the raised brows might have a sense of bewilderment that I should make such decisions, but there are others, I know, who will sympathise because of my tragic dilemma which has reached classical proportions: he could have been a truly great commentator on lower league football but for his tragic flaw – his penchant for poetry.

So it was, I consigned myself to an afternoon of sneaked glances at my phone while neglecting my duties of promoting creative writing which I do enjoy, and self-promotion and bookselling at which I am truly awful. But fear not, those sneaked glances first of all revealed that owing to injury, Dylan McGeouch would not be playing, which was a shame as his recent defence splitting pass still lingers in the memory, and also that Jon Mellish would be starting on the bench. This second fact being much more worthy of discussion. Is it possible to read too much into this or has Mellish, who has talismanic status, reached a point where his star will begin to wane? If there is to be a new era of flowing, attractive football, does he have the necessary finesse to hold a place in the side?

It is a thinking point which doesn't sustain as a later discreet glance at the phone confirms that Carlisle are one nil up after a Sam Lavelle header found the net after only twelve minutes. An early goal and match statistics that suggest everything is going to be okay – it is the new era after all, and one hundred plus miles away from the action in a South Yorkshire new-build academy, I can concentrate on the important matters to hand like asking children, "If this lion could speak, what would it say?"

That Grimsby equalise is of little concern because with ten minutes to go to half time Carlisle are leading thanks to a Dominic Sadi right-footed shot into the roof of the net. Saturday afternoons should always be this easy.

Hubris though is an element in tragedy which features well before Shakespeare started putting his quill to the form. My confidence in the fact that we had victory in the bag was a case of me defying the football gods. My next surreptitious look at my phone was timed to take place well after the final whistle would have blown. It was planned to confirm a victory; nine league points for Carlisle now and a hefty jump up the table to boot. But the awful truth was revealed: two late goals for Messrs Cass and Rodgers meant that the points would be going elsewhere. Nemesis had arrived in the form of Grimsby Town.

It's not a new sensation, a Sunday morning sifting through the ashes looking for some form of consolation. On-line I found a few reports and a nine-minute video of highlights from the game from which the following points are made:

- *Carlisle played well in the first half, refreshingly fluent after much which has been presented for the fans over a lengthy period now.*

- *Harry Lewis was reported to have made a fine one on one save but the video also revealed that there were two other saves of note from the Carlisle keeper.*
- *Insufficient credit was given to Grimsby for their first equaliser where a player created some space for himself in a tight situation on his own defensive touchline before making a break with the ball and releasing a fine pass towards two fast running forwards who were creating havoc. One of these players produced the accomplished finish.*
- *The Grimsby keeper received a sporting round of applause as he was stretchered off. This shouldn't need saying but that is how it should be. The Carlisle crowd, the Paddock cognoscenti, have always had a reputation for fairness and sportsmanship. That shouldn't be traded for the boorishness which has been present on some recent occasions.*
- *When all is said and done, Carlisle lost two goals in the final ten minutes. When this happens, whatever level you are playing at, fingers are pointed and always the question in the air is, are you fit enough? The answer can be uncomfortable.*

So that is that, then. Still three points and still third bottom and a long time before anything can be done about this. All of three days in fact when Notts County, currently sitting in fourth place are the visitors. Well, bring it on.

Now, where have I heard that before?

Chapter 4
CLUTCHING AT STRAWS

Tuesday 1 October. Carlisle United v Notts County. Brunton Park. EFL League 2.

I'm getting a little weary of writing yet another account of yet another dispiriting defeat. I know Mike Williamson has only had three games in charge, and it's going to take considerably longer than that to place his stamp on the team and turn things round, but after the purgatory of last season, I yearn for even a short spell of sustained success.

I should start by admitting that I wasn't actually at the game. I hadn't realised until Sunday that the next home match followed so quickly and wasn't sure that I fancied a second drive from Wakefield to Carlisle and back in four days. The fact that Lisa had a parents evening at school the same evening clinched my decision not to travel. John decided that he didn't fancy "flying solo" so, for the first time this season, a United home game kicked off without any of the Wakefield Blues in attendance (I don't include the discredited EFL Trophy).

However, I was still able to watch the game. The EFL's new deal with Sky, and my existing subscription to Sky Sports package, meant that I was able to access the match at no extra expense, unlike the previous deal with i-Follow. It did mean that I was deprived of the commentary and comments of James Philips and Chris

Lumsdon with their Radio Cumbria feed, though the Scottish commentator did a decent job and was noticeably less partial!

The telly may have been on, but I didn't see a great deal of the first half because I was in the kitchen preparing meals. That meant that I missed both Notts County goals, but the cries of, "Oh, for fuck's sake" each time I popped my head round the lounge door and saw another goal had been conceded quickly alerted Lisa and Imogen to how things were going.

The starting line-up featured two changes from Saturday. Terrell Thomas replaced Ben Barclay in defence, and Jon Mellish returned in place of Charlie Wyke, who dropped to the bench. The game appeared to be pretty much a mirror image of Saturday's game. This time it was the first half that was dire, while the second half saw significant, but insufficient, improvement. The commentator was spot on when he said that Notts County toyed with Carlisle for much of the first hour.

The first goal was Route One football at its most basic: a massive kick from the goalkeeper, Terrell Thomas caught on his heels and the County striker finished clinically. It shouldn't be that easy. The second goal was a bit more considered in the build-up but was significantly aided by a defence that merely reacted to situations rather than anticipating them.

The final half-hour of the game was dominated by Carlisle, but with no end product. Some of the match stats are telling, but deceptive. Carlisle had twenty-one shots compared to County's seven. Seven of Carlisle's shots were on target and only three of County's were. Carlisle won fourteen corners compared to County's three. Yet it was County who departed with a comfortable 2-0 victory and three points.

I'm not going to join the torrent of abuse of the team and individual players that is currently prevalent on social media. I believe that many of the squad are the equal, if not better, than the team that won promotion a couple of seasons ago. But a losing mentality is far too strongly embedded in the club. Heads drop far too quickly, and the team seems to be incapable of getting back into a game once it goes behind. I think the problem is psychological rather than one of skill or ability. A strike force of Charlie Wyke and Luke Armstrong should be terrorising League Two defences. We'd have dreamed of such an attack just a year ago. What the team needs is someone who can break the losing mentality, restore self-confidence, and find a formation and style of play that brings the best out of the players we have at our disposal. I fervently hope that Mike Williamson and his rapidly expanding team of coaches are the people who can do that.

The attendance was down by almost 2,000 on Saturday's figure. Time will tell whether that fall is due to an evening fixture in early October, or growing disillusionment amongst the core support which has hitherto remained solid in some testing times.

When the gods of football wish to punish us, they make an attractive fixture imminent. After missing three games during my visit to the States, including the notable victory at Swindon, and missing an additional match due to a commitment made twelve months earlier, now the gods were putting in prospect a night match against Notts County. An attractive night match as this will be a good game surely, with County whose start to the season has seen them rise to fourth place in the table against Carlisle United on the brink of their brave new world. No more speculating from afar for me as this will be the real thing. Get down to the ground and witness firsthand the developing understanding between the players and the new philosophy taking hold. County should be wary as they may be among the first to take away the message that Carlisle is no place to be on a Tuesday night. It's a long uncomfortable journey to take home with your tail between your legs. And thus, when the gods wish to punish us, they load the scales marked hope very heavily.

Following that, to mix the classical allusions with the idiomatic, the gods are prone to whip the rug from under your feet. I hope I haven't foreshadowed this too heavily but attractive fixture or not, in the end I wasn't able to attend. For one reason or another the planned trip fell through. Well, it had rained very heavily all day on Monday and Tuesday morning wasn't much better. Although the rain eased on Tuesday afternoon in Wakefield, that was absolutely no guarantee that a drive over Stainmore would be a pleasant one. I was rationalising this turn of events, seeking some comfort from the new situation. I don't have Sky and I didn't feel inclined to chase up a radio commentary. I would divert my attention elsewhere and pick up the score when the battle was lost and won. I would also make a resolution to stop littering my writing with weak quotes from Macbeth.

As things turned out, I was able to log on to an on-line short story writing course which did in fact lead me to a super quote from the American writer, Frankie

*McMillan and her story Coming Towards Her, a
Thoroughly Decent Man off Bumble:*

*"She thought if they met, something terrible
would cross her face, some arctic flare in her eye."*

*A brilliant metaphor; trying to keep a normal face but
betraying the fact that all is not well by the "arctic flare"
in her eye. This may be a further digression on my part
but it did lead me to think about the situation at Carlisle
after huge investment, massive player recruitment and
a new coaching team installed after the crucial decision
to sack a World Cup winning manager. Are the new
arrangements beginning to bed in, or are optimism and
patience becoming redundant? Eight games in and a
mere six points gained. All is well, is it? Or is the look in
anyone's eye being betrayed by an arctic flare?*

*Surely not. I decided to ignore these thoughts and
continue to sail in the good ship Optimism keeping
myself fully occupied in pursuit of Hemingway's "one
true sentence." I would check out the score when it
would be a done deal.*

*When the gods wish to punish us, they build up hope
and anticipation and then hand out a two-nil defeat at
home. They also load the match stats in our favour:
possession, shots on target, corners etc making it look
like we gave the opposition a good game before going
under but watching highlights footage later and casting
a wary eye over social media responses it turns out that
this was not the case. Apparently, Notts County bossed
it, taking two first-half chances clinically and then
protecting their lead. Their first goal came from what
refined football commentators might call a "massive*

welly" down the middle, the sort of goal my college team used to concede quite regularly, while the second was from a cut back from the dead ball line, something of a regular sight this season.

More despair then. Well not quite. Carlisle had sustained spells of creating pressure forcing Notts County to defend. This may have been the result of huff and puff on Carlisle's part but a more generous interpretation would be that the team was showing fight and not just meekly falling to another defeat. Also, in a blink and you'll miss it moment in the second half, Carlisle altered their corner routine. For corners from the right-hand side, they had been depending on in-swinging crosses into the box, but with this variation they played it short and instigated a sharp passing move towards the corner of the penalty area which almost resulted in a shooting opportunity. Unlucky, yes, a planned move doesn't quite pay off. And that's what it was as eagle-eyed viewers will have spotted that this was almost a carbon copy of the move which Tranmere used for Omari Patrick's second goal against Carlisle earlier in the season, the significance being that work on the training ground is taking place and there isn't just a blind acceptance of continual defeats. Talented players have been recruited, and they are being drilled so put away any thoughts of lighting flares. Such thoughts fuel optimism which is, of course, just what the football gods desire before they make their next play.

Even so, it is time to check on the fixture list and take a bearing. Who's next? It turns out to be Colchester, 195 miles away from Wakefield followed by Wimbledon which remarkably is 196 miles from Wakefield and it's time to take stock.

Saturday 5 October. Colchester United v Carlisle United. Colchester Community Stadium. EFL League 2.

Well, at least I don't have another dispiriting defeat to reflect upon.

The distance to Colchester meant that in-person attendance at this fixture was never a possibility, but all credit to the 350 or so who made the even longer journey from Carlisle and made up about 10% of the overall attendance. The Premier League embargo on live football at three o'clock on a Saturday afternoon meant that I was unable to watch the game on Sky Sports Plus. It seems that we can't risk live football on TV affecting match attendances when Premier League teams, with their untold millions, are playing, but when they're not, during international breaks, it's perfectly acceptable to risk reducing crowds at much smaller, cash-strapped clubs. So, I was reduced to pinning the score on my phone and taking frequent glances at it. Consequently, this post is largely based on match reports and post-match interviews.

Even so, I'm not sure how much there is that one can write about a goalless draw one didn't attend. The match stats for the first half suggest that Carlisle bossed that part of the game, dominating possession, completing significantly more passes, winning more corners and having more shots. The figures at the final whistle were less marked, but Carlisle still had 56% possession over the game as a whole and made almost a hundred more passes. All of which serves to highlight just how misleading statistics can be, as United came away from the game with no goals and a measly point to show for this apparent dominance.

The issue of statistics and data emphasises a clear line in the sand between the previous coaching regime and the current one. Paul Simpson was quite happy to concede a majority of possession when it was in unthreatening defensive and midfield areas. His focus was on Carlisle making effective use of the possession they did have. This approach was seen to best effect in the 2022-23 promotion campaign, when United frequently lost the stats contest but came away with the points. Mike Williamson favours a possession-based style of play, and is obviously big on data, with plenty of talk of expected goals and the like in his interviews. Adam has patiently tried to explain expected goals to me – I nod knowingly and still don't really get it. I always expect goals when I watch Carlisle, but they don't always materialise.

The match reports all indicate that Harry Lewis made some outstanding saves and has received deserved praise on United Facebook groups. That's good to hear, given some of the intemperate criticism he's received on social media. It's not his fault that for most of his time at the club he's been behind a defence with more holes than a colander. Talking of intemperate criticism, I've seen both Josh Vela and Luke Armstrong described in recent weeks as "running around like headless chickens". I take issue. Both were successful at their previous clubs and didn't suddenly become bad players on signing for Carlisle. Players have to adapt their play to the pattern and style of the team they play for; I have no argument with that. Similarly, while it's good for coaches to have a clear philosophy and style of play, it's their responsibility to make the most effective use of the playing resources at their disposal. Simpson failed to do that in the case of these two, so let's hope Williamson is more successful in that respect.

The injury list is an ongoing and growing concern. Not a week seems to pass without at least one new name being added to the list of walking wounded, whether for the short or longer term. We could field a damn good team from those currently unavailable. It's not as if this is a new phenomenon. This is the third successive season in which injuries have played a major part. Exactly what has been/is going on with the training and fitness regime? Equally concerning are the comments about players failing to maintain levels for the full ninety minutes. I appreciate that those players who are currently fit are bearing a disproportionate playing burden, and that the idea of squad rotation is a distant dream at the moment. But surely well-prepared professional footballers should be able to keep standards up for a full game when the season is less than a quarter complete?

Still, it's a point and a clean sheet. The three games in which we've earned points this season have been the same three games in which we've kept a clean sheet. It's not exactly rocket science, is it?

Tuesday 8 October. Carlisle United v Wigan Athletic. Brunton Park. Football League Trophy group stage.

This won't take long! I've previously made clear my disdain for this competition. Adam was verging on dismissive when I told him that I was even going to watch the game. But since I'm currently undergoing a three-week furlough from attending a game, and because it cost me nothing in addition to my usual Sky

Sports subscription, I decided I might as well have a look. My first impression was that I was pleased that both coaches were treating the competition with the contempt it deserves. The commentator made it clear that Wigan's team was a second string. As far as the Carlisle team were concerned, only three of the team could be considered to be front-line players. And neither Jon Mellish, Ben Barclay or Harrison Neal can be considered automatic first-team choices under Mike Williamson. Tonight's team was basically a youth team with a smattering of first team experience. Predictably, we lost 2-0. An early Wigan penalty and a second goal that sliced open our defence meant that Carlisle's interest in this competition was effectively over by half-time. I'll take just three minor positives from this game. In goal, Gabe Breeze did nothing to suggest he won't be an able deputy to Harry Lewis, should he be called upon. Dan Hopper made his first senior appearance as a second half substitute. Dan's dad Tony was a former Carlisle full-back, who was taken far too early due to motor neurone disease. It was a touching moment for Carlisle supporters of a certain vintage. And finally, it was disproportionately encouraging to see Taylor Charters, and particularly Callum Guy, make much needed returns from injury as second half substitutes.

Saturday 12 October. AFC Wimbledon v Carlisle United. Plough Lane (currently known as The Cherry Red Records Stadium). EFL League 2.

Oh dear. This was utterly dreadful. I can't recall seeing a worse performance from a Carlisle United team in a long, long time, and that's saying something after last season's car crash.

I was joined in my afternoon of suffering by John Clarke. Being a man of principle, John does not subscribe to Sky Sports, because of the network's links to Robert Murdoch. However, his principles are not rigid enough to preclude him from watching Carlisle United on Sky Sports + via my subscription!

I really don't know where to start with this shitshow. I'm fully aware that the Piataks (and Mike Williamson) believe in a data-driven approach to football. Shortly before half-time I checked the match stats that revealed that Carlisle had had almost two thirds of possession to date, had made more than a hundred more passes than Wimbledon and had a higher percentage of pass accuracy. Yet Wimbledon were already 2-0 up and about to score a third. Dominating the stats does not win games and points, preventing and scoring goals does, and Carlisle were woefully inadequate in both respects today. I finally brought an end to my teaching career because I was disillusioned with everything being driven by data rather than people and their needs. I don't really want to see my football team go the same way.

Today we fielded three centre backs, none of whom appeared to have the ability to make a constructive forward pass. They were obviously making earnest efforts to deliver the coach's mantra of playing the ball out from the back and were determined not to resort to just hoofing it long, as happened so often last season. But what was the outcome? Invariably it led to a pass to a teammate who was in no better a position and was immediately under pressure from Wimbledon's high press. The wing backs have the ability to look good going forward, but I remain to be convinced by their defensive qualities.

In midfield Harrison Neal's movement and passing are increasingly crab-like, either sideways or backwards while Biggins struggled to make any impact. I still believe that there's a good player hidden inside Josh Vela waiting to emerge, but there was no sign of that happening today. He committed a series of niggling fouls and was fortunate it took so long for the referee to brandish a yellow card. His substitution, relatively early in the second half, was probably to pre-empt the likelihood of the yellow card being upgraded to red.

Up front one player (Sadi) struggled to get more than half-a-dozen touches, and there's obviously something seriously wrong when your main striker as well as captain (Wyke) is substituted at half time. As for our goalkeeper, I've not been as vocal a critic of Harry Lewis as many on Facebook have been. But I'm yet to be entirely convinced by him. He's playing behind a woeful defence, which makes his job much harder. But he seemed to be rather slow to move across his goal to save what wasn't the most powerful of headers for Wimbledon's first goal. And should he have done better than parry the shot that led to an easy tap in for their second goal?

Having trashed Saturday's performance, what is to be done? If I had the answer to that question, I'd be at Brunton Park tomorrow morning, banging on the door and demanding a job. But I would suggest a couple of things that need to be urgently addressed. One is set pieces. Our defending of corners and attacking free kicks is woeful. And when we win a free kick, even in a relatively forward position, the current attitude seems to be to knock it sideways to begin another phase of successful but ineffective possession. And secondly, there needs to be a balance between patience as a new style of play is introduced, and the urgency of addressing the current perilous situation. I saw a post on Facebook recently which included a chart showing that it took Chris Beech twelve games to affect a significant turnaround when he took charge. My worry is that if we wait that long for Mike Williamson to have a similar impact, the situation will be irretrievable.

Just over thirty months ago, we were in a similar position, in the League 2 relegation zone. It beggars belief that we now find ourselves back there following a dramatic escape from relegation, a glorious promotion season, and an ownership takeover that gives us resources we could only dream of in the previous history of the club.

As season ticket holders, John and I will be there on Saturday for the Harrogate game. I will probably be at Walsall for the away game next Tuesday, because I've said I'll go via Nottingham University to pick Adam up. But I can't say I'll be devastated if he decides he's got better things to do.

It's not easy being a man of principle. Many a time my noble attitude to life has left me sitting squarely on those massively uncomfortable horns marked dilemma. Amazon, for instance, I have no truck with Amazon as they pay little or no tax. Well, I say no truck but there have been times when I've urgently needed a book, and their speed of delivery has been utilised. And yes, there have also been occasions when I've been seduced by a cheaper price online rather than in the bookshop. But on the whole, it's a case of no truck with Amazon, it's just that occasionally small commercial deals do take place between us. Principles are best when they are flexible.

I have a similar relationship with Sky TV. I will have no dealings with them. Sky is part of the Murdoch empire, the people who, amongst other things, have been involved in phone tapping the phone of 13-year-old murder victim Milly Dowler. Before the body was discovered, the hackings gave hope to the anguished parents that their daughter might still be alive. A despicable act in the name of journalism; how could they sleep? So, no, the Clarke household exists with tv watching habits centred around the mainstream channels and a Netflix subscription. Leading such a virtuous lifestyle only presents a problem on occasions such as when Howard Falshaw invites me to his house to watch the Wimbledon versus Carlisle game on his tv. His tv with the Sky Sports channel. I immediately accepted and rationalised my situation later. I would not be paying a penny to the evil Empire, I would be watching on Howard's subscription. Thus, my conscience was clear, and my virtue undimmed. As Grouch Marx once said, "These are my principles, and if you don't like them...well, I have others."

By this guidance, I also forswear eating crisps and chocolate unless there are some easily to hand on offer.

To the game in question then, Wimbledon versus Carlisle and possibly the worst experience I have had as a Carlisle supporter. I say possibly because I also witnessed a 4 – 0 defeat by Orient at their place some ten or so years ago. It was a game in which Carlisle did not manage a shot at goal until the final few minutes when Paul Thirwell broke with the ball towards the Orient area before deciding to let fly. Please note here that the term "let fly" is a monstrous exaggeration in the circumstances. The shot was certainly on target, but it dribbled across the turf before eventually being picked up by the goalkeeper in what looked like an act of kindness more than anything else. Let's put this pitiful effort out of its misery.

The other memorable feature of that day was passing the Carlisle bus parked outside the ground as we left. The engine was running, as is the wont of coach drivers, and the door was open offering the old guy in front us the opportunity to berate the bus driver about the team's performance. Quite why the bus driver had to receive this tirade was beyond me, but it typified the sheer frustration of fans when they have witnessed a totally ineffective performance from a team of whom they expect so much more.

So, Orient away a decade ago or the Wimbledon debacle? Both jostle for the title of worst experience watching Carlisle ever and do you know what, I think I'm going to present the award to the encounter at Wimbledon. Try as I might, it is too soon to expunge the memory. Conceding an early goal is never a good thing, an uncontested header from a corner which evaded two ineffective attempts to clear from two Carlisle defenders and then the despairing dive from Harry Lewis in the Carlisle goal. This was followed by another corner where the Carlisle defenders opted not to jump at all and then a third came when a Wimbledon player advanced on goal clearly intent on lining up a shot and no-one managed to mount a block.

Lewis parried the resultant low shot straight back to a Wimbledon player who had the simple task of diverting the ball into an unguarded net.

Half-time and Carlisle were 3 – 0 down without offering the slightest suggestion that the second half would offer any improvement. Passing the ball out from the back was not paying off. Wimbledon eagerly mounted a press happy in the knowledge that the ball would soon be theirs again. Four times in the second half Carlisle were unable to retain possession from their own throw in. A free kick just inside the Wimbledon half to Carlisle resulted in the ball ending up with Lewis in goal. Without exception, the Carlisle players looked incapable of controlling the ball and making a penetrative pass. There was the tedious sight of Carlisle players repeatedly passing the ball along the back line without any pace to stationary players thus building up the possession stats but offering nothing at all in the way of a threat.

A second half revival never looked to be on the cards and defeat was confirmed when Wimbledon scored an early fourth goal. Second phase play from another corner saw a ball floated into the six-yard box and with Carlisle defenders once again declining to get a head on the ball, it was an easy task to score with a header past Lewis who was rooted to his line.

If there had been any doubt about the outcome of the match, it had now been finally removed. Wimbledon were happy to play a training ground game and Carlisle were happy to let them. Fight? Desire? Pride? What are these qualities of which you speak?

If there was any consolation to be drawn at all from this dismal sight, it came with the introduction of

Taylor Charters who showed flashes of spirit and then Callum Guy making a very welcome return from a long-term injury who several times managed to get on the ball and, lo and behold, get his head up. There was no-one to pass to but still. Thin gruel perhaps, but Carlisle fans would have to take nourishment from such meagre offerings.

To compound the misery of the afternoon, as the last few minutes were being dragged out, I realised I had neglected my promise to pick up my wife's prescription and with the chemist's closed it was too late now for any remedial action. It had been remiss of me and I would have to bear the consequences.

As the full-time whistle blew at Wimbledon, results elsewhere confirmed that Carlisle were now placed firmly at the foot of the fourth tier of English football. In the parlance of the game, Carlisle had not turned up. I was not alone in my laxity, but the Chemist would be open on Monday and amends could be made. A similar opportunity would face Carlisle the following Saturday when they were due to face Harrogate at Brunton Park. Notoriously tricky opponents for the Blues, there will have to be a performance which restores some optimism. Some passion, some belief and an evident willingness to get stuck in would also be good to see.

Who knows, some cherished principles of playing fine possession football may also have to be abandoned.

Saturday 19 October. Carlisle United v Harrogate Town. Brunton Park. EFL League 2.

The Harrogate hoodoo continues! We've played seven league fixtures against them now and have only three draws and four defeats to show for our travails. Let's not forget that two seasons ago we contrived to lose to them despite them not having a single shot on target (more about stats later). Our one win came in a meaningless EFL Trophy game.

At least I wasn't the only Wakefield Blue making the journey this time. John was back on board and had offered to drive into the bargain, which meant I had the rare pleasure of being driven from Wakefield to Carlisle and back. Having said that, by the time we reached Scotch Corner my legs were aching from lack of movement, and I was more than happy to take a break and quite literally stretch my legs. We left Wakefield in steady rain but were bathed in bright sunshine by the time we parked in Carlisle.

The pre-match experience has improved immeasurably in recent seasons, with the introduction of the main fan zone and more recently the giant video screen, meaning we can watch the lunchtime Premier League game. Yesterday we soon bumped into two old high school friends of John, and once he'd introduced us John did a fine job of convincing them that they should buy my book. We entered the ground a bit later than usual, meaning that to have a crush barrier to lean on we were much closer to the Warwick Road End than usual, where we soon encountered John's sister and brother-in-law. I also spotted Ron Maddison close by, a member of the Carlisle Collective, the group of supporters largely responsible for gathering memorabilia and putting together the Carlisle United exhibition currently on display at Tullie House Museum.

Ron is currently helping out at the Dementia Café, which is hosted at Brunton Park on the last Friday of each month. The café aims to create a supportive and welcoming space for people living with dementia, and their families, by providing opportunities for people to engage in conversations and activities while feeling supported through meeting people who are going through similar experiences. Ron takes along some of his personal collection of souvenirs and memorabilia, in the hope that they may prompt positive memories for dementia sufferers in attendance. It was good to catch up with him again. There were a number of changes to the starting line-up. Terell Thomas was back after his absence on international duty for St Lucia (he got sent off!) and Luke Armstrong replaced Charlie Wyke in attack, starting against his former club. Both Callum Guy and Taylor Charters made their first start after lengthy absences through injury, having come on as substitutes last week.

Guy's calming influence and authority in midfield was immediately evident as Carlisle dominated the early stages of the game. The first opportunity came after just thirty seconds and by the quarter hour Carlisle had already had six shots to Harrogate's none, though the only one that seriously threatened the Harrogate goal was a Harrison Biggins free kick which cannoned off the crossbar. Harrogate were struggling to make any incursions into threatening territory.

It appeared that we were getting the response to from the players to last week's debacle that Mike Williamson had demanded and that the supporters deserved. The same patient passing out from the back was still apparent, but now it tended to be to players who were on the move rather than static. Neal and Guy were finding space in midfield, which meant that defenders had increased options to pass the ball forward rather than laterally. Dominic Sadi was giving the left side of the Harrogate defence a torrid time. On the rare occasions that Harrogate gained possession, Carlisle were quick to execute a high press, often winning back control of the ball.

Given all that, it was a sobering slap in the face, though perhaps predictable, that Harrogate took the lead in the 38th minute. Possession was given away in midfield, Harrogate moved the ball quickly, and a cross from the left was efficiently side-footed home. Fortunately, it took only seven minutes for Carlisle to equalise, and fittingly Luke Armstrong was the scorer, prodding home at the second attempt, after his first effort had been blocked. He had received a fair amount of abuse from the travelling support (all 220 of them), and there was only one place he was heading to in order to celebrate. He raced to the away section and stood in front of it, hands cupped to his ears. The match report on the club website described it as a "fine celebration in front of the travelling supporters".

Given Carlisle's first half dominance, it was disappointing to reach half-time only on equal terms, though it was better than being in arrears. At the back of my mind was the Grimsby game three weeks ago when an excellent first-half performance was followed by a dismal second half that resulted in defeat. And so it proved. Once again, the team failed to produce the same levels for a full game. At least we held onto a point, though with fifteen minutes left I turned to John and said, "I think we're going to lose this". Fortunately, I was wrong, but the same momentum was lacking. Too many passes were to stationary players. The press was less effective.

Understandably Guy and Charters were substituted after sixty-five minutes, given their recent return from injury. But their absence meant that the shape of the team was less clear. Their replacements were Ethan Robson, making his first league appearance for the club following pre-season injury, and Tyler Burey, who I have to admit I'd never heard of. It transpired that he was an unattached player, with Championship experience, who had been signed just hours earlier on a short-term contract until January. It says much about the thinness of the current squad that he went straight onto the bench. It would be unfair to judge either player on the basis of twenty-five minutes at the end of a game that was dying a death, but Robson certainly displayed some good touches. Let's hope he lives up to Paul Simpson's description of him as having "a wand of a left foot". Further substitutions followed in the 76th minute when Wyke and Robinson replaced Armstrong and Sadi. The latter substitution was a little surprising, particularly given that he was subsequently named Man of the Match. By this time Carlisle were increasingly going long, and it was a little concerning that Wyke failed to win many clean headers and was found a bit wanting for pace on a couple of occasions. Ultimately the second half and the result were anti-climactic. A draw was better than a defeat, and at least the point moved us off the foot of the table, but it really should have been a win. The attendance was 8,297, and the paltry away support meant that over 8,000 Carlisle fans had turned out to watch a team that started the day at the bottom of the EFL. Admittedly, the crowd was probably boosted by a cheap ticket promotion, but I'm sure there are plenty of League One clubs that would give an arm and a leg for that kind of attendance.

And so to the stats, if only to emphasise the point that I made last week. They support the saying that there are lies, damned lies and statistics. Yesterday's data is as follows: shots 23-4; shots on target 9-2; possession 71%-29%; passes 609-256; pass accuracy 83%-67%. In other words, significant dominance but only one point. Stats count for nothing if the results don't follow. A recent Facebook post pointed out, supported by charts and data, that it took Chris Beech twelve games to start turning things around after he succeeded Steven Pressley. Get a move on Williamson! Results matter, not statistics. A word on Harrison Neal. I was less then complimentary about his performance last week and was a bit surprised that he retained his place in yesterday's starting line-up. To be fair, he challenged Sadi for the Man of the Match accolade yesterday. He was tenacious in defence, winning possession and making one goal-saving intervention. He also offered much more going forward, finding space to receive passes in midfield, making forward passes and even firing off the odd shot at goal. Credit where credit's due.

Yesterday's crowd included a delegation from "Visit Jacksonville" which I assume is something like what we would call a tourist board. The Piataks are keen to develop links between the two cities, of all kinds – sporting, commercial, tourism related. There is talk that nest summer's pre-season may involve a tour of Florida, rather than the more prosaic usual trips to Kendal and Penrith. Heady days indeed.

Tuesday will see me heading south for the Walsall game, diverting via Nottingham University to pick up

Adam. It'll be good to see him again – I just hope our faith is not misplaced.

Hang out the flags and let the trumpets sound. It's a Saturday, Carlisle have a home fixture, and I am able to make the hundred plus mile journey to take up my position in the Paddock at Brunton Park. That season ticket will not be sitting in my wallet mocking me as today it will be put to its full and proper use. Come On You Blues!

It seems odd to drive up the A1 past the turn off to Harrogate when it's Harrogate Town we are due to watch as opposition, but no matter. At Scotch Corner the Yorkshire drizzle gives way to a break in the clouds and by the time we pass the county boundary into Cumbria, the sun is shining and the sky is blue. This is an omen surely because today is the day when Carlisle are going to get a result which will herald the long-expected turnaround to the whole season and the new era of attractive football can begin. In that scientifically infallibly proven process, I can feel it in my waters.

A pause to consider today's opponents. Harrogate is a town of elegant crescents, a town of enviable wide-open space adjacent to the centre in the form of the Stray. A spa town where people of refinement go to take the waters. The beautiful Harlow Carr Gardens are in Harrogate, as is the Old Swan Hotel where Agatha Christie turned up after a mysterious eleven-day disappearance. Harrogate has Betty's Tea Shop where Alan Bennett would share a pot of Earl Grey and a macaroon with Thora Hird. Harrogate is a hotbed of football fervour with an awe-inspiring stadium and a massive fan base.

One of the above statements is not true. Although the club was founded in 1919, they did not gain football league status until 2020. They are not held in the same light as Accrington Stanley, say, with a long and notable tradition. Industrial Lancashire or genteel North Yorkshire as a football base? It is undeniable that Harrogate Town is often thought of in patronising terms. And yet, since their accession to the footballing elite of League Two, Harrogate have yet to be beaten by Carlisle in a league fixture. They are, after all, a Yorkshire team and they don't give owt away. They don't have any stars, but they are workmanlike, well-organised and they don't give up. These were the only thoughts that troubled my otherwise confident demeanour. Harrogate would not want to turn up and be marked as the team against whom Carlisle won handsomely and started their season.

When we checked the starting line-up, we were surprised to see the naturally gifted left footer, Dominic Sadi in the right wing-back position. Our number one choice, Archie Davies is out injured, and his replacement is a twenty-one-year-old midfielder, a loanee signing from Bournemouth. Was this a sign of desperation or evidence of some thinking out of the box? Time would tell.

Following the kick off, Harrogate surprised us with their somewhat supine manner. They were holding off, battening down the hatches in order to see what Carlisle would throw at them. In the first two minutes, that man Sadi broke down the right and reached the byline from where a successful pull-back would surely have resulted in a goal. So soon in the game, this was a reassuring sight, Carlisle on the attack, but any realist will tell you that in situations like that you need to be clinical and score. Put the ball in the back of the net. Don't hope to, but expect to score. The creation of chances in itself is not rewarded with points. Sadi produced another couple of exciting runs as Harrogate, surely, had not been prepared for such a threat from right wing-back. But it didn't produce any goals. Likewise, a free kick from outside the box from Harrison Biggins smacked against the crossbar as the Harrogate keeper flailed across his line and so the scoreline remained nil, nil. It is a football truism that you should score while you are exerting pressure. Otherwise...

Exactly. A ball was given away cheaply in midfield and Harrogate launched an attack down the left wing (into a space left by Sadi by the way) and an excellent cross was not effectively cleared. Daly, the Harrogate player, showing commendable ambition, arrived in the box to side foot home.

It is to Carlisle's credit that they got back on terms before the half-time break. Finally, Luke Armstrong got the service he needs when Biggins picked him out with a thirty-yard pass to meet his intelligent run across the box and he bundled home the chance at the second attempt. For once, the immutable law of the returning former player scoring had been enacted in Carlisle's favour.

The statistics after the game will show that Carlisle had seventy percent possession and they massively outnumbered Harrogate in terms of shots on target. But as always, statistics can be misleading. Harrogate were more assertive in the second half. They were well-drilled in getting men forward when there was even a sniff of a chance around the Carlisle goal, and when Callum Guy and Taylor Charters were taken off, they contested the midfield much more effectively, so much so that they did look as though they would be the side to "nick it".

But they didn't and neither did Carlisle. They won a point at home against a team in the lower half of the table. Is that good enough? Probably not, but it is clear now that the transformation, in whatever form it takes, is going to take some time and the habit of not losing would be a good one to pick up at this point.

Picking out some positives, the welcome return of Guy and Charters after lengthy injuries is a big plus, Cameron Harper at left wing back was energetic and competitive, Biggins seemed determined to impress and 8,297 people were tempted down to Brunton Park to watch the game. There were signs, there was a semblance of a team there who can work to prove that Carlisle are in a false position.

Also, there is the lingering hope that one day we will beat Harrogate Town.

Tuesday 22 October. Walsall v Carlisle United. The Bescot (Poundland) Stadium. EFL League 2.

How much worse does it have to get before things start to get better? This was utterly dreadful.

At least we were spared the full horror of the evening. Having checked the logistics, I'd realised that it wouldn't add too many miles and minutes to the journey to go via Nottingham and pick up Adam from uni. And that's where things started to unravel. Adam called me on Monday afternoon to say that a tutorial had been added to his timetable on Tuesday afternoon from five until six. After brief consideration I reassured him that we could still make it to Walsall on time. I was at Nottingham University promptly at quarter to six, only for Adam to inform me that his tutorial was running over. By the time it had finished, and Adam had grabbed a hurried tea, we were up against the clock. This was when forward planning came into play. I'd pre-booked car parking at the ground and when we reached the Bescot Stadium at twenty to eight, we were promptly directed to the away parking zone by the friendly and helpful stewards. It was our third visit to Walsall and we've yet to see Carlisle win, but every time we've been impressed by the warmth and good nature of the stewards. It must be a Midlands thing, because the other stewards who stand out from away games are at Port Vale.

Having parked, it was less than a minute to the away entrance. I was literally pushing my way through the turnstile when a loud roar erupted inside the stadium. Yes, that roar meant that Carlisle had failed to hold out even long enough for us to reach our seats, conceding in just the second minute. And to be honest, it was all downhill from there. We reached half-time still only a goal behind, but without ever seriously threatening the Walsall goal. During the break I bumped into Eric Hornsby and Liz Appleby, contemporaries from my primary school days in Orton. We were remarkably unanimous in our assessment of just why things are so crap at the moment, of which more shortly.

After the restart, it took Walsall only a minute longer to score than it had in the first half. When they scored a third just seven minutes later Eric had had enough and headed for the exit. I feared the worst, expecting a five or six goal thrashing. Thankfully that didn't transpire, and we even managed to grab a consolation goal when Jon Mellish prodded home a corner at the far post, but I don't think that by that point anyone believed it was going to spark a late revival and comeback. Or that anyone believed that from the moment the first goal was conceded in the second minute.

So, what exactly was wrong? Bear with me because this may take some time!

Firstly, both Neal and Vela were selected in midfield. I've been fairly critical of Neal's crab-like tendencies and overall limitations, while acknowledging that he had a decent game against Harrogate on Saturday. I'm beginning to re-assess Josh Vela. My initial impressions were positive before injury intervened, a player with plenty of energy, a potential box-to-box midfielder. He's done little to vindicate that opinion this season. I have no clear idea of what his position and role is meant to be, and I suspect that neither does he. Whether that's his fault or that of the coach is not for me to say. What I do know is that he and Neal do not function as a pair in midfield. Dominic Sadi was dropped to the bench, a little surprising following his man of the match performance last Saturday (not that that was a particularly high bar). Aaron Hayden returned from injury to a defence that appeared to include four central defenders. To be fair, Jon Mellish moved to left wing back, not his natural position, while Cameron Harper was switched from his usual left wing back role to right wing back. You're probably beginning to get the picture. Luke Armstrong appeared to be playing the lone striker, with no-one clearly playing off him. Charlie Wyke didn't even make the bench. The explanation was that he was ill, though rumours circulate that he had a bust-up with coach Williamson at half-time of the AFC Wimbledon game, when he was substituted.

I was amazed to discover that Carlisle had twice as much possession as Walsall, more than twice as many passes, and almost 20% higher pass accuracy. Given the number of times they haplessly conceded possession, one is tempted to say sod statistics. We were never even in this game.

After the third Walsall goal, the Carlisle fans noticeably turned against their team. Chants of "You're not fit to wear the shirt" rang out, and, less prominently, chants of "We want Simmo back". There were even sarcastic chants of "We made a pass" on the occasions when that actually happened. When supporters who have travelled for hours on a Tuesday evening to attend the game turn on the team like that, something is seriously wrong. These are the hardcore supporters that are being alienated.

In his post-match interview Gavin (sorry, Mike – Freudian slip) Williamson talked of "controlling the controllables". Apart from that being meaningless mumbo jumbo, he needs to focus on training his players on how to control a football and make accurate controlled passes. Some fans have compared his interviews to those of the hapless Keith Millen, and last night's performance was strongly reminiscent of Millen's final game in charge, the 3-0 home defeat to Swindon. I know that Williamson has only been in charge for eight games, and I don't expect an instant upturn, but he needs to wake up and smell the coffee. This group of players do not possess the ability to play the style of possession-based, quick passing football that he advocates. He needs to confront the situation that faces him here and now. We have a team that is currently on a fast-track to relegation to the National League, and he needs to reverse that decline as a matter of urgency. That done, he can start to recruit players who suit his chosen philosophy. Right now, survival is paramount.

Paul Simpson inherited a similar situation. He took over a squad assembled by previous managers that was staring relegation in the face. By playing to that squad's strengths, he engineered a remarkable surge to safety, and, following some judicious additions, led them to promotion. The less said about what followed the better. There are plenty online who are calling for Williamson to go now, saying that he's the wrong man for this situation. I disagree but my patience is running thin and will disappear if he doesn't urgently address the realities of the current situation.

Some are suggesting that we need a "disciplinarian" of the likes of Neil Warnock or Steve Evans in charge. To be honest, the moment either of those two or their like arrives at Brunton Park will be the moment I return my season ticket and start watching a more entertaining and virile sport like dressage.

The natural optimist has been cast aside for a while in view of the lowly position in the league, the number of injuries to crucial players and the lack of any kind of run of form to speak of. The realisation has dawned that these are worrying times. But against Harrogate a point was gained, not the three points which would once have been expected at Fortress Brunton Park, but it was a point, a draw and not a defeat despite the Yorkshire side's resurgence in the second half, and during the Harrogate game there had been signs, had there not? Signs, you say? Well, yes, there's the return of Callum Guy and Taylor Charters. Harrison Biggins looks as though he is ready to put in a shift, and for me at least, Cameron Harper is an asset, as is Dominic Sadi who has undoubted talent. Maybe the natural optimist has not been jettisoned too far. A point against Harrogate is a start, now to the more serious challenge of Walsall away on a Tuesday night.

I should perhaps have accepted the protocol of football writing and referred to "high-flying Walsall" because they currently occupy a top three position and this fixture represents a real opportunity for Carlisle to demonstrate that they are indeed setting out on that long journey towards Bringing on Back the Good Times. But be warned, a Tuesday night match at Walsall will call for resilience before free-flowing football. Nevertheless, the appetite is whetted, and the optimist has wormed his way back in from the cold. Except for the fact that due to a triumph of disorganisation I have ruled myself out of attending the game. Some weeks ago, I signed up for an on-line short story writing course, calculating the four-week course would be over before Walsall away sailed into view. Miscalculated as it happens as the final session was scheduled for Tuesday 22nd October and instead of aligning myself with the travelling Blue Army and pledging "Carlisle till I Die," I would in fact be on the trail of Hemingway's "One true sentence."

This would be a shame, but not a real problem as the course was due to finish at eight-thirty and I could immediately check on affairs at the Bescot stadium or, as it is currently known as, the Poundland Bescot

Stadium which would be quite cool if it meant that everyone could get in for a quid.

A little bit of levity is needed as what follows is grim and those of you of a nervous disposition should leave the room now. Predictably enough, I didn't wait until the end of the course to take a surreptitious look at my phone to pick up the ominous news that Carlisle were one-down after two minutes. There was a time when such a situation would have led me to think that this wasn't so bad as there is still plenty of time to mount a fightback. But these are not those days my friend. We rarely score goals and coming back from behind is even rarer. After only two minutes, I knew that as far as this game was concerned, we were doomed. A snippet from my writing course is timely here; the American writer Kurt Vonnegut once offered the suggestion that authors should make bad things happen to their characters. Well, thanks for that Kurt, why not make your characters fans of Carlisle United? There is no sugar coating this particular pill as the facts are that Carlisle lost 3–1, with two further goals conceded in the 49th and 56th minute. John Mellish's 82nd minute goal barely qualified as a consolation although watching the highlights later on YouTube, Mellish was seen, in an act of either defiance against fate or just misguided hope, retrieving the ball from the back of the net and running back to the centre spot with the ball tucked under his arm. I suspect it was the former and I hereby salute Jon Mellish.

But the rest of the highlights package should be given an x certificate. It showed goals conceded after losing possession when playing out from the back and the all too familiar sight of a porous defence. Whether witnessed live or on-line, these scenes were the signal for the social media sites to go into overdrive. The consensus among those posting was that the recently appointed Head Coach, Mike Williamson didn't have a clue, he was a clown while his players without exception, were "wage thieves" who were not prepared to show any spirit or fight. They were according to a chant heard at the ground, "Not fit to wear the shirt." Some on-line commentators compared this result to the notorious one of three seasons ago against Swindon when notice of Carlisle's imminent demise was writ large on the wall. Was it really that bad?

Your absentee correspondent, weighed down by his optimist angel on one shoulder and pessimist angel on the other, thought long and hard about it all and then went to bed.

Saturday 26 October. Carlisle United v Cheltenham Town. Brunton Park. EFL League 2.

There were a couple of crumbs of comfort to be derived from this latest defeat that make it marginally less bad than Tuesday night's debacle, but that's not saying much. One of the worst things about a run of results like this is that, if you're writing about it, you have to relive the agony of the event a day or two later. One wouldn't want to be accused of only revelling in the glory days. Once again it was just John and myself making the trip, and a significant proportion of the journey was taken up with me recounting to John all the trivia and vitriol from Tuesday night that I didn't deem worthy of inclusion in my last post. In response, John asked me if I knew someone called Alistair

Kirkpatrick. John and his wife were in Carlisle the day before for a funeral, and Alistair had delivered the eulogy. It turns out he and John go back many years. It happens that Alistair and I go back a fair few years as well. In the late nineties Alistair initiated and chaired a Yorkshire branch of the Carlisle United Supporters Club. We used to meet in the upstairs room of a pub in Otley, and I distinctly remember a meeting, full of doom and gloom, just three days before the Jimmy Glass miracle. Three days later Alistair was on the pitch at Brunton Park to present Ian Stevens with the Yorkshire branch's player of the season award. He commented afterwards that Stevens appeared largely disinterested. Perhaps he was worried that he was missing out on the contents of the hip flask that Nigel Pearson was offering around the dressing room at the time, if Jimmy Glass is to be believed (and why shouldn't he be?). Anyway, the upshot is that we spent a very enjoyable ten minutes renewing old acquaintance in the fan zone before heading into the ground. And that was about as good as the afternoon got. Mike Williamson had shuffled the starting deck again (or would rearranged the deckchairs on The Titanic be a more appropriate metaphor?). Mellish and Hayden were out, Barclay and Robson were in, the latter making his first start for the club. Perhaps the constant chopping and changing is one of the reasons for the current lack of cohesion? The game started pretty much where Tuesday night finished. Carlisle struggled to retain possession and string any coherent passing movements together. The one noticeable difference was that there was less passing out from the back, with Harry Lewis frequently clearing long. Whether that was due to a change in tactics by Williamson or Lewis ignoring instructions is anybody's guess.

It mattered not. In the seventeenth minute Lewis parried a shot at his near post and then floundered helplessly by the post as the ball span back and nestled in the net. Lewis had an afternoon that he will want to forget. He struggled to make a clean catch all afternoon, invariably opting to punch rather than catch crosses, usually leading to renewed pressure. He also struggled to catch shots cleanly tending only to parry the ball, frequently towards another opposition player, rather than divert it away from danger. I've rarely seen a Carlisle goalkeeper show so little control of his area. When he cleanly gathered a misplaced Cheltenham through ball, the ironic applause was unhelpful but predictable. When Carlisle won a corner deep into the eleven minutes of added time, some supporters urged Lewis to go forward. I disagreed. He'd probably have soared above the Cheltenham defence to make his only clean catch of the day.

The team was roundly booed off the pitch at half-time. The majority of online comment both before and after the game is that Williamson's appointment has been a massive mistake, and that he should be dismissed before the situation is irretrievable. I'm not quite there yet, but I'm not far away. He seems incapable of getting the best out of players like Mellish and Armstrong (or any of the squad at his disposal for that matter), even though he should know their strengths better than most, having played with them at Gateshead. I think his days may well be numbered.

So what are the crumbs of comfort? Charlie Wyke was brought on at half-time in an attempt to change the pattern of the game. Just fifteen minutes later he was fouled, suffering a serious ankle injury in the process, and was stretchered off after a lengthy delay, receiving gas and air and with his leg in a splint. He was taken to hospital for x-rays, but no further information is forthcoming.

Wyke's injury prompted a triple substitution and for the final half-hour we were at least treated to a bit of honest effort and endeavour, though not a great amount of skill. From the free kick that eventually followed Wyke's injury Carlisle immediately went on the attack and created a half-decent chance. That galvanised the crowd, and they got behind the team for the rest of the game. As a result, the reaction at the final whistle was less negative than I expected, though relatively few waited behind to acknowledge the players.

The crowd was down by about 2,000 to just over 6,000, which might be largely explained by the lack of a cheap ticket promotion for this game. And, of course, most fans yesterday hadn't witnessed the true horror of Tuesday night's shitshow. But 6,064 (Cheltenham only brought 134 fans) isn't bad for a club in the League 2 relegation zone. On Tuesday night Walsall, who are flying high at the opposite end of the division, only attracted 4,500 when the travelling support is discounted.

There have been a number of comments on fans' forums about struggling through to the January transfer window, when Williamson can bring in players suited to his playing style and philosophy. Have these people learned nothing from the experience of the last three windows? Who will want to come for the right reasons to a club languishing at the foot of League 2? The last three windows have been dreadful. Recruitment following promotion was woeful, with none of the new signings making a significant impact, and a number moved on in the last window. Last January the Piataks' money was meant to bring in players who would steer us to League 1 safety. That didn't happen, did it? And of the numerous signings this summer I can't think of a single one who has stamped their authority and personality on the team yet or become a fan favourite. The signings from the last two windows may eventually do so, but there's little sign yet.

The last really successful transfer window for Carlisle was January 2022. Keith Millen, for all his shortcomings, brought in Kris Dennis, Omari Patrick. Jamie Devitt, Dynel Simeu and others who played significant roles in the surge to safety. The next two windows saw good additions, but not on the same scale: Huntington, Moxon and Back in summer 2022, Garner and J.K. Gordon in January 2023. Is it unreasonable to point a finger of blame at the same Head of Recruitment who oversaw the last three windows and is still in post?

A couple of familiar gripes in conclusion. The refereeing was woeful – from the early minutes Cheltenham players were holding Carlisle attackers whenever the ball was played forward and went entirely unpunished. I'm not talking about a little tug on the shirt. I'm talking about both arms around the chest, often wrestling the player to the ground. All it needed was one early whistle to make it clear that the referee wouldn't tolerate such blatant foul play. He probably thought, mistakenly, that he was allowing the game to flow. Yet he seemed perfectly happy to stop the game and brandish yellow cards for relatively innocuous trips by both sides.

Supporting Carlisle at the moment offers hardly any positives, but I'd hate to watch Cheltenham every week, with their cynical foul play and time wasting, fully supported by their manager.

These are desperate days.

"We saved the country from boredom." So said George Harrison when he was reflecting on the achievements of the Beatles. He may well have been right as the four lads from Liverpool, on top of their musical talent also showed an impatience with social protocol and any deference to the establishment. Alongside attitudes developed in the liberated sixties and student-led protests, perhaps the Beatles were instrumental in giving people a voice and shifting the social dynamics of the country. People became much less likely to "know their place" and behave accordingly. Consequently, those professions which previously relied on an assumed authority: doctors, teachers, police and so on suddenly found that their actions would be questioned. Accountability came to the fore as did the inalienable right people felt to voice an opinion.

This is cod social science, I know, grasping at straws to find an explanation as to why, we as a country seem to have become angry and intemperate. Why such rudeness towards those people serving the public? When and why did road rage become a feature of British life? How to explain the existence of keyboard warriors?

A clue lies in that very term keyboard warriors. It's the internet, of course. We can let the Beatles off the hook as the establishment did not take lasting offence. To the contrary, honours up to and including a knighthood were handed over to the erstwhile mop tops. No, it is definitely the internet which is the villain of the piece, allowing all and sundry to exercise their right to free speech without the obligation of respecting responsibilities not to harm others, not to promote hate and not to lie. We have reached the stage where the keyboard warrior can peddle ill-informed, insensitive twaddle to his or her heart's content in more or less complete anonymity without fear of any sanction.

Following the Tuesday night debacle at Walsall, the online atmosphere was febrile. Social media comment regarding the state of Carlisle United both on and off the pitch was running wild and unchecked. And now, Dear Reader, your hunch has been proved correct as you knew, didn't you, that eventually, I would get to the point. Just to get this straight, the people had spoken and according to some of the more extreme of the wired-up gurus passing comment, all of the players are content to pick up their massively inflated wages without showing any commitment to the shirt, the team or the club. The team coach and his assistants don't have a clue and even the Piateks, the financial saviours of the club, are misguided Americans who don't know how English football works. All of the people mentioned above are clowns lacking commitment.

Just let that settle for a moment as we consider the case of Dominic Sadi who, in an attempt to benefit his career, has opted to leave Premiership outfit Bournemouth and travel the length of the country to further learn his trade in a loan spell at a club playing three levels lower than his parent club. Include in your consideration how this naturally gifted left-midfield player has been asked to play at right wing-back without, as far as I can see, any complaints. His team mate, Sam Lavelle, broke his nose for the cause. (Later he would play in a face mask and still contest every header that came his way.) And finally, if we are considering whether or not there is any commitment amongst the players, I offer you two words: Jon Mellish.

There is no guarantee of course that those passing comment online are bona fide fans and there's no certainty that they even attend games, so they, with their ill-considered, sometimes farcical, opinions, should be ignored. A view with which I agree as I well know that you can't reason with the unreasonable.

But the trouble is that views aired online are pervasive and they soon gain traction. Look at how words and phrases are picked up and loaded with malign intent, how for instance a direct style of football can soon be characterised as "hoofball", how a player considered to be important to the club and offered a two, or three, year contract becomes a "wage stealer". And most pitiably, those supporters who choose to applaud their team at the end of the game are deemed to be "happy clappers."

Unburdened by any sense of responsibility the trolls continue to pursue their pestilent agenda and as the Brunton Park faithful gathered for the encounter with Cheltenham a toxic atmosphere was discernible. After a telling defeat in midweek, you might expect fans to be a little hesitant, fearful maybe and world weary in their outlook, but prior to kick off attitudes were already formed and there was to be no giving of the benefit of the doubt. Five home games earlier as the final whistle blew against Tranmere some fans gathered around the tunnel to shout vile abuse against Paul Simpson, and now entitlement insisted that more vitriol directed at players and coaching staff from the terraces was a right.

I had the misfortune to be standing against a crash barrier next to the Paddock's Mr Sweary. He was making liberal and tedious use of the "F word" in every utterance. Now, I know the rejoinder here - football is a working-class sport where the working-class man can vent the frustrations of his working week by paying his money at the turnstiles, by verbally letting off steam - it is his paid for right. But gratuitous swearing in the presence of a lot of kids? Unacceptable, I would say, realising immediately that such a suggestion in itself is enough to put me in the bracket of fuddy-duddy. Lighten up a bit, John, there was no harm done. So, I won't make the further suggestion that this guy was also debasing working class culture.

He was in full flow as soon as the ref's whistle blew for the start of the match. Players passing the ball in their own half were derided for "fannying" about, and when a longer ball was attempted, they were scorned for "just booting it anywhere." Please note that if I included all of his swear words, this report would be twice as long. And maybe his commitment to airing such a level of profanity blinded him to what was actually happening on the pitch. The team had suffered a chastening experience at Walsall and another such performance wouldn't be at all acceptable. There had to be a reaction, and indeed there was. Carlisle looked promising in the early stages as Sadi forged a great chance on six minutes and Cheltenham didn't look to be any great shakes at all. Things were looking promising but once again there was the feeling that Carlisle were failing to take advantage of such a spell.

And so, it proved when on seventeen minutes, the Cheltenham forward, Ethan Archer, was able to burst in from the left to set up a one against one situation against Ben Barclay. To be fair to Barclay, for all of his merits and achievements, being faced up against a player with a trick doesn't show him in his best light. Archer's trick was to drop his left shoulder as a feint and then cut in onto his right foot and Barclay obligingly bought it to leave Archer with a clear shot on goal from no more than eighteen yards. The chance was there and he could choose his corner and claim his goal without any blame being attached to Harry Lewis who was horribly exposed in the Carlisle goal. Archer though lacked the necessary composure and instead he blasted his shot directly at Lewis who couldn't fail to, as they say, "get something on it." This "something" was insufficient to clear the ball which spun up off the hapless Lewis before bouncing and spinning wickedly and agonisingly into the empty net. Oh Harry Lewis! He shouldn't have stood a chance against such a clear opportunity, but a chance was exactly what had been offered and he failed to take it. Later, he would make a very good save, as he had in previous games, but the damage had now been done by that spinning ball and the trolls could gear up for a renewed onslaught. Indeed, Mr Sweary must have felt as though he had been thoroughly vindicated and he could now enter Sweary Nirvana.

What a difference a goal makes. Cheltenham could now see, even at this early stage, three points for the taking. They were a goal up and didn't need to score again as long as they didn't concede. They could set up their defensive shield, fall back whenever danger threatened and slow down the game as much as they pleased. For the remainder of the half, they played with immeasurably more confidence and then as the teams left for the break, the Carlisle players were met with what is best described as a mixed reception.

Carlisle had to emerge with a much more spirited approach. They had to generate some passion, some energy and evident commitment. Could Mike Williamson engender this with his half-time talk? In the event there was insufficient time to provide the evidence either way because the game then turned on the worst sort of incident in football. Charlie Wyke was felled with a tackle over a loose ball in midfield. It looked like a bad 'un and it merited a yellow card from the ref. But worse than that, the players in the immediate vicinity recoiled in horror while others gestured for immediate assistance from the trainers.

Wyke was eventually stretchered from the field. A bad one indeed as it was later confirmed that he had broken his ankle. The incident necessitated a long suspension of play and as always there was the question of how everyone would respond. It's not easy to put something like that from your mind. Was Harrison Biggins affected when he slid in on a cross along the deck in the penalty area? He looked certain to score but he managed to lift his effort over the bar. Was the ref affected as his decisions became increasingly erratic? This bad injury had occurred on his watch, and he had only issued a yellow card. Meanwhile, Carlisle possibly fired up by the injury to their captain, or the ref's inconsistencies generally played with more vigour and dominated without the vital goal being scored. The final whistle blew on another home defeat.

We trooped out of the ground with that odd sense of knowing that when you are down at the bottom, things don't go for you. So much to reflect upon but the bare bones of the game were: a terrible goal to concede, an awful injury and a glorious chance to take three points squandered.

I had learned a lesson though and I was firm in my resolve. I would never stand next to Mr Sweary again. Fucking idiot.

Chapter 5
SEARCHING FOR A
SILVER LINING

Saturday 2 November. Carlisle United v Wigan Athletic. Brunton Park. F.A Cup Round 1.

I think the decision not to travel to this game was probably made about a week ago, having travelled over 800 miles in the previous week for the meagre return of a single point and some dreadful performances. A ticket would only have cost a fiver, given my status as a season-ticket holder and senior citizen, but I really couldn't be bothered to commit the time and effort required to travel to a game where I saw little, or any, possibility of a positive outcome. Given all that, I'm not sure why it took me until Thursday morning to confirm to John that I wouldn't be going. Given that no live stream of the game was available, I decided to follow the game via Jon Colman's online "As It Happens" online posts for The News and Star. This report is largely based on that and online post-match comments. A 2-0 defeat would appear to justify my decision not to travel, though it perhaps wasn't quite as simple as that. There were a number of changes to the starting line-up that suggested that Mike Williamson was prioritising the league over the cup, something I have no problem with. However, his selections appeared to prompt one of the most promising performances of the season, judging by post-match online comments. The most significant selection decision was that of Gabe Breeze in goal. Many fans have been calling for Harry Lewis to be dropped for some weeks now. This game gave Williamson the opportunity to select Breeze under the pretext that he was "resting" Lewis. Whatever the reasoning, it appears that Breeze seized the opportunity with both of his capacious hands, coming for crosses, commanding his area and making a number of excellent saves. It'll be interesting to see who Williamson plumps for next weekend. The game seemed to pivot around a controversial incident in the fourteenth minute. Following what was widely described as a 50-50 challenge, Ethan Robson was issued with a straight red card. The overwhelming opinion was that the Wigan player had made a meal of the challenge. I wouldn't presume to make a judgement on the referee's decision, based on the highlights I've watched, but there has been extensive online comment on the referee's strong connections with the Wigan area and the appropriateness (or otherwise) of his appointment for this particular fixture.

Whatever the rights or wrongs of Robson' dismissal, it seemed to have a galvanising effect on the crowd who proceeded to vent their anger on the Wigan player in question and the referee for the rest of the first half. It also galvanised the remaining ten players, who made light of the numerical disadvantage. Ironically, in a rare instance of Carlisle not having the majority of possession, the team managed to create more good chances than in any recent game. The Wigan goalkeeper had to be at his absolute best on more than one occasion to keep the scores level. As the second half wore on the extra man began to tell, as Wigan began to fashion more and better chances. But Carlisle demonstrated sufficient resilience to take the tie to extra-time. No replays of course – we've got to create space in the fixture schedule for the big boys to fit in a couple more money-spinners. It took until the second half of extra time for Wigan to finally break the deadlock. Their second goal, in the final minute, was an irrelevance. It came when Gabe Breeze went up field for a last-gasp Carlisle corner, perhaps trying to channel his inner Jimmy Glass. Wigan cleared and raced to the other end to score into an unguarded net.

Post-match online comments were full of praise for the spirit and determination shown by the players, some going as far as to suggest that this game might mark a turning point in a dreadful season to date. It does rather beg the question as to why that fight has been conspicuously absent in previous games. Perhaps Mike Williamson should think long and hard before he restores some of the "rested" players to the starting eleven for Saturday's game at Salford. At the end of the day, we still lost – again. It reflects badly on the situation we are in when supporters are getting so animated by a 2-0 defeat. Clutching at straws? The crowd was 4,532, the second home game in a row that has seen a significant drop in support, particularly when the 1,257 Wigan fans made up almost a third of that figure.

Saturday 9 November. Salford City v Carlisle United. Moor Lane (currently known as The Peninsula Stadium – stadium?). EFL League 2.

In the corresponding fixture two seasons ago, we had a fantastic afternoon at Moor Lane. We were right behind the goal as three second half strikes in eleven minutes, all scored in front of a jubilant travelling contingent, secured a superb victory, one of the best wins of the promotion season. Was it too much to expect a repeat this time round?

Well, it was in at least one respect. We didn't even make it across The Pennines to Salford on this occasion. We were a bit slow off the mark when tickets went on sale, and before we knew it the away allocation had sold out. That brings me back to an old and familiar theme. The official attendance was 3,737, with 1,366 away fans, meaning that Moor Lane was about 1,400 below capacity. I have little doubt that Carlisle could have sold most, if not all, of those remaining tickets if they'd been given the opportunity. I appreciate that an increased away following would have incurred extra policing and stewarding costs for Salford, but surely those costs would have been far less than the thousands of pounds of extra gate money the club would have earned. The same applies for Carlisle home games. The away section at Brunton Park is larger than most in League 2, particularly when The Waterworks End is opened up, but if certain clubs can bring three or four thousand supporters, than why not let them. It would improve both the atmosphere and the income. Maybe Salford were worried that if Carlisle sold the remaining tickets, home fans would be embarrassingly outnumbered by away ones. They were comfortably out sung as it was!

So, John and I settled down on the sofa to watch the game live courtesy of Sky Sports +. Mike Williamson made just two changes to the side that performed creditably in the F.A. Cup defeat a week earlier. Callum

Guy came back in for the suspended Ethan Robson, and Luke Armstrong replaced Taylor Charters. Perhaps most significantly, Gabe Breeze kept his place in goal.

To be honest, there weren't any early or obvious signs of a positive carry-over from the previous game in the first half. Salford dominated most of the statistics, most significantly possession and attempts on goal. The defence looked a little bit more robust in dealing with opposition attacks, but no better when in possession and trying to build an attack. Too often the ball was passed laterally to a teammate who was in no better position to initiate an attack, or the ball was hit long, largely failing to find a Carlisle player. There seemed to be no real strategy for building movements through midfield, as Guy and Neal frequently watched the ball sail over their head before being required to resume defensive duties. Carlisle created only one meaningful chance in the first half, Luke Armstrong hitting a shot over the bar from near the penalty spot when he should have at least hit the target. Now that Harry Lewis has been dropped in favour of Breeze, the online boo boys seem to have switched their vitriol to Armstrong. I'll be the first to admit that he hasn't lived up to the high expectations that accompanied his signing nearly a year ago, but I'm not sure that's entirely his fault. I've argued before that he's not a conventional target man, which is the role he's largely been played in since joining United. I was hopeful that he'd be more effective playing off Charlie Wyke, with Wyke the target man, but the latter's season-ending injury put paid to that hope. Perhaps if Georgie Kelly ever achieves full match fitness that might provide a similar pairing. Another minority online voice pointed out that the service Armstrong has received since his arrival has been pretty dire. That's absolutely right – he's been feeding off scraps. The criticism of him is a bit like expecting Harry Lewis to be an impregnable barrier in goal behind such a porous defence. In the case of both players, there's no benefit for anyone in their confidence being undermined by mindless criticism online and from the terraces.

I mentioned earlier that Salford dominated the first-half statistics, as they did for the game as a whole. Now here's a thing. Carlisle have been dominating most statistics for the last few games, with bugger all points to show for it. In this game the stats were against us and guess what? We came away with all three points. Memo to Mike Williamson – I don't want to see again a member of your coaching staff thrusting an iPad in front of you to highlight a particular piece of in-game data. Focus on what's happening on the pitch in front of your very eyes.

Things did improve in the second half. Although John rightly commented after about an hour that there appeared to be no clear pattern of play from either side, some well-judged substitutions from Williamson saw a gradual shift in the balance of play. While the Sky commentator seemed to be preoccupied with a narrative of whether Salford could find a way to break down Carlisle's defence, we both commented around the seventieth minute that the momentum now seemed to be shifting in Carlisle's favour. They were winning more possession and attacking with greater purpose and penetration. Kadeem Harris, only signed on a short-term deal a couple of days earlier, had a distinct impact when he was brought on in the 72nd minute. Good chances fell to Daniel Adu-Adjei and Aaron Hayden before the breakthrough finally came in the 88th minute.

Carlisle owed the three points to two of the substitutes. A Harrison Biggins corner from the left curled in towards the edge of the six-yard box. There it was met by Ben Barclay, only on the pitch for three minutes, who timed his run to perfection. Not only that, but he also showed real determination and bravery to thrust himself into a dangerous area, scoring with a spectacular diving header. The more I watch the goal, the more I'm convinced that it's my goal of the season to date. Not that there's a lot of competition to be honest.

I'd love to have been there to celebrate in person, but it was great to see the away fans behind the goal erupt in wild celebration as the ball hit the back of the net. One win doesn't spell a resurgence, but it'll do nicely to be going along with.

The decision to buy a season ticket for the 24/25 season wasn't one that was ever based on financial prudence. Any advantages of paying upfront for all the home games are soon cancelled out when you begin to miss a few matches. Even before the fixture list was released, I knew in advance that I would be unavailable for three weeks in September on account of my holiday plans to visit Brooklyn and then Denver, Colorado; the call of the wild as it were. And there are any number of other reasons why making the round trip to Carlisle on any given Saturday might not be feasible.

Bill Shankly once said,

"Some people believe football is a matter of life and death, I am very disappointed with that

attitude, I can assure you it is much, much more important than that."

Shankly, who was famously an ex-manager of Carlisle United and one or two other clubs as well, was speaking tongue in cheek here, or else he was quite wrong. Read David Peace's excellent book Red or Dead and you will encounter a Shankly who was reliant upon and devoted to his wife, and who realised late in life that by relegating her role in the partnership he had done her a great disservice. He was hugely committed to football and he was passionately involved, but ultimately there are human responsibilities which matter more than playing or watching the game. Another quote, this time from former Liverpool manager Jurgen Klopp,

"Football always seems to be the most important of the least important things."

And I'm with Jurgen on this one. Due regard should be paid to weddings, funerals, and general family commitments, and football fandom should take its ordered place from where it can thrive. Let it entertain and fascinate us, provide magic and fantasy to buoy our spirits, but by the same token let it keep us humble. Football is a sport and there's nothing like sport for providing hubris, for leaving a huge bite imprint on our derriere. More important than life and death though? No, but with its massive highs and desperate lows it's a very good medium through which to reflect upon life in all its complexities. Lay out for a season ticket but recognise that there are perfectly valid reasons for taking a hit on your investment.

All of this is by way of explaining that a run of three games took place where for a number of reasons the Wakefield travelling faction was missing but thanks to the hospitality of Howard, I was able to further trample on my principles and sponge off his Sky subscription. It's a measure of the kind of man I am though that not content to live off freebies, I turned up with a packet of biscuits as a token of my gratitude towards my generous host. A decent packet too, none of your boring rich tea stuff, we're talking Tesco brand double choc cookies here. But don't let that distract you from the main issue here as football is more important than biscuits.

The match can be dealt with quite succinctly. Salford City's Moor Lane, the scene of a magnificent victory two seasons ago when a rampant Carlisle scored four goals to register a significant victory on their charge towards promotion, once again became the venue for Carlisle to pick up three points. Yes, a win! Sound the trumpets and bang the drums! Up the football league we go! Note the three consecutive sentences ending with exclamation marks written in an attempt to gloss over the turgid nature of the match, but this was what was needed; pick up the points and dispatch mediocre opposition and turn that metaphorical corner. But if this was a resurgence, it made for grim viewing. The Carlisle passing was pedantic, slow in delivery and often made to stationery players showing little or no urgency in mounting attacks. There was no discernible pattern of play and no evidence of an understanding between players. In short, there was very little threat towards the opponent's goal.

Data seems to be so important at the moment, so let's take a look at this match's vital statistics. Carlisle *had seven shots, one of which was on target. They made 258 passes, 59% of which were deemed to be accurate and they were awarded four corners throughout the game. Statistical analysis gives me no joy whatsoever but from this data readers may be asking about how Carlisle managed to take three points from the game as their figures were inferior to Salford's in all respects except for yellow cards where we had two to their three. Well, the win came from an eighty-eighth minute goal from Ben Barclay who launched himself horizontally through a crowd of players at one of the four Carlisle corners and planted a header into the net. It was the sort of goal which puts me in another dilemma over principles, this time about avoiding the hackneyed phrases of television pundits as it was clear that Barclay wanted it more.*

So, there it is. After writing that I need to go and lie down in a darkened room.

Tuesday 12 November. Morecambe v Carlisle United. The Mazuma Mobile Stadium (?). The Bristol Street Motors Trophy.

You know what I think of this competition from previous posts, so this won't take long. If a Carlisle game is available to watch free on TV than I find it difficult to stay away, but I can't claim that I was making a beeline for the sofa for this one.

With Lisa at a parents' evening, I was on cooking duties when the game kicked off. When I checked the score about twenty minutes into the game I wasn't surprised to find that we were a goal down, but was a bit pissed off to see that yet another former Carlisle player, Hallam Hope, had scored against his old club. When I eventually saw a replay of the goal, it was a dreadful illustration of the dangers of playing out from the back when you don't have players with the ability to do that. Ben Barclay, the goal-scoring hero on Saturday, was the villain in this instance.

I was able to watch the final fifteen minutes of the first half, and it wasn't particularly encouraging. There was far too much sideways passing to another player who was under immediate pressure and was invariably reduced to hoofing the ball aimlessly up field, giving the strikers precious little chance of winning possession. Not quite the entertaining, front-foot football we were promised when Williamson arrived.

Domestic duties completed, I settled down to watch the final half hour of the game. It was Sod's Law that the moment I chose to take a toilet break was the moment that Carlisle equalised. Fortunately, I was back in place when Carlisle scored what proved to be the winner just three minutes later.

It's a meaningless win in a meaningless competition from which we'd already been eliminated. A crowd of 788 said it all. But a win is a win. And two wins in a row is in danger of being described as momentum.

Incidentally, I'm less than impressed by the standard of commentary on Sky Sports +. The commentators tend to rely on current cliches about the clubs in question and be about ten minutes late in noticing changes in the dynamic of the game. In the good old days of i-Follow the commentary tended to be a feed of the coverage on regional radio. That meant that you got a commentator and summarizer who were extremely well-informed about the home team, and, with a little bit of homework, could do a decent job on the away side, and their players' strengths and weaknesses. A little bit of bias towards the home team was to be expected and didn't really matter too much.

Wednesday 13 November. Barnsley U18s v Carlisle United U18s. Oakwell. F.A. Youth Cup Round 2.

I don't normally make a habit of watching Carlisle's age-group teams, but when John suggested going to this game last Thursday three factors came into play. It's only twenty-five minutes' drive from Wakefield to Oakwell; admission was a princely £3 (£1 for concessionary old gits like us); and John's nephew, Tom Randall, was in goal for Carlisle.

I'm really glad we went. We were treated to a very entertaining game, and more importantly we saw a Carlisle team win for the third time in five days. Barnsley dominated the first half, controlling possession and looking pacy in attack. Carlisle struggled to create a meaningful attempt on goal and had to rely on a couple of excellent saves from Randall to reach half-time on equal terms.

A half-time substitution led to a slight change in formation and Carlisle looked distinctly livelier in the opening minutes of the second period. They took the lead in the 51st minute with their first attempt on goal was horribly mishandled by the Barnsley keeper, who managed to fumble the ball over his own line. John rather unkindly described it as an error of Harry Lewis proportions. Barnsley came at Carlisle strongly in the immediate aftermath of the goal and Randall made a brilliant double save to keep them at bay. John ventured that the rest of the game would probably be like The Alamo. But, having weathered that initial storm, Carlisle increasingly dictated the pattern of play, as Barnsley became more ragged. There was the worry that at 1-0 it only needed one mistake or moment of skill to turn the game on its head, but as the game entered the final stages it was Carlisle who looked more likely to score the game's second goal. Five minutes of added time were successfully negotiated to close out an excellent win.

All credit to those members of the team who put in a full shift just twenty-four hours after featuring in the senior side's win at Morecambe. Following a post-match huddle the players came over to acknowledge the small group of United fans who had remained behind (largely family I suspect!) and we were able to grab a couple of minutes with Tom, who probably earned my vote as man of the match.

There have been times when setting out for a game that either Howard or myself have said words to the effect that what we were about to do did not sit well with our notions of being intelligent men. A long drive, a cold afternoon/evening in prospect and very little chance of seeing our favourite team stage a thrilling performance. Let it be said, we have questioned our own behaviour and have been far from comfortable with the answers that turned up.

However, this particular evening did not lead to any such disquiet. Was it because of the close proximity of Oakwell, Barnsley's ground, which was a mere 9.8 miles away according to google, or the fact that no vital

League 2 points would be at stake? Or was it because we knew that the attendance would not stretch much beyond three figures? and those that were there would be seated together in the one open stand; no segregation, with tribal enmities laid to rest. Or was it just the prospect of watching two sets of talented young lads pitching their skills against each other? Whatever the reason, we shouldered the economic burden of paying our one-pound entrance fee and settled down to watch this F.A. Youth Cup round two fixture.

I acknowledge partiality in my writings on football as I am a Carlisle fan and have been since before the time when England won the World Cup, back to the year in fact that the poet Philip Larkin said sex was invented in Britain. This is an entirely unrelated fact, and an irrelevant one as far as my seven-year-old self was concerned, but it does mean that I have been a Blue long enough to see Carlisle play in all four divisions and, whisper it, in one division below that. They have reached Wembley finals on six occasions (with Cardiff standing in for Wembley twice) and they remain unbeaten in Europe thanks to their exploits in the Anglo-Italian Cup in 1972. Yes, and among the many ups there have also been a lot of downs, and such things cause an inextricable bond. Consequently, whenever I put pen to paper on football, my writing comes out in a distinct shade of blue. This is not always becoming or honourable. Without a degree of objectivity, writing can lose credibility which is why I recognise my various leanings and strive for a detached viewpoint untainted by bias or family allegiance. It is also why I will abide by this stricture in reporting a match where a stunning man-of-the-match performance, including several *brilliant saves, was turned in by the Carlisle goalkeeper; a fearless achievement from Thomas Randall who just happens to be my nephew.*

Down to business then, as the two teams lined up, Barnsley looked to be the bigger, stronger team and that proved to be the case as the game began and the South Yorkshire side were quick into the tackle in midfield denying Carlisle space or time to play. Rare forays by the Carlisle forwards were quickly snuffed out by some aggressive tackling and the visitors struggled to gain a toehold. The few goal attempts came from Barnsley but resolute tackling, and alert sweeping from Randall kept the scores level. The clearest chance on goal came with a drive from just inside the angle of the penalty area but the keeper pushed it competently wide to safety.

With the scores level at half time, it was evident that Carlisle should be pleased with that, but it was equally obvious that unless the balance of play altered, it looked odds on for an eventual Barnsley win. If Carlisle were to go through to the next round, they would need to step up their neat play in midfield, take the game further forward and look to nick a goal. And while, in boxing parlance, it would be foolish to try and "trade punches" with the team in red, they would need to mix it a bit more. Get in amongst the back four and prevent them from playing easy balls out from defence.

From the restart, Barnsley had a great chance within thirty seconds when a cross from the left created an opening, but the resultant poorly controlled shot landed on top of the United net. Even so, it looked as though it was Barnsley who had been fired up at the break and who were now intent on settling things. But Carlisle's careful persistence paid off on fifty-one minutes when substitute Lewis Lambert worked his way forward to get a shot on goal which the keeper fumbled allowing the ball to trickle into the net. One-nil to the Blues with a goal which was celebrated with a massive pile up of blue-shirted players by the far corner flag.

Whether it was conceding a goal or the celebration which was deemed to be provocative no-one will ever know, but Barnsley looked rattled, and they began an all-out assault on the Carlisle goal. With the best part of forty minutes to play it looked as though Carlisle would have to hang on and mount an Alamo-style defence. A fierce drive was finger-tipped onto the post by Randall before he was called upon again to save another fierce shot and then throw himself at the feet of the onrushing forward to smother and then hold the ball when a goal had looked certain. Brilliant and brave; the Barnsley fans around us acknowledged as much but they probably thought it would only be a temporary reprieve.

But it was not to be. Carlisle weathered the storm and played increasingly measured football along the length of the pitch. A lovely move from a corner ended with a fierce shot which hit a defender and rebounded to safety, but the young Cumbrians looked the most likely to score a second goal in the game as Barnsley's game unravelled. Constantly rebuffed, they lacked a plan B. Their last chance was a corner delayed by the referee's intervention following some intimidatory tactics as the players jostled in the box for position. When the ball was finally played in, it was Randall again who took control of the situation by punching clear.

And that was it. The final whistle blew and it was the cue for more massive celebrations on the pitch.

A well-deserved win, the significance of which had clearly not escaped the attention of these lads.

Let's not get carried away though and sentimentalise the encounter. This wasn't a salutary reminder of the joy and innocence of youth, of how the beautiful game could be enhanced by such evident pleasure and exuberance. This had been a proper, hard football match with some thundering tackles, some late challenges, time wasting and, on occasions, disrespect shown to the referee. But the team which was most manifestly a team, the team which had stuck to their craft and belief, was the team which had come out on top, and how satisfying was it to come away from a game where the winning team had shown such commitment to individual and group performances. Pride in the blue shirt shared by the smattering of Carlisle fans in the East stand.

Oh! and did I mention that the young lad in the Carlisle goal had an absolutely brilliant game?

Saturday 16 November. Bromley v Carlisle United. Hayes Lane. EFL League 2.

I need to start this report with an apology and a correction. When John arrived this afternoon to watch this game on Sky, he was at pains to point out that I'd misquoted him in my report on the U18s win at Barnsley on Wednesday evening. I'd said that he'd described the Barnsley goalkeeper's fumble that gave Carlisle their goal as "an error of Harry Lewis proportions." What he'd actually said was that the Barnsley keeper had experienced "a Harry Lewis moment", a reference to the home game against Cheltenham when, to quote myself, "Lewis parried a shot at his near post and then floundered helplessly by the post as the ball span back and nestled in the net." My apologies John, though I don't think the corrected version is much less damning!

The attendance for the game was 3,741, with the away allocation sold out well in advance, which is frequently the case. The capacity of Bromley's Hayes Lane ground is 5,000, meaning 1,250 tickets went unsold. You know what my feelings are about this recurring scenario, so I won't bore you by repeating what I said about a similar situation at Salford just a week ago. I'm not suggesting that a higher allocation of away tickets would necessarily have persuaded John and me to make the long trip to Bromley, but there may have been plenty more who would have been willing to do so.

There were eight changes to the starting line-up from the team who beat Morecambe on Tuesday night. The youth players who played two games in twenty-four hours on Tuesday and Wednesday were understandably not part of the match day squad. A whole host of others were absent through either suspension, injury or, in one case, an international call-up. It was telling that the starting eleven contained five players who are either loanees or on short-term contracts until January.

The early stages of the game followed a familiar and predictable pattern. Carlisle dominated possession but largely in their own half, failing to create any meaningful chances. Bromley made much better use of their limited possession to produce better opportunities. Gabe Breeze's handling and positioning in goal were a little suspect on a couple of occasions, but for those online trolls who are ridiculously quick to lay into him, let me point out the following. He's barely reached double figures in terms of first team starts, so he's still learning, and he's the best option we've got at the moment. He made a fine save to tip over a goal bound header.

As the half progressed Carlisle began to show more going forward. This may have been due to the fact that with no height up front, the players needed to play the ball on the ground, rather than lumping it long and high. Kadeem Harris showed an encouraging willingness to take on and beat defenders. Funny, we released players like Patrick and Gibson who had exactly that ability. The Bournemouth loan pair of Dominic Sadi and Daniel Adu-Adjei also impressed with their close control and direct running. In the last fifteen minutes of the half the momentum was definitely with Carlisle.

Bromley started the second half brightly and were gifted the lead in the 54th minute. After a weak challenge by Jon Mellish, Ben Williams then slid in with a rash and late challenge which led to an inevitable penalty. Breeze went the wrong way, and we were up against it.

One of the positives of today's performance was the evidence that Callum Guy is getting back to his best after a lengthy lay off. He broke forward with purpose and delivered some beautifully judged long passes. It looks like he's getting his radar back, even if it failed him on a couple of occasions.

Carlisle were gifted a way back into the game in the 82nd minute when Bromley substitute Leigh flailed a wild elbow into the face of Sam Lavelle and was issued with a straight red card. Lavelle, who is currently wearing a face mask to protect his broken nose, understandably reacted angrily and duly received a yellow card. Which is cue for yet another digression on the standard of officiating. A lot of Carlisle fans seem to think that the referee did a decent job and he certainly got the big calls right, the penalty and the red card. But both were so blatant that anyone could have called those two decisions. I can fully understand someone with a broken nose reacting to an elbow in the face and don't think he should have received a yellow card. If the original offence hadn't been committed there would have been no reaction. One red card and eight yellows suggest a pretty dirty game and it certainly wasn't that. And the fact that Carlisle received seven yellow cards to Bromley's one is, to be honest, preposterous. So no, I don't think the referee did a decent job. He was far quicker to punish the struggling away team than he was the newly promoted home team. Read into that what you will.

At least Carlisle made the extra man count. They created a number of chances in the remaining ten minutes though they failed to convert any of them. Shortly after seven minutes of additional time were signalled, Carlisle won a throw in on the right. As if in response to my calls from the sofa, Ben Barclay took the ball and launched a long throw into the Bromley penalty area. The ball ricocheted around for a moment before falling to Daniel Adu-Adjei who turned deftly and poked the ball home just inside the left-hand post. Carlisle fashioned a couple of further chances, but the winner was not forthcoming.

As for the post-match interviews, I think it's fair to say that Mike Williamson isn't the world's greatest communicator. In evidence I offer quotes such as "we wanted to make sure we didn't come away from our levels.", "we have got to just review the intention." and "Quality varies throughout the season and confidence and things like that, but the actual intention of what we tried to do was really good." I think nineteen-year-old Daniel Adu-Adjei achieved more clarity in his interview!

I suppose I should be reasonably happy with four points from two away games, plus a meaningless midweek win in a meaning less competition. But I'm not sure I am. Too many of the familiar failings are still in evidence; too much lateral passing to no effect in our own half; inaccurate forward passes; poor ball control; no clear pattern or style of play; the failure to convert chances into goals; no consistency in selection. We may be starting to pick up points, but I see no real sign that we've turned the corner yet.

What's this, an unbeaten run starting? Sure enough, Carlisle travel down to Bromley and earn a share of the spoils. Clearly that lie down in a darkened room did not do me any good. Nor was the game much of a spectacle with the same problems being evident i.e. too little in the way of fluent football. Quite frankly, Bromley looked there for the taking but this task appeared to be beyond Carlisle. They did manage to pick up seven yellow cards and from the fifty-fourth minute they trailed after Ben Williams gave away a penalty following his rash challenge in the box. The long trip to Bromley looked like being a fruitless one until the second minute of time added on, when Bromley failed to clear a corner and Daniel Adu-Adjei with his back to goal turned sharply to hit a ball into the bottom corner of the net. This was fair enough for Adu-Adjei who had looked lively throughout in the lone striker role but it did not

*cue the kind of madness you might expect from a late
equaliser, not in the Falshaw front room anyway. Relief
would be nearer the mark and the feeling that after ten
games with the new coaching regime, signs of the
promised intensity and excitement should be more
evident. Mike Williamson as Head Coach is on the
record as saying, "We want to attack the back line at
every opportunity, and we want to connect that with the
fans." Well Mike, the fans are waiting for the
connection.*

Saturday 23 November. Carlisle United v Doncaster Rovers. Brunton Park. EFL League 2.

It feels like an age since I've seen a Carlisle game in
person, and indeed it's a whole month since John and
I were at Brunton Park to witness Charlie Wyke's
season-ending injury. This game was meant to mark our
return to front-line supporting duties, but parental
responsibilities intervened. Imogen, who has already
accepted an offer of a place to study Sociology at
the University of Sheffield, had booked a place on an
open day, with a particular interest in checking out
accommodation options. So instead of spending the
afternoon at a rain-sodden Brunton Park I spent it in a
rain-sodden Sheffield.

Given that the game was a goalless draw, it may be
the case that Providence was shining on me. I probably
gained more from the day in Sheffield than I would have
from the long trip to Carlisle for limited reward. My
direct involvement with the game was limited to regular
glances at my phone for score updates. In fact, that
process began well before three o'clock, with frequent

checks to see if the game had survived the weather. I was half hoping it hadn't, to assuage any residual guilt at not being there.

On the surface of things, a draw against a team in one of the automatic promotion places is a decent result, even though it meant that we sank to the bottom of the table. It's another game unbeaten and another clean sheet. There was some consistency of selection in midfield and attack, though Ben Barclay's suspension and Terrel Thomas's injury while on international duty with St Lucia meant yet more changes in defence. That scenario will be repeated next weekend due to Jon Mellish's suspension. It's impossible to comment on the detail of the game, but the impression I've gleaned from match reports and the dreaded statistics is that Carlisle had the best of the first half while Doncaster came back strongly at them in the second half. Apparently, Carlisle thought they'd won the game with yet another last gasp goal when Cameron Harper netted, only for the inevitable offside flag to be raised. Having just watched the brief highlights, I'm not sure where the offside occurred. As the final minutes ticked away, we were sitting on a grossly overcrowded Northern Rail train from Sheffield to Wakefield, with me glued to my phone. When I saw that Doncaster had had a player sent off in the 96th minute I fleetingly hoped it was for giving away a penalty. Alas, it was not to be.

Mike Williamson's post-match interview largely consisted of the usual platitudes and meaningless phrases. Whatever his coaching credentials might be, he's certainly no master of the media.

In a positive footnote, there was a nice Facebook post from a couple of Ipswich Town fans. They found themselves without a game on Saturday, as the Tractor Boys' game against Manchester was being shown on Sky Sports on Sunday teatime. I would have seized the opportunity to rail against Sky's pernicious control over fixture schedules. They saw it as an opportunity to tick off another ground on their way to the Holy Grail of visiting all 92 league grounds, a target they're both tantalisingly close to. Despite a fairly tortuous journey in both directions, they apparently enjoyed their very long day.

Now here's a story, an anecdote if you like from the Clarke archives. Way back in the early sixties, my father began to take my brother and me to watch Carlisle United play. Very often we'd call for his friend Jim to come with us and the four of us would set off from Currock to walk amongst the crowds crossing St Nicholas Bridges, past Cowans Sheldon crane works, along Woodruffe Terrace, across London Road to eventually join Greystone Road before crossing Warwick Road to enter Brunton Park and take up our places as close to the half way line in the Scratching Pen side of the ground as possible. My brother and I wore our blue and white scarves and walked at a fast enough pace to keep up with the adults and fall in with the general air of excitement. We were going to the football match. Or in the vernacular, we were gan ower Nicky Bridges to gan to the match.

We were indeed going to watch Ross, Caldwell, Neil, McConnel, Passmoor, Thompson, Brayton, McIlmoyle, Livingstone and Kirkup. There were occasional variations on this as sometimes Joe Dean would appear in goal, Johnny Evans would make an appearance at inside-right and a local boy by the name of George

McVitie was being marked out as a very promising prospect in the reserves.

This was the general pattern on every other Saturday afternoon, we would set out to watch Division Four football against teams with names redolent of that level: Darlington, Halifax, Hartlepool, Bradford, Stockport, Lincoln, Rochdale, Southport and Workington among others. But the fixture I particularly remember was against Doncaster Rovers. On that afternoon, as Jim closed the front door behind him, he made the astonishing statement, "I think it will be six-nil to Doncaster today."

Even with the naivety of a seven-year-old, I knew this to be a wind-up and kept my counsel. Losing? My heroes in blue folding to Doncaster Rovers by a six-goal margin? Unthinkable. It would go right against the natural order of things.

In the event, there was a six-nil scoreline but in Carlisle's favour. Four nil up in the first half and a further two added in the second. Hugh McIlmoyle scored, of course he did, but I would have to look it up to provide more details.*

I only mention this because coming right up to date, the game against Doncaster Rovers looked like a good one in prospect. Rovers, having a good early season, were lying third in the table. Carlisle were hopefully taking confidence from their recent haul of four points from two games. Getting to the match though was no longer a case of skipping across St Nicholas Bridges. It is now, according to Google, a hundred and thirty-two-mile road trip. Daunting at any time, but Howard had already declared his unavailability owing to a University Open Day for his daughter and so I was faced with the solo journey. It was a prospect which paled even further in the face of a weather forecast saying bad and getting worse.

So, I settled for an afternoon in front of Grandstand and the teleprinter. Yes, you have spotted the distinctly nostalgic tone of this post already. Regardless, I stayed at home to discover later that the A66 had been closed since early morning, so travelling up would have been folly.

What was rather more pleasing was when the score came through and it was not the six goals of yore, obviously, but it was a creditable goalless draw. From all accounts a well-merited draw as possession was shared equally, and although Gab Breeze was called upon to make some fine saves, Carlisle had a goal ruled out for offside when, as the saying goes, it looked well onside on Ceefax.

A crowd of 6,837 with 704 away fans watched what appeared from the highlights, to be an entertaining game. Carlisle held the high-flying visitors, created chances along the way and they could now proudly point towards a three-match unbeaten run. Is the bright light at the end of the tunnel beginning to emerge? Can Carlisle fans now look forward to a bright future, or do they still need to take comfort in tales of the good old days?

*A team of highly dedicated researchers has in fact been engaged in checking details of this game and alongside the fallibility of your correspondent's memory the following emerged:

Carlisle United (6) versus Doncaster Rovers (0). H.T. (3-0) March 21st, 1964.

Scorers: Evans (3) McIlmoyle, Davies, Taylor.

Attendance 4,753. It is not recorded how many away fans were in attendance nor indeed, how many spectators arrived at the ground after gan ower Nicky Bridges.

Saturday 30 November. Carlisle United v Crewe Alexandra. Brunton Park. EFL League 2.

This is becoming more than a little embarrassing. For the second week in a row I had to message John to tell him that domestic duties would prevent me travelling to Brunton Park. Lisa was doing a poetry recording at Chapel FM in Leeds, and Imogen needed transporting to her Saturday shift at Wakefield RSPCA. I wouldn't have minded so much if it hadn't been John's turn to drive.

A 12.30 kick-off meant that the game was available to stream on Sky Sports +, but the aforementioned domestic duties meant that I could take only limited advantage of that opportunity, Imogen and I had just begun our journey to the RSPCA in East Ardsley when Radio 5 reported that Carlisle had taken an early lead, thanks to a second minute strike from Dominic Sadi. By the time I finally got home, the score was still 1-0, with just over twenty minutes left to play.

That was sufficient time to see Georgie Kelly, finally fit again and on as a substitute, narrowly fail to get on the end of two teasing crosses to the far post at the Warwick Road End. Unfortunately, it was also sufficient time to see him commit a rash challenge at the other end of the pitch that led to a penalty and the Crewe equaliser. Some online comments suggested that Kelly hadn't touched the Crewe player. Having watched the match highlights, I wouldn't like to pass comment on whether it was indeed a penalty, but I'm quite happy to comment that neither the referee or the linesman were in the best position to make a decision. I did like the online comment that Tom Daley must have been playing for Crewe today. I hesitate to pass judgement based on the limited amount of the game I saw, but some familiar failings persist. One is the tendency to concede penalties through intemperate tackles – that's two in three weeks now. A lot of hard work can be rendered irrelevant by a moment of rashness. The main issue though is the mantra of playing out from the back. It's evident that the players are becoming more comfortable with and accustomed to the strategy, but there were still occasions in those last twenty minutes (I should say 30 given the 10 minutes of added time) when possession was conceded in dangerous areas. There were also times when players received the ball under pressure and had little option but to hoof the ball hopefully forward.

It's not that long ago that I used to mock League 2 teams who persisted in playing the ball out from the back, when it was patently obvious that they didn't have players with the skills to execute that strategy. It worries me that Carlisle seem to be becoming one of those teams. Pep Guardiola's coaching genius may have transformed the way football is played by highly talented multi-millionaires in the Premier League, but I'm not convinced that his influence further down the football pyramid has been entirely positive.

Again, I'm loth to read too much into the thirty minutes I actually watched, but I don't recall Gabe Breeze kicking long on a single occasion. When he first replaced Harry Lewis in goal he appeared to exercise good judgement in mixing long clearances with the short pass or throw to a defender. I get the distinct impression that someone's had a word with him and told him that he should only go long when there's absolutely no other option. To end on a positive note, this is the second game in succession where we've played a top three team and come away with a point. It's also four games unbeaten, even if three of those games have been draws. Carlisle's best moves came when the ball was played to feet, and when players like Jordan Jones and Dominic Sadi had the confidence to take on and beat defenders. Jones and Kelly, both returning from lengthy injuries, both did enough as substitutes to suggest that they could make a significant contribution in the long term provided they stay fit.

This result means that we've moved out of the relegation zone, even if that may be temporary. But it's a very long way from where we expected to be at this stage when the season kicked off.

Chapter 6
WHEN WILL THERE BE GOOD NEWS?

Saturday 14 December. Carlisle United v Chesterfield. Brunton Park. EFL League 2.

It felt like a long time since John and I had made the journey to Brunton Park together, and indeed it was. One day short of fifty since we'd travelled up for the Cheltenham game that saw Charlie Wyke's season ending injury. Adam should have been joining us but, to his eternal shame, he'd chosen to go with his sister to see Sam Fender live in Birmingham, rather than come home from university on Friday so he could travel with us. One day he'll grow up and act his age!

I wouldn't say that we travelled bursting with optimism, but I think there was a sense that, after a couple of decent draws against top three teams, this might be the day that we picked up a much needed three points against less challenging opposition. We both talked positively about the fact that there finally appeared to be some consistency in selection over the last three or four games. That positive was blown out of the water just after two o'clock, as we turned onto the M6 and the line-ups were published. The midfield was entirely reshaped, with Guy dropped to the bench and McGeouch and Vela starting for the first time in a while. Jordan Jones also started, after a couple of substitute appearances, not that I had any problem with that. I can only assume that Callum Guy was rested rather than dropped, since he's put in a fair shift since he returned to action after nearly a season's absence.

There was a silver lining when my eyes dropped to the small print of the substitutes. I said, "John, Tom's on the bench for today's game!" If you didn't read my piece on the Youth Team's win at Barnsley a few weeks ago, Thomas Randall is the U18s goalkeeper and just happens to be John's nephew. When we finally arrived and made our way into The Paddock, it didn't take long to meet up with two very proud parents.

And there was a special moment (for those of us of a certain vintage) in the build-up to kick off when a number of the surviving members of the Carlisle United squad that graced the First Division fifty years ago were introduced to the crowd and welcomed with generous applause. It's a sad fact that probably only a minority of Saturday's crowd appreciated just how important these men were to the greatest era in the club's history, and how special it was to see so many of them together again at Brunton Park. Les O'Neill, Bobby Parker, Ray Train, Peter Carr, Bobby Owen, Tot Winstanley and Peter McLachlan all appeared. And I should also mention the members of that squad who are sadly no longer with us – Chris Balderstone, Allan Ross, Bill Green, Joe Laidlaw and Frank Clarke.

I'm not going to attempt to give a coherent account of the game. It seems a bit pointless when there were so few signs of coherence on the pitch. That's not to say that there weren't moments of encouragement, particularly in the first half. Three times Jordan Jones made impressive runs through midfield from a deep position. Three times his final pass was woeful, hit into empty space, many yards from where another blue-shirted player might have or should have been. On a similar number of occasions Arron Hayden brought the ball confidently out of defence, rather than settle for an easy sideways pass, only for his positional sense to desert him in the second half. Dylan McGeouch strived manfully to make himself available to defenders, but often in a position as deep as the defenders themselves. The bottom line is that we lost 2-0, both goals the result of defensive errors, and we remain rooted to the bottom of League 2. So, what exactly is wrong at Brunton Park at the moment?

The players are clearly doing their best to play in the style that the coach asks of them, even if they're not doing it very well. I suspect that we don't currently have the quality of players to execute the style of play that Mike Williamson demands. It's all well and good having a clear view of how the team should play, but it's pointless adhering slavishly to that philosophy when it clearly isn't working at the moment. Williamson's vision of how the game should be played may well bear fruit in the long term, but I don't want to see that happen in the surroundings of the National League.

I am yet to be convinced that Mike Williamson knows how to get the best out of the players at his disposal, or how to set up a team to play effectively, whether that adheres to his philosophy or not. It was disappointing that his post-match interview waffled on about things like the expected goals data. I now have a slightly better understanding of expected goals, thanks to Adam's ever-patient explanation, but at the end of the day there's only one statistic that really matters, and that's position in the league table. I struggle to find any sign of improvement since Paul Simpson was dismissed.

Simpson is long gone, but Greg Abbott unfathomably remains in post as head of recruitment. Which brings me on to transfer windows. I'm not going to waste time on the summer recruits, since so many of them are currently injured. But let's go back to last January when we had added buying power thanks to the Piataks' takeover. I still retain a slender hope that Luke Armstrong will rediscover his mojo at Carlisle, but he's currently not even making the match-day squad, so I think the writing is on the wall there. Harry Lewis in goal is playing second fiddle to Gabe Breeze, a fairly recent product of the Carlisle Academy. Harrison Neal impresses with his energy and endeavour, but in a rather limited way. I had high hopes of Josh Vela after watching his first couple of appearances for Carlisle. He looked tenacious and aggressive in defence, and speedy and incisive in attack. Potentially a well-rounded box-to-box player. On Saturday I saw a series of niggly fouls, yet another early yellow card and an entirely predictable half-time substitution. Georgie Kelly has been injured for most of the last year, and when he came on at half-time on Saturday his performance was mainly notable for the number of crosses he didn't quite get on the end of. When he did finally connect, he spooned the ball over the bar. He may be a little rusty, but he needs to start producing almost immediately. Given his recent recruitment record, Abbott needs to produce some rabbits out of his hat if he is not to be gone by the end of January.

It's easy to criticise defenders for playing easy sidewise passes to a teammate who is immediately under the same pressure as they were. Some of the criticism should also lie with the players further forward who are failing to find the space to offer the option of a forward pass. It was noticeable that when Callum Guy came on as a substitute on Saturday, he was quick to provide that option. I feel that this all re-enforces my belief that Williamson does not know how to set up a team effectively with the players he has in front of him.

I'm going to conclude this post with a few quotes from Carlisle supporting friends. Ron Maddison, a stalwart of "Old School Carlisle United" and a significant contributor to the "Backing the Blues" exhibition had this to say. "At the risk of being labelled as negative I have to say I have no faith in our coaching set up and that team is rubbish. Time to scrap this three at the back before it is too late. Not because the system is flawed but because we don't have the players to play it. I'm a fan of Aaron Hayden but yesterday he looked like a first-year pro, way out of his comfort zone. At the moment we are making players look far worse than what they are and I believe that is down to the coaching staff and the way they are asking the players to play."

When I messaged Peter Scholes, author of "The Place I Belong", his account of his life as a Blues fan, for his reaction to the game, he responded thus. "It was awful. Like the game v Cheltenham. Selection was a mystery, players out of position, awful passing, no goal threat, suicide defending etc. Hard to find any moments of the day. Desperate stuff. A lot of these players aren't bad players but in this system with this pressure they are looking like complete strangers playing National League North level. I'm sure they are better than this but not on current showings."

Saturday 21 December. Port Vale v Carlisle United. Vale Park. EFL League 2.

Was this going to be a day when Carlisle presented us with an early Christmas gift, in the form of a long overdue win? I ventured as much to Adam as we battled our way across the windswept summit of the M62, a view based far more on hope than genuine expectation. I suggested that we might manage a scrappy 1-0 win.

The Wakefield Blues travelled at half-strength for this game. John was on airport duty, in Manchester to collect his son and partner who were flying in from New York for Christmas. Ben was on a short break with his mum, having just returned from university. However, our numbers were bolstered on arrival at Vale Park, where we were joined by Peter Scholes. Peter is yet another former teacher, currently a driving instructor, and fellow author of a book on Carlisle United (and much more). We'd been trying to arrange a proper meet-up ever since I contributed a small piece to his book 'The Place I Belong', and this was the first proper opportunity. Peter's seat in the main stand at Brunton Park is almost directly above where we normally stand in The Paddock.

Nearly seven hundred Carlisle fans had made the journey, an impressive turn-out for the Saturday before Christmas. It's interesting to note that Port Vale, second in League 2 at the beginning of the day, are attracting almost exactly the same size of crowd as Carlisle, bottom of League 2 at the start of the day. Since Adam and I last visited Vale Park the away section has been switched from one end of the ground to the other.

There were one or two surprises in the match-day squad. There were predictable changes in midfield, with McGeouch and Vela from the previous week's team both injured. We appeared to be playing four centre-backs, though it quickly became clear that Jon Mellish was playing as left wing back. Luke Armstrong, not even on the bench for the previous game, returned to lead the attack, while George Kelly, a half-time substitute a week earlier, remained on the bench. Callum Guy wasn't even on the bench. My comment to Peter was, "If he's not injured, then Mike Williamson really doesn't know what he's doing." Apparently, the explanation was that a sickness bug had swept through the squad and Guy was one of the victims. Our favourite youth goalkeeper, Thomas Randall, was on the bench for a second week in succession. My pre-match optimism wasn't entirely unfounded. We appeared to have hit paydirt as early as the second minute when Luke Armstrong forced the ball home from close range, only for the referee to rule it out for a foul on the goalkeeper. Having watched the match highlights, I can't see that Armstrong did anything wrong. His rueful smile spoke volumes. It proved to be the first of a number of poor decisions. Nonetheless, Carlisle had the best of the first half (a view endorsed by Radio 5 Live according to John), playing some pacy and direct football, with not too much laborious playing out from the back. Jordan Jones is beginning to look like a player around whom Williamson can build his team. Pacy, confident in taking defenders on, and a good crosser. It was noticeable that when he and Mellish found themselves together in advanced positions on the left, Mellish would usually feed the ball to Jones, knowing that his final delivery was likely to be better.

There was less laboured passing out from the back than has often been the case, with the ball being moved more quickly and with more urgency. This was due in no small part to Harrison Neal who, despite his ungainly running style, frequently sought space to make himself available for a forward pass out of defence and is starting to display an improved range of passing. Jon Mellish made a handful of his trademark surging runs forward, but all too frequently conceded possession due to poor ball control.

As the second half wore on, the game increasingly took on the appearance of that rare entity, a relatively entertaining goalless draw. That wasn't necessarily reassuring! While it held out the prospect of possibly snatching all three points with a late goal, it also embraced the possibility of a good afternoon's work being undone by a single error or momentary lapse of concentration. Neither outcome happened, leaving us to savour a hard-won point away to one of the best teams in the division. The ability to grind out draws against high-flying opposition offers some slender hope, though not when it's followed by the failure to put on a decent performance against less elevated teams, as was the case against Chesterfield. Let's hope that the pattern is not repeated against Morecambe on Boxing Day, in what is an absolutely crucial match.

It transpired in a post-match interview that Jon Mellish had thrown up during half-time, which might explain his less than impressive performance in the first half. Nonetheless he emerged after the interval and played the full ninety minutes plus. Maybe some of his sick colleagues need to show the same commitment to the cause.

Thursday 26 December. Carlisle United v Morecambe F.C. Brunton Park. EFL League 2.

Where do I start? Okay, with an admission that I wasn't actually at this game. Already committed to the Accrington game on the 29th, and with the strong possibility of trips to Tranmere and Crewe in the early days of the new year, plus John's unavailability for travel, I made the decision to spend Boxing Day 2024 in the bosom of the family. In most respects I'm glad I did, though there's a tiny bit of me thinks that I really should have been at Brunton Park to share the pain.

I don't need to have been there to be able to comment on the events that unfolded though. Jon Colman's "as it happens" posts, and the hundreds of online comments, plenty of them from people whose opinions I value and respect, give me a perfectly clear picture of what happened. The bottom line is that we lost abjectly to the one team below us in the table, in what was justifiably described as a must-win game. We are now bottom of the EFL and staring relegation to the National League in the face.

The obvious point of reference for me is the day in February 2022, less than three years ago, when Harry McKirdy returned to Brunton Park in the colours of Swindon Town, twisting the knife against his former club with a goal and two assists. That game featured chants of "Sign him on" following two pitch incursions by disgruntled supporters, and post-match chants of "Hello to the National League". Yesterday sounded even worse. Apparently season tickets were thrown onto the pitch in disgust, while chants of "You're getting sacked in the morning" and "You don't know what you're doing" rang from most sections of the ground. The difference is that the Swindon game took place in front of 4,345 fans. Yesterday's shitshow was watched by a bumper Boxing Day crowd of 9,225, with 8,500 plus being Carlisle fans.

I'm not going to waste time attempting to comment on the details of a game I didn't even watch. What I will do is attempt to assess the parlous situation the club finds itself in and offer some (reasonably) considered opinions.

I've read hundreds of comments on Facebook groups over the last couple of days, many of them saying that this is the worst Carlisle team and performance they can remember seeing. Any support for Mike Williamson was very difficult to find. I stated some weeks ago that Williamson has a responsibility to get the best out of the players at his disposal. He obviously disagrees. He's persisted with a style of play to which his players are patently unsuited, and while he drones on about expected goals and the number of incursions into the opposition area, he appears to ignore the most basic bit of data imaginable – the league table.

Until now I've refrained from openly condemning Williamson, but I think my previous posts have made my scepticism perfectly clear. So, cards on the table time. His appointment has been an unqualified disaster. He's been even more incompetent as Carlisle coach than his political namesake Gavin was as Education Secretary during the pandemic. And believe me, coming from a recently retired teacher who taught through the pandemic, whose daughter's A-Level results were almost fucked up by his incompetence, that really does take some saying. I really did not believe that I would ever encounter anyone less capable of doing their job than Gavin Williamson. For god's sake, I had two letters published in The Guardian about his incompetence!

If Mike Williamson is so big on data and analysis, why doesn't he spend a bit of time watching videos of Luke Armstrong in a Harrogate shirt (particularly against Carlisle) to work out how to bring the best out of him. Williamson played with Armstrong at Gateshead and yet still can't deploy him effectively. I've said it before, and I'll say it again, Armstrong is not a target man, particularly in a team that gives its strikers such meagre scraps to feed off. Armstrong playing off Kelly in the channels, with Kelly as the conventional target man has enormous potential. Or it would if anyone could rely on Kelly's fitness and availability. In just three months Williamson has achieved the remarkable feat of making a group of competent League Two players appear much worse than they are. I'm going to go off piste for a moment here. Pep Guardiola has been rightly lauded for transforming the way in which football is played. I have immense respect for Guardiola as both a football coach and a decent human being. But his success has been achieved at three elite clubs, where he has had access to almost unlimited funds to recruit outstanding players capable of playing the style of football he demands. Meantime managers and coaches at lower levels have striven to emulate his philosophy, with much poorer resources at their disposal. What it leads to is slow, sterile football which is incredibly boring to watch. Two seasons ago Paul Simpson managed a squad that was highly adept at countering that style of football and won promotion as a result. I don't want to watch my team endlessly making lateral passes across the defence. I want to see them moving forward with pace and urgency to put the opposition under pressure.

Some comments have suggested that Paul Simpson would be the ideal person for this situation. I can understand why, given the transformation he achieved just under three years ago, but there's a significant difference to the situation he inherited then. He took over a squad entirely inherited from previous managers and worked wonders. If he were to return now, he'd inherit a squad that was entirely assembled by him, with the exception of Guy, Mellish, Burey and Harris. Much as I'd like to see him back, he's already failed with the same group of players.

We will be travelling tomorrow, because hope springs eternal. I desperately hope that we win, because it's so long since we've enjoyed a home win. If we don't, Williamson has to go. I have to admit that I'm disappointed he hasn't gone already. And Abbott should have gone ages ago. As manager he used to complain about lack of resources. Now that they're available, he's made a woeful job of recruitment in the last three transfer windows.

A brief footnote. The game featured an initiative to promote awareness of autism. Players of both sides were asked to walk out for the game wearing ear defenders. Almost every Morecambe player did so. All credit to Sam Lavelle and Luke Armstrong for doing the same. Shame on the other nine Carlisle players who obviously couldn't be bothered and shame on Mike

Williamson for not insisting that they all did so. I have a child who is autistic.

Sunday 29 December. Carlisle United v Accrington Stanley. Brunton Park. EFL League 2.

Sod waiting a day for sober reflection before committing my thoughts to paper. I want to savour the warm (and rare!) feeling of success and victory while it's still coursing through my veins. For the first time in ages all four Wakefield Blues were able to make the trip. Our numbers were further reinforced by Anna, Adam's girlfriend, who was not only attending her first Carlisle game, but she was also attending her first ever football match. Would she prove to be a lucky talisman? Lisa had already told her about her first, and to date only, experience of attending a Carlisle game nearly thirty years ago. Her account of her afternoon at Doncaster Rover's dilapidated former Belle Vue ground was underwhelming to say the least. Adam had warned Anna that the Brunton Park atmosphere might be fairly toxic after the Boxing Day debacle. A 12.30 kick off meant an early departure from Wakefield, and we parked in the Riverside car park just after 11.30. In the fan zone we bumped into Alistair Kirkpatrick. He reassured us that the Boxing Day game was every bit as bad as the online comments suggested.

When we finally made our way into the ground, the atmosphere was surprisingly calm. The line-up looked relatively attacking, with Kadeem Harris and Daniel Adu-Adjei restored to the starting team. The subs bench was worryingly weak, including three youth players and

Anton Dudik, recently recalled from a loan spell. With such a large squad, how can we be so short of players? A close look at fitness and conditioning is called for, alongside closer scrutiny of players' injury record before signing them.

Someone had obviously failed to do due diligence on the pitchside advertising. As the teams walked out the electronic boards brightly proclaimed "The region's biggest panto returns"! Fortunately it referred to a genuine pantomime and not the Boxing Day horror show.

The early signs were encouraging. Gabe Breeze in goal invariably went long with his clearances, and there was encouraging pace and movement further forward. Pay-off came as early as the 12th minute when Jon Mellish overlapped down the left flank, and his low cross from the byline was slammed into the roof of the net by Kadeem Harris, his first goal for the club. The sense of relief on the terraces and in the stands was palpable.

The rest of the first half saw a more direct and entertaining style of play than we have become accustomed to in recent weeks. Who knows whether that was a result of instructions from the coaching team or simply the players doing their own thing? I don't think that a 2-0 half-time score would have flattered Carlisle. As it was, we were lucky to go into the interval ahead. Twice in the final minutes of the half Accrington hit the woodwork. The first was a long-distance shot that rebounded off the crossbar. The second was a close-range header that hit the post.

They would regret those missed chances early in the second half, when they proved to be authors of their own downfall. As Accrington attempted to play the ball out from the back on their right flank, Kadeem Harris and Luke Armstrong pressed them hard. A loose pass from a defender to the goalkeeper gave Harris the chance to surge forward and although he couldn't reach the ball he made an excellent block on the keeper's attempted clearance. The ball fell to the feet of Armstrong who had the simple task of side footing it into an empty net. Boy did he celebrate!

A few minutes later Harris had the opportunity to put the game to bed when one-on-one with the goalkeeper, but put the ball over the bar. It was good to see stand-in captain Jordan Jones to go straight over him to have a quiet word. I was impressed by Jones in his new role. He was frequently talking to the referee, though in a slightly less aggressive manner than was Paul Huntington's habit, and he was constantly encouraging and cajoling his teammates.

Accrington pulled a goal back in the 73rd minute when Aaron Hayden carelessly let an attacker get the wrong side of him. That set the nerves on edge, with plenty of time for an equaliser. Fortunately, that didn't transpire as Carlisle showed sound game management to see the game out, despite a couple of dodgy attempts to play the ball around at the back while under a high press from Accrington. The crowd were quick to voice their disapproval. Nerves were further shredded when the six minutes of time added on quickly doubled when Jon Mellish suffered a head injury that required lengthy treatment. The one thing that was clear was that there was no way he was going to come off at that stage of the game. Predictably the bandage was whipped off the moment the final whistle went.

The game also had its own comedy moment in the second half. After a Carlisle set-piece was cleared, Accrington broke forward and Carlisle defenders raced to get back into position. In doing so, Ben Barclay clipped the heels of referee Thomas Parsons sending him sprawling full-length on the turf, to widespread hilarity on the terraces. That was no doubt compounded by the fact that it was Parsons who issued Jon Mellish with a ridiculous red card for pushing Salford's Nathan Watt in the chest two seasons ago, a decision that caused Mellish to miss the last game of the season and both play-off semi-final ties. His performance wasn't much better yesterday, issuing ten yellow cards (five to each team) in a game that was never particularly dirty.

This was a day when the result was everything. The fact that the performance included a few positive signs was a bonus. I know it's only one game, and we may be back to doom and gloom after the New Year's Day fixture at Crewe, but it's a lovely feeling while it lasts. I still don't think Mike Williamson is the right man to take the team forward, but this result has probably bought him a bit more time. Interestingly, Tom and Patty Piatak were in the crowd at Queen of the South (managed by Carlisle legend Peter Murphy) the day before, and Murphy was in the crowd at Brunton Park yesterday. The crowd was a remarkable 7,130 of which only 288 were away supporters. I say remarkable because the club started the day at the very bottom of the EFL, after a performance that many supporters described as the worst they'd seen in decades. John, as a native of the city, commented, rather cynically, "Howard, it's a Sunday in Carlisle. What else do people have to do?" Neither the management, the players or the owners should take such support for granted. Not only did they turn out in numbers, but they also got right behind the team vocally. I feel privileged to be part of such a dedicated fan base.

Chapter 7
SQUARE PEGS (AND NEW ONES) IN ROUND HOLES

Wednesday 1 January 2025. Crewe Alexandra v Carlisle United. Gresty Road (or The Mornflake stadium if you prefer – I don't). EFL League 2.

Well, the warm feeling generated by Sunday's win over Accrington was nice for the three days it lasted. It actually endured for the ninety minutes of this game. It was the seven additional minutes that were problematic.

I did have thoughts of travelling to this game but wasn't too disappointed to learn that the away allocation had sold out. Gresty Road would have been another ground ticked off the EFL list, but with Tranmere a likely destination on Saturday I didn't mind foregoing a third long trip in seven days, particularly when the game was available to watch on Sky Sports +.

My initial reaction on seeing the team selection was to wonder why Mike Williamson had tinkered with the line-up that had ground out a deserved win over Accrington just three days earlier. I know that the games come thick and fast at this time of the year, and that any coach has to be mindful of the physical fitness of his players, but it seemed a little perverse to relegate Jordan Jones, captain against Accrington, and Kadeem Harris, scorer of one goal and instrumental in the other, to the bench, altering the shape of the team. Despite those reservations Carlisle started the game brightly against a Crewe team very much in the promotion picture. United were creating the better chances and took a deserved lead after twenty-one minutes. Harrison Biggins curled a free kick towards Crewe's right-hand post where it was met by Jack Ellis, whose downward header bounced up and over the flailing arms of the Crewe keeper into the far corner. It was Ellis's first senior goal for the club.

Carlisle continued to have the better of the exchanges, but gave Crewe a route back into the game, thanks to a bad error by Ben Barclay in the 32nd minute. He slipped and fell a few yards outside the Carlisle box, allowing Crewe's Long to fire a shot at goal. Breeze parried it onto the bar from where it bounced down and span into the net, despite Barclay's last-ditch attempt to clear it off the line. United were definitely the better team over the first forty-five minutes and could consider themselves unlucky not to be ahead at the interval.

The team struggled to regain their momentum in the early stages of the second half, and it began to look like yet another example of failing to string together two decent halves in the same game. Williamson did attempt to change the shape of the game in the 58th minute, bringing on the attack-minded Jones and Harris in place of Ellis and Harper. Nonetheless, the game looked increasingly likely to end in a slightly disappointing draw until Kadeem Harris got to work again in the 78th minute. As against Accrington he harried defenders and won the ball deep in Crewe territory. He played the ball through to Armstrong, who squared the ball perfectly for Harris to slot home from about ten yards. Suddenly we were looking at the unlikely scenario of wins in successive league games, as the game reached the end of normal time. I groaned as seven minutes of added time were indicated, and if I'd known what was about to happen, I'd have done a lot more than groan. In a mad five minutes poor game management and slack marking allowed Crewe to score twice, entirely turning the game on its head.

I'm not sure where we go from here. It wasn't just the defeat that was so dispiriting, it was the manner of it. When Williamson made his second set of substitutions in the 82nd minute, I can't for the life of me understand why he brought on Tyler Burey. Not that I've anything against Burey. He looks promising in attack, but defending is not one of his strengths. Having just retaken the lead the situation cried out for Aaron Hayden to be brought on to bolster the defence. If I can see that, why can't Williamson? His earlier decision to take off Ellis, another defender, also came back to bite him.

Two new signings have already arrived early in the transfer window, both midfielders, but I'm really struggling to find any cause for optimism in the current situation. I'm way past clutching at straws.

Saturday 4 January. Tranmere Rovers v Carlisle United. Prenton Park. EFL League 2.

This was a first for John, as in a first trip to Prenton Park. There were a couple of minor jeopardies attached to this trip. Firstly the weather forecast was not good, with amber warnings for snow and ice. Given the fact that we would be crossing The Pennines twice, this was not a minor consideration. But snow was not forecast until about nine in the evening, so despite Lisa's reservations, we sallied forth. The second jeopardy was that we didn't have tickets for the game. The initial away allocation had sold out, but I'd been reassured by the Brunton Park ticket office that a further 400 tickets would be on sale at the Prenton Park office from 1.30 p.m. It didn't prove to be quite that simple, but more of that later.

A brief digression on satellite navigation. This was my third visit to Tranmere, and not once has the satnav taken me by the same route in both directions. The first time it took me along The Wirral Peninsula on the outward journey, and through the Birkenhead Tunnel and the centre of Liverpool on our return. The second time it conducted me along the same routes but in opposite directions. Before you dismiss this as a quirk of my Hyundai's satnav, we travelled in John's Ford Focus yesterday and the same thing happened – outward journey through the Birkenhead Tunnel and return along The Wirral.

We even experienced a brief 'Gavin and Stacey' moment on our outward journey. On exiting the Birkenhead Tunnel, we had to pay a toll. The machine rejected our coins but failed to return them. I momentarily contemplated leaping out of the car and raising the barrier manually, Smithy-style, before John did the sensible thing and pressed the help button.

And I'm afraid that's as entertaining as this post is going to get.

On arrival, we duly made our way to the ticket office, only to be directed to go and join the queue we'd walked past two minutes earlier and pay on the turnstile. The 400 extra ticket limit was clearly a fiction – the away end had sufficient capacity for Tranmere to take the money of all supporters who'd travelled without a ticket. As we queued patiently a steward informed us that they hadn't expected many extra away fans and were urgently trying to find someone to staff an extra turnstile for us poor souls without tickets. Had no-one at Tranmere bothered to check the size of away following that Carlisle regularly attract? There were eventually two turnstiles to process about 1300 supporters.

Once inside the ground we soon hooked up with Peter Scholes and enjoyed the pre-match atmosphere as the away end filled up, illustrating the old adage that hope springs eternal. Anticipation was heightened by the inclusion of two new signings in midfield, Callum Whelan from Gateshead and Elliot Embleton from Blackpool.

Carlisle started reasonably brightly, probably having the better of the opening exchanges, despite an apparent reluctance to get early balls into the box. Whelan showed an encouraging willingness to make himself available for the ball, and to initiate forward moves. But then slack marking allowed Tranmere to open the scoring in the 22nd minute with a goal that was all too easy, and it all went downhill from there.

The current group of players seem to lack any sort of resilience. Once Tranmere had scored the performance disintegrated. The passing deteriorated, often because players were not making themselves available to receive the ball. Carlisle never seriously threatened to get back into the game. To quote Mike Williamson's post-match interview, "But, you know, 18 shots, 11 shots in the box, we don't really lay a hand on the keeper." By the final fifteen minutes he was again being regaled with chants of "You don't know what you're doing" and "You're getting sacked in the morning". When the players came over to acknowledge the supporters after the final whistle, they were greeted by a chorus of boos and chants of "Fucking useless, you're fucking useless," from a significant number of fans. Personally, I don't think that's particularly helpful for the group of players that we're relying on to rescue us from this situation, but I can understand the frustration.

I'll restate my belief that Mike Williamson is not the man to rescue Carlisle United from the situation they find themselves in. That belief is based on three reasons, carefully considered ones, not kneejerk, emotional responses voiced in the heat of the moment.

Firstly, he does not appear capable of inspiring and motivating the players at his disposal. His post-match interview included the following comments - "I think the emotional pressure on some of the lads is too much" and "We've got the weight of the world on our shoulders, every single player." Does he not accept that it's part of his role to help the players deal with that pressure? Paul Simpson inherited a group of players who had been performing woefully under Keith Millen, and almost immediately transformed the way they thought and the way they behaved on the pitch. Peter summed up things nicely at half-time when he said, "I'd love to hear Williamson's half-time team talk. He's probably showing them a Powerpoint presentation."

Secondly, he is failing to get the best out of the players at his disposal, which is a basic expectation of any coach. Far too many players are being played out of position. Cameron Harper was signed as a wing-back and is currently performing less than impressively in midfield. Meanwhile Dominic Sadi, an attacking midfielder, is played at wing-back. Likewise, Kadeem Harris. Right now, the club's EFL survival is far more important than slavish adherence to a particular philosophy of how football should be played.

Thirdly, I don't buy into Williamson's philosophy. We were told that he favoured a possession-based, front-foot style of football. We've seen plenty of the former but precious little of the latter. I've not checked the stats (I'll leave that to Williamson) but I'm pretty sure that the three games we've won under his stewardship have all come in games where we've had a minority of possession. Most of the football I've watched during his tenure has been dull and unexciting. Some fans have said he should be given time to bring in players suited to his style of playing. I disagree. His style of play is uninspiring and doesn't work very well, particularly at League 2 level.

I accept that he's unlikely to be moved on. He's already been given licence to sign three new players, all midfielders, when what we really need is more defenders and attackers, given our horrendous injury list. But after yesterday, I really can't see where the next goal is coming from, never mind the next point.

Saturday 18 January. Carlisle United v Bradford City. Brunton Park. League 2.

A lot has happened in the fortnight since the last post, but the end result is depressingly familiar – another dispiriting defeat.

There have been major changes in personnel since the defeat at Tranmere. A whole raft of new players have been brought in, either as 'permanent' signings or on loan. I'm not going to attempt to assess the new signings on the evidence of one game (or an appearance as a substitute), though I may make reference to their performance in this particular game. But I will take a little time to consider a couple of significant departures.

Harrison Neal has departed to Fleetwood Town. His earnest endeavour, determined running, robust tackling and somewhat limited distribution initially earned him the respect of fans, but was never going to make him central to Mike Williamson's plans (whatever they are). More significant is Jon Mellish's decision to join Wigan Athletic in League 1. Mells was Carlisle's longest serving player, having been signed by Steven Pressley, meaning he worked under five different managers during his time at Brunton Park (excluding caretakers). Like Neal, he had his limitations. His passing and final ball sometimes left something to be desired. His positioning in defence could sometimes be suspect, without Paul Huntington to marshal him. But there was something irresistible about his tireless running, his surges out of defence and midfield, his goalscoring record and his general commitment to the cause. It feels as if a little bit of the club's current DNA has left with him.

Furthermore, all the loan players signed at the beginning of the season have returned to their parent clubs. In the case of the Bournemouth pair, Dominic Sadi and Daniel Aju Adjei, that was due to something of an injury crisis at the Premier League club. They immediately found themselves on the bench for Bournemouth's first Premier League fixture after their return.

Meantime there have been numerous new arrivals: permanent signings: short-term contracts; loan players. No-one can argue that the owners are failing to back the coach, allowing him to bring in players who he believes are suited to the style of play he espouses. But that also increases the pressure on Mike Williamson. He can no longer claim that he is working with a group of players inherited from the previous manager. If results fail to improve, he will now have to shoulder a much greater proportion of the blame.

The postponement of the MK Dons game the week before was a bit of a blow for John and me. That day was John's birthday, and unknown to him, his wife Julie had booked a hospitality package for the two of us as his birthday present. The package has now been rebooked for the Swindon game on 1 February. We're fervently hoping that the ex-player in attendance isn't Harry McKirdy!

And so to the game itself. The scale of the change in playing personnel was emphasised by the fact that four of the starting eleven were making their debut for the club, and a further two were making their home debut. Only three players were at Brunton Park at the beginning of the season. It was difficult to have any clear expectations of the game, with what was essentially a scratch side, who had very little time to train together and develop any understanding. New signing Paul Dummett was unavailable, having been involved in a car accident the day before. That pretty much sums up Carlisle's fortunes at the moment. We could probably field two pretty decent teams if all the players signed over the last twelve to eighteen months were fit and available. Luke Armstrong wasn't even in the squad. Rumour has it that he refused to be involved, ahead of a possible move to Motherwell. If that comes to pass, Armstrong's time at Brunton Park will have been a sad waste of a talented footballer. Both Paul Simpson and Mike Williamson have failed dismally to find a formation and style that play to his considerable strengths.

When the line-up was announced I was more than a little concerned to see that Jordan Jones and Kadeem Harris were being played as wing backs, meaning the team only contained three 'proper' defenders. Mercifully, my worst fears were unfounded, but bear with me while I make my case. I think it is easier for a defensively schooled wing back to make significant attacking contributions than it is for attacking wide players to put in a decent defensive shift (someone like Ashley Young is probably an honourable exception, though Leighton Baines would support my case). Jones and Harris are potentially exciting players, with the ability to beat defenders and deliver a telling pass or get a shot away. They should not be overly burdened with defensive duties. Cameron Harper should be returned to the position he was signed to fill, and if Archie Davies continues to be unavailable then a new wing back signing is a priority before the transfer window closes.

Given all these caveats, the first half was surprisingly encouraging. Callum Whelan again looked the business in midfield, making himself available to defenders for a forward pass and driving forward. He has a slight appearance of Luka Modric about him. If he proves to be half the player for Carlisle that Modric has been for Spurs and Real Madrid I'll be more than happy. Alongside him Will Patching also impressed. I was a bit surprised by some online critics who suggested he was off the pace. That might have been true of his second half performance, as he visibly tired before being substituted, but he contributed well before the interval. In attack, Joe Hugill, on loan from Manchester United, looked strong and mobile, but suffered the same problem as all United strikers over the last season and a half, namely poor service.

With the score at half-time being 0-0 and Bradford not doing a lot to impress, a rare win did not seem beyond the bounds of possibility. That was until the 54th minute. Young Newcastle loanee Charlie McArthur had looked good in defence before the interval, justifying the description of him being 'comfortable on the ball'. On this occasion he was a little too comfortable, being robbed of possession in the move that led to Bradford's goal.

Thereafter it was a depressingly familiar scenario. The team seemed to lose its shape and heads went down. None of the substitutions made any impact. Jack Ellis, having replaced Ben Barclay, looked all at sea positionally and his distribution was poor. Cedwyn Scott, another debutant, ran gamely up front but suffered from the same dearth of supply as Hugill. Sean Fusire, the final debutant, on loan from Sheffield Wednesday, was woeful, appearing to be playing at a different pace from everyone else on the pitch. The last half-hour saw far too much lateral passing across the back line, suggesting a worrying lack of urgency when there was still a game to be won, or at least saved.

There are obvious tactical issues, the main one being the failure to play players in their best position. But I suspect that the problems are as much psychological as strategic. Once we have gone behind, there seems to be a lack of belief in the players (and fans) that the situation can be retrieved. It seems like a case of new players, same mentality. I'd hate to think that the new squad is being assembled with promotion from the National League next year in mind, rather than League 2 survival this season.

Mr Williamson, the owners and fans deserve better than you're giving us at the moment.

Saturday 25 January. Fleetwood Town v Carlisle United. Highbury Stadium. EFL League 2.

Three weeks ago, I pondered where the next point and even the next goal was going to come from. Well, my question has been answered, in the short-term at least. Predictably the goals and points came in the one game this month that I couldn't attend. On Saturday afternoon I was in Birmingham with Lisa and Imogen, helping Ellie to celebrate her 23rd birthday. That means that this post is largely based on Jon Colman's 'as it happens' posts for "The News and Star" and online comments from those who were there.

The game saw two further debuts, both for defenders, Paul Dummett and Josh Williams. The early signs weren't good. Dummett suffered an injury after just two minutes, and after a couple of minutes' treatment was replaced by Terell Thomas. You really couldn't make it up. Dummett was involved in a car accident a couple of days after signing for the club which meant he couldn't make his debut against Bradford. And now he makes what must be the shortest debut in the club's history. Am I alone in thinking that Dummett has arrived at Brunton Park with a curse hanging over his head? And is it the same curse that has afflicted Dylan McGeoch, Georgie Kelly, Josh Vela, Charlie Wyke, Archie Davies and Ethan Robson, all of whom have been available intermittently at best since joining the club?

Fortunately, Dummett's injury didn't upset the balance and shape of the team, if there was any at such an early stage of the game. Reports suggest that Carlisle had the best of the first half, and fortunately for once they managed to convert their superiority into a goal, when Cedwyn Scott prodded home a low cross from Kamal Harris at the far post in the 19th minute. I suspect if I'd been at the game I'd have spent half-time worrying that the team didn't have another goal to show for their dominance.

Predictably the tide turned after half-time, and Fleetwood started to increasingly dominate the game. Currently Carlisle seem unable to sustain their first-half level of performance for a full ninety minutes. Who knows who is to blame for that? Fleetwood eventually equalised in the seventieth minute and looked the likelier team to clinch a winner.

But in the 82nd minute Hugill went close and three minutes later he set up Harris, whose shot was put behind for a corner. The set piece found its way to Lavelle, whose initial header was saved before it bounced back off the centre-back, hit the post and then went over the line. It's one of those games when I'd have loved to be in the away end to celebrate a late goal and then the win as United held out for a fraught eight minutes of time added on.

It's notable that despite being bottom of the league, Carlisle's travelling support of 1,087 constituted almost a third of the total attendance of 3,517.

I don't care how the win was achieved, whether it was down to Williamson's tactics or due to the players ignoring instructions and doing their own thing. All that matters at this stage is getting the three points. I'm far from convinced by Mike Williamson, but I have some sympathy with the online comments that say it's ridiculous to heap all the blame on him for defeats and then deny him any credit when the team eventually win. At the moment this is a one-off result. The real test will come on Tuesday night at Meadow Lane. Two successive victories for the first time since the promotion season might just start me believing that we can actually survive.

Tuesday 28 January. Notts County v Carlisle United. Meadow Lane. EFL League 2.

This was a first of sorts – the first time I'd visited Meadow Lane, home to the oldest club in the English League. So that's another ground ticked off the list of ninety-two, though a handful of the grounds I've been to no longer exist – Ayresome Park, Roker Park, Elm Park and Highbury for starters.

It was John's turn to drive, which was a relief, because I'm getting a bit weary of driving down the M1 to Nottingham, and sometimes beyond to Birmingham, and back. The plan was to meet up pre-match with Adam, his girlfriend Anna, some other mates, and Ben who had travelled up from Cardiff University to see the game and spend a couple of days with Adam. One or two issues finding our way to the ground put paid to that plan, but we did manage to hook up during half-time.

I was quite impressed by Meadow Lane. It's now an all-seater stadium (yes, it just about justifies that description!) and I'd rank it alongside Tranmere's Prenton Park as one of the best grounds in League 2. The ground was a little under half full, and the division was quite marked. The home end and the stand facing us were both pretty full. The opposite end was sparsely populated, and the other side was empty apart from the just under five hundred of us away fans who were contained in a section to one end of the ground, much like at Brunton Park. I think just under 500 away supporters is a creditable showing for a Tuesday evening in January, when most of the fans had had a considerably longer journey than us. The total attendance, for a team in the automatic promotion places, was just over 8,000. That's only slightly more than we attract to our struggles in the League 2 basement. I think you know what I'm saying! Carlisle's support is truly remarkable.

Once again there appeared to be an element of selection tombola about the starting line-up. Terrel Thomas, despite impressing as a very early substitute for Paul Dummett on Saturday, was again on the bench. Meanwhile, Aaron Hayden, not even a substitute on Saturday, was in the starting eleven. Surprisingly Kadeem Harris, having just extended his contract until the end of the season, was also on the bench.

Carlisle started the game positively, moving the ball quickly and making some early inroads without creating any bona fide chances. Gabe Breeze dealt efficiently with a couple of early County shots before being beaten by a header in the 19th minute. Perhaps he should have come to claim the cross. But he's still a young lad who is learning his trade in far from ideal circumstances.

It would be easy to say that United reverted to type after going behind. But that would be unfair. We took one of the top teams in the division the full distance. If a Joe Hugill shot in the second half had gone in rather than hitting the post who knows how the rest of the game might have developed? Hugill impressed again, with his strength and direct running, but he suffered the same curse as every Carlisle striker for the last eighteen months – poor service. Callum Whelan again provided ample evidence in midfield that he is the best of the signings in the current transfer window, always making himself available and looking to move forward when in possession.

The final fifteen minutes were very frustrating. Carlisle constantly attacked down the left flank, directly in front of us, repeatedly channelling the ball to Jordan Jones. He appeared to be up for the challenge, taking on defenders, but in that period only one real chance transpired when he cut inside and curled a shot just wide of the far post. I'm not looking to make Jones a scapegoat. His final pass or cross could often be better, but it's also the responsibility of his teammates to give him better options.

I'm not too dispirited by this defeat. There were plenty of encouraging signs as we ran a decent team close. The response from the fans at the final whistle was overwhelmingly positive despite the result. But the reality is that it was another defeat, and time is starting to run out. A win against Swindon on Saturday is essential.

So, is this it? We've got beyond the Christmas period with seventeen games still to play and fifty-one points

*still up for grabs. Over the transfer window we've
assembled a new team, if not a whole new squad. The
most significant features of this activity are that Jon
Mellish, embodying the spirit of never say die, and
record buy striker Luke Armstrong, have both left for
Wigan and Motherwell respectively. Also departed are
Harrison Neal, (Fleetwood) Taylor Charters (Queen of
the South) and Anton Dudik (South Shields) and this is
just to scratch the surface of the dealings of Carlisle
United in the transfer window.*

*The New Jerusalem of the Piatak takeover was
heralded by the Own the North slogan and as if to
support this aspiration, Carlisle United from English
football's lonely North-Western outpost, have emerged
as major wheeler dealers, presumably paying out big
money to attract players to the hitherto "unattractive"
outpost. While this is gratifying to an extent, it does
not sit easily with some of the Blues' faithful who
remember the days of recruiting from the lower levels
of English football, coaching players extremely well
(Thank you, Dick Young) and eventually selling those
players because that is what the club had always done.
A modest club maintaining very high standards of
playing performance and governance, but essentially a
selling club.*

*This is when we were in what could easily be called
football's dark ages when clubs could retain the
registration of a player even if his contract had expired.
Clearly not a healthy situation and, as Johannes Bozman
went on to prove, not one that was sustainable in law
either. More equitably, clubs playing away from home
were entitled to a share of the gate money which was
great for smaller clubs when they went to play against*

teams who attracted a larger following. This system did not survive the eventual muscle flexing of the big clubs though and the argument that two teams providing entertainment should both benefit from the raised revenue of such entertainment was easily lost in the face of football's growing avarice. What! all clubs having a responsibility for the general health of the national game? Poppycock.

Nevertheless, this is the climate in which from the 1965/66 season to 1973/74, Carlisle United flourished with playing performances which sustained a healthy existence in the second tier of English football and culminated in an historic season in what was prosaically called the First Division. Over those nine seasons, without moneyed benefactors, Carlisle averaged a finishing position of ninth and this might give some indication of why amongst some of the fans there is a sense of unease. Carlisle United with a Sugar Daddy doesn't sit easily, does it?

Or does it? Beyond the American marketing razzmatazz, the Piateks have done nothing but be entirely supportive, putting money where the mouth is, so to speak. This is no ego trip on their part, Look! We own an English soccer club! *But it might be time to roll out that cliché about money not always guaranteeing success and also point out that having hitherto unknown fabulous wealth can easily lead to unrealistic expectations. Expectations which might account for a tendency of some supporters to respond to results rather than performance, of subjecting the team coach Mike Williamson to intemperate criticism over his perceived inflexibility over tactics, lack of charisma and a demonstrable lack of passion. Get your hands out of your pockets, Man! Maybe even it has caused them to lose sight of what it means to be a supporter. There is insufficient time and space to explore this fully now but being a supporter should certainly rule out booing and swearing at your own team.*

More positively, after my veiled comments about what constitutes supporting your team, over 450 Carlisle fans turned up on a cold January night for the game against Notts County. Second bottom of the league with a measly twenty-one points to their name, whatever motivated those 450, it wasn't glory seeking, was it? Notts County on the other hand with forty-four points in the bag began the game in sixth place knowing that a win could take them into the top three. Even so, the mood amongst the Carlisle fans seemed to be buoyant but not unrealistically optimistic. This wasn't a "must win" game in prospect, it was more of a "it would be good to get something from this" game. Something like a point, for instance.

In the event, a point for Carlisle seemed quite possible as they settled into a passing game which sent a message to the opposition that this was not a bottom of the table clogging team they were up against. The style is not universally popular among the Carlisle fans as it seems to invite danger. One slip here and you're a goal down, but the benefits are that inviting a press is to draw players out of their own defensive formation resulting in gaps to exploit. Passing the ball to colleagues as you cross the halfway line, thus retaining possession, is another benefit. With possession, in order to exploit any gaps, pace and accuracy in passing are then required and the good news here is that Carlisle now appear to have players within their ranks who can provide these qualities. Callum Whelan has been a busy midfielder and talismanic figure since his arrival. He is never afraid to show for the ball and given time and space he can use it very effectively. In a quieter mode, drawing less attention, Elliot Embleton has played tidily, unfazed by receiving the ball under pressure and also showing a good eye for a pass, not unlike John McGovern whom older readers might recall playing for Nottingham Forest and Derby. Further forward, Joe Hugill has made a very impressive start to his Carlisle career showing a willingness to close down defenders and put them under pressure. More importantly he has very impressive pace; bend a ball around defenders into space and he will chase it down and cause problems. But as always with young strikers, the feelings persist that a couple of goals are needed to set him on his way.

It was Hugill who forged the first clear cut chance for Carlisle when he used his pace to latch onto a through ball to bear down on goal from the left-hand side. His shot appeared to beat the goalkeeper but agonisingly it also evaded the far post. But he had served notice and in these early exchanges Carlisle appeared to be the more composed team, something which an apprehensive home crowd had not missed. The Blues fans meanwhile were happy to keep up sustained chanting and cheering for their team.

How often though does a spell of dominance not result in a goal? And how detrimental to your chances can this be? The point was proved in the nineteenth minute when a neatly worked move from County resulted in a tempting cross for their in-form striker, Jatta. It was too tempting for him not to score, and his header was duly dispatched into the far corner of the net.

It is always dispiriting to concede a goal and current punditry suggests that all goals are avoidable. There was a feeling that Gabe Breeze in the Carlisle goal might have come out to claim the cross, but this feeling was not supported by a later viewing of the television highlights. Credit where credit is due, it was a good goal, well-taken by a dangerous opponent, but the bigger lesson is that it should have been an equaliser or a goal to reduce arrears and not the opening goal.

The goal inspired the home fans who began to make more noise, galvanised as they were by their expectations being matched. From here their team could go on to win the game perhaps with one or two more goals and the lowly opposition would fold.

But that didn't happen. As the second half opened Hugill hit the post with a shot which looked certain to go in. Four hundred Carlisle fans were waiting for the net to bulge but instead the ball rebounded back into play and was cleared. It's the fine margins of football. A goal at that point would certainly have rattled County. As it was, their second half performance deteriorated and the previously dangerous Jatta was starved on any meaningful supply. Carlisle continued to play and their Nottinghamshire opponents were happy to camp eleven players behind the ball with their performance descending into the unpalatable when players frequently dropped to the pitch with injuries which required attention. Surely it is time for a rule to be brought in which requires a mandatory five- minute spell on the sideline for any player who has disrupted the game's flow to be treated by the physio. Such a rule might have spared us the sight of the Notts keeper lying prone in his area after making a token dive for a ball which went beyond his far post, feigning an attack of cramp and thereby causing further disruption to the game's momentum. Even more farcical was the triple substitution made by County which took an age to perform.

There are some people in the game who refer to tactics like this as "game management" when the more apposite term is cheating.

Sour grapes from your correspondent? Possibly, as despite doing most of the attacking in the second half, Carlisle were unable to break through County's eleven-man defence. The ball was frequently fed out to Jordan Jones on the left who, to his credit, kept to his task in trying to make the all-important breakthrough. He cut inside once to shoot narrowly wide of the far post and played another cross into the box along the floor without a Carlisle player getting on the end of it. He also forced a corner which led to a goal chance, but for the most part his delivery was disappointing, and the final penetrative cross/pass eluded him.

Full time. A one-nil scoreline and a defeated team magnificently supported by the four hundred plus. The despondent players in turn applauded the fans and amongst their number was the manager, Mike Williamson who must have realised that in terms of winning hearts and minds, he has a lot of ground to make up.

Chapter 8
OF HORSES AND STABLE DOORS

Saturday 1 February. Carlisle United v Swindon Town. Brunton Park. EFL League 2.

This was quite possibly the strangest day I have spent at Brunton Park in well over half a century of supporting Carlisle United. The primary reason is that this is one of the worst defeats I have witnessed on our hallowed turf. The only worse result I can recall watching was the 6-0 home defeat against Southampton in January 1977. But that was against a team that included Alan Ball, Peter Osgood, Mick Channon and Ted McDougall. Yes, they may have been past their best, but they still possessed a potent threat.

Swindon's starting line-up yesterday included Dan Butterworth for god's sake! Here is a player who was only spared the ignominy of being the worst signing of the summer 2023 transfer window by the presence of Sean Maguire in the Carlisle squad. Given the relative strength of the opposition, while yesterday's scoreline may have been marginally better, it was probably a worse defeat. Predictably, Butterworth fulfilled the curse of the returning player, opening the scoring a minute before half-time and displaying an ability to find the back of the net that was woefully lacking for the vast majority of his time at Brunton Park. This was particularly galling as Carlisle had started brightly, moving the ball well and quickly and creating a decent handful of chances, though none that required a significant save from the Swindon goalkeeper. More of the game itself later.

The other factor that made it such a strange day was the fact that most of it was highly enjoyable. John and I were finally enjoying the hospitality package that was originally intended as a birthday surprise for John three weeks ago (the weather put paid to the Newport game that day). We arrived at Brunton Park at about 12.15 and were able to park close to the East Stand, free of charge. From there we made our way to the West Stand fan zone, where we'd arranged to meet John's sister Cathrine. The purpose of the rendezvous was to hand over a birthday present for John's nephew Thomas, who just happens to be Carlisle's U18 goalkeeper (I may have mentioned this before!). Unsurprisingly, Thomas is currently on the injured list. The Brunton Park treatment room must be busier than the changing room at the moment.

Handover complete, we retraced our steps to the East Stand and the hospitality entrance. From there we were directed upstairs to The Cumbria Lounge, the venue for our hospitality package. I must admit that I was impressed. We were escorted to our table, and informed that everything was table-service, meaning we didn't have to lift a finger. The lounge was spacious and airy, no attempt to cram in the punters to maximise profit.

I was driving, so that John could enjoy a couple of drinks as part of his birthday treat, but the availability of Guinness Zero meant that I was able to indulge as well. The food was excellent: Katsu chicken burger;

Chilli con carne; smoked haddock fishcake with prawn and lemon dill cream sauce; vegetable and chickpea curry with mini naan. They were served as small bowls, meaning that we could have as many different dishes as we liked, as many times as we liked. A couple of pudding choices were also provided.

The lounge had a couple of large-screen TVs, showing the Premier League lunchtime game. That happened to be Nottingham Forest v Brighton and Hove Albion, so we were royally entertained by Forest's 7-0 win. We were further entertained by the presence of current player Dylan McGeoch (currently injured – what a surprise) who was interviewed for about ten minutes about his time at Carlisle and his pre-United career. A complimentary gin and tonic followed, and then we were ready to take our seats. A short walk along the corridor and through a door and we were in the top of the East Stand, in a dedicated hospitality seating area, replete with padded leather armchair seats. I could get used to this!

I've already summarised the first half, so let's fast-forward to the break, when we returned to The Cumbria Lounge to enjoy our pre-ordered half time drinks. The TV screens were displaying the first half stats, which indicated, predictably, that while Carlisle dominated the stats, we were actually losing the game. A few minutes later we looked up again to see that both teams were already back on the pitch. It's surprising how quickly fifteen minutes passes when you're enjoying a pint. Unfortunately, we weren't quite quick enough to get back to our seats. What we assumed was the second half kick-off was actually the restart following Swindon's second goal. I had the distinct feeling that we were guilty of prawn sandwich syndrome, despite there being not a prawn sandwich in sight.

And from there it was pretty much all downhill. The team reverted to type, with too much passing across the defence, to other defenders who were immediately under pressure, and struggled to generate forward momentum. Things got even worse in the 66th minute when Jordan Jones received a second yellow card and was dismissed. Both cards were for simulation which is ridiculous. His first card came in the first half and was a travesty. It wasn't a bad foul, but he was clearly tripped. The referee, in his infinite wisdom, chose to award Swindon a free kick and book Jones. The second card was less clear cut. From our position I couldn't be confident that his going to ground was the result of a foul, but it certainly didn't look like a dive. Neither incident was as blatant as the dive for which a Swindon player later received a yellow card.

To be fair to Mike Williamson, he did at least try to be proactive, making a couple of attacking substitutions in an effort to redeem the situation, but it was probably too little too late. The writing was on the goal when Swindon scored their third in the 83rd minute, prompting a significant exodus of Carlisle supporters. Joe Hugill did pull one goal back in the 88th minute, with what was probably the best finish of the game. When Carlisle won a corner a minute later, I said to John that it might get interesting if Carlisle scored from the set-piece. Instead, strong appeals for a handball in the Swindon penalty area were rejected and they broke away to score their fourth in the ninetieth minute. Even worse was to follow when they scored their fifth in the final seconds of time added on.

I'm overwhelmed by a depressing sense of déjà vu. It must be about a year ago when I questioned how I could find new ways to describe another dispiriting defeat as the League 1 campaign wended its way to a depressing conclusion. I feel exactly the same right now. My feeling is that we've got a host of new players but are still beset by the same old problems.

Even worse, it's almost three years to the day since Carlisle suffered another awful defeat at home to Swindon, with Harry McKirdy the chief executioner on that occasion. The atmosphere in the ground yesterday wasn't as toxic as on that occasion, but I couldn't help feeling that despite a subsequent promotion and new ownership, we're back where we were three years ago, with the very real threat of relegation to The National League. Three years ago, the situation prompted drastic action and fortunately that happened. Keith Millen and he who shall not be named were sacked and Paul Simpson returned to provide the best fifteen months in the club's recent history. Equally drastic action is required now. Facebook rumours suggest that Carlisle have approached three clubs for permission to speak to their managers, and that Williamson was due to have a Zoom meeting with the owners at ten o'clock this evening. I hope the rumours are true. I've avoided saying it until now, but Williamson has to go.

I haven't got the time or inclination to trawl through the data (though I'm sure Williamson would), but I'm pretty sure that every game Carlisle have won under Williamson's tenure (and there haven't been many!) has come in matches when we've had less than 50% possession. And I'm similarly sure that in almost every game we've lost we've had a majority of possession.

Surely a data-driven coach like Williamson should see what that suggests.

I'm sure that Mike Williamson is a decent individual and human being, and I don't wish to attack his personality. But he's the coach of my beloved football club, and he's failing dismally in that capacity. The charge sheet against him is as follows: he is failing to bring out the best from the players he has at his disposal; some players are clearly ill-at-ease with the style of play imposed on them; he is tactically inflexible, unwilling to change formation and style of play, either between games or during games; he appears to be lacking in motivational skills. As John and I adjourned to The Cumbria Lounge for the final time to enjoy a hot meat pie post-match, we had witnessed both the best and the worst of the new regime at Brunton Park in a single afternoon. We had enjoyed the benefits of the massive investment in the club's off-the-pitch infrastructure. Brunton Park may be an old ground, but with the new lounges, the fan zones, the giant screens and much more, it is a venue of which supporters can be justifiably proud. At the same time, we witnessed on the pitch the consequences of a series of bad decisions over player recruitment and the management of the playing staff.

Some keyboard warriors are pointing the finger of blame at CEO Nigel Clibbens. One can only speak as one finds. I met Clibbens last summer at the official opening of the Tullie House exhibition on Carlisle United, and I have to admit that I was impressed by him, both as a member of the panel who were interviewed about the exhibition, and also in personal conversation later. I suspect he played a bigger role in the Piatak takeover than us ordinary punters will ever realise. I have a friend who supports Huddersfield Town and he speaks very highly of his time at The Terriers.

Since I started writing this piece, events have moved on dramatically. At ten o'clock on Monday morning the club announced that "head coach Mike Williamson has this morning been relieved of his duties and has left the club with immediate effect." I have no doubt that this is the right decision. I just wish it had been made sooner, at the very least at the beginning of the transfer window rather than at the end. The first chants of "You don't know what you're doing" had rung out more than three months earlier, on a dismal evening in Walsall.

Feelings of déjà vu are strong. Just as three years ago, Carlisle have dismissed their manager/head coach following a demoralising home defeat by Swindon Town. Just as three years ago, the club are looking for their third manager/head coach of the season. Is it too much to hope that history will repeat itself again in Carlisle ultimately climbing out of the relegation zone and achieving League 2 survival?

All sorts of names are being bandied around as Williamson's successor including, remarkably, Steven Gerrard, recently "relieved of his duties" in Saudi Arabia. I'm not going to get involved in the name game other than to repeat my familiar mantra of "anyone but Warnock"! To be honest, I don't think that Warnock or Sam Allardyce, who has also been mentioned in dispatches, would even get out of bed to answer a call from Carlisle United, let alone take the job.

So here's my job spec for what it's worth. The appointment should be short-term until the end of the season, with avoiding relegation the only priority, and a healthy bonus awarded should that target be achieved.

The lucky individual must be able to motivate and inspire the current crop of players; they must be capable of making the most of the players at their disposal; they must be flexible, in terms of formation, style and strategy. And ideally, they should be in place before Saturday's game against Grimsby.

That will then give the owners time to assess whether the interim appointment is suitable for the long-term and to also explore other options. I wish them luck!

I know it's not a good thing to read significance into unrelated matters. Signs and symbols, it's the stuff of superstition – not to be trusted at all he says, fingers crossed. Nevertheless, our early start for the drive to Carlisle for this fixture meant that we saw the gentle sun breaking through the cloud over North Yorkshire. Red kites were in evidence, as were buzzards, circling overhead as we left Scotch Corner behind on the A66. The single bird flapping across the road as we passed the turn off for Brough was merely the pointer to a whole field of lapwings on our right. Oh, for a sight of the whole flock taking flight! But it was not to be and the very minor ornithologist in me was content to know that the threatened species exists in good numbers along this stretch of road.

It was a good omen surely on the day we were due to play Swindon Town at Brunton Park. Today there were ghosts to lay and spectres to banish; Harry McKirdy and all that, and a healthy victory would do the job nicely.

We had a chance to express our confidence as we were introduced to the pre-match competitions in the Cumbria Lounge as part of our hospitality package.

Predict the scoreline, the Man of the Match and the match attendance to be in with a chance to win something or other. Howard and I did a quick summoning up of our immediate thoughts. Two football gurus, wise in their knowledge and perceptive in outlook, how could they possibly go wrong? Off the cuff we came up with the following predictions: a 2-1 home victory, Callum Whelan Man of the Match and an attendance in the region of somewhere above seven thousand. Afterwards we both admitted that when we made our individual entries to the competition, we gave more optimistic predictions. My reasoning was that after a thrilling hat-trick, Joe Hugill would have to be man of the match. Forget wisdom and perception, this was a classic case of heart ruling the head. And we were both, spoiler alert here, well wide of the mark.

The perils of trying to tell the future though? It can only lead to tragedy and that lesson should have been learned long ago. We may as well have chanted around a cauldron dropping in the eye of a newt and the toe of a frog while foretelling a future kingship. Or we could have used a Ouija board, but you shouldn't dabble with those either. Whatever, Fortune would not be smiling upon us as Carlisle resumed their football rivalry with Swindon Town.

But let me digress a little further as eagle-eyed readers will have spotted my subtle reference to a hospitality package in the Cumbria Lounge. Yes, it's true, a benefactor whom I love dearly, bestowed such a package upon me for my birthday and rather than leave Howard to maintain a lonely Paddock vigil she included him in the deal as well. So, off we trotted to enjoy a totally different match experience.

A very civilised experience it was too as we were warmly greeted and shown to our places. It was table service for our drinks to arrive and then food was served tapas style in small bowls. Four main courses were on offer and I managed to sample the Katsu Chicken Burger, the Smoked Haddock Fishcake with Lemon Dill Cream Sauce and the vegetable and Chicken Curry with mini-Naan. The only one I missed out on was the Chilli Con Carne served with Rice and Nachos but Howard assures me that it too was delicious. I've never really been one for buying food at football matches. There was a time when I would put an apple in my pocket for half-time and I have a faint memory of the wooden hut at the end of the Waterworks which had a supply of mars bars, kit kats, crisps and a massive hot water boiler to serve the demand for tea and Bovril. I was never tempted to sample from the array of dubious looking pies and sausage rolls.

Times have moved on. They've taken the laces out of the balls and the food offering at football has taken on a more sophisticated air. Purists may well sniff at the betrayal of the "working man's sport," but I thoroughly enjoyed myself, even if I wasn't "keeping it real." There was only one drawback to this experience, a really massive one, you might say, and that was the football itself.

Only four days earlier we had watched Carlisle perform very creditably at Notts County losing somewhat unluckily against the promotion chasing contenders and the suggestion was that confidence would be on a high, particularly as the new players would have had a few more days to bed-in. The early signs were that this was indeed going to be the case.

*Carlisle came out and passed the ball well, and it took
Swindon twenty minutes to get any kind of toe-hold
in the game. Once again though, Carlisle didn't take
advantage of a spell of dominance and despite the
chances made it looked as though the sides would be
going in level at half-time.*

*Not so. It was the second minute of time added on
that a familiar weakness showed itself. A long ball from
the Swindon keeper was headed on by an unchallenged
forward to an unmarked teammate who in turn passed
it on to Dan Butterworth, the ex-Carlisle player who
had been allowed to leave earlier in the season.
Previously noted for making flashy runs with the ball
with no discernible positive end product, on this
occasion he advanced into the area and smacked a left-
footed drive into the top corner of Breeze's net.*

*Inquest time. Why was the first header unchallenged?
Why was the second ball not contested? Why was
Butterworth allowed complete freedom to drop off
from the back four and pick up the ball without any
hindrance from a Carlisle player? Lastly, and this may
be a bit harsh, but why didn't Breeze get within sniffing
distance of the goal-bound shot? For this is the time
when you want your keeper to stand up. Okay, it's
nearly half-time and the defenders have taken a
premature rest, but this is when your keeper shows he
has superior concentration skills, he is more than
competent, and he can produce a "worldie" out of the
blue and the clean sheet stays in place and hero status
beckons for the local boy with the gloves.*

*It goes without saying that the toilets in the Cumbria
Lounge are way beyond what used to be the Brunton
Park offering in this regard and this is no time for*

further graphic recollections as some readers may be eating. Still, a visit to what we can now call the washrooms and then a return to the lounge where a pre-ordered pint sits begging to be supped makes big inroads into the fifteen minutes break and sure enough, we were a few minutes late in returning to our seats and our panoramic view in the East Stand where something was clearly amiss. It was the steward's look of dismay which made me look to the scoreboard and realise that Swindon had scored within two minutes of the restart.

It is seriously unprofessional to concede a goal at either side of half-time. In Brian Clough's glorious phrase, "For that you want bloody shooting!" But let's also call out the two spectators who had enjoyed their hospitality to the extent of missing a goal. Oh, the shame! John and Howard had joined the Prawn Sandwich Brigade.

If it reads as though I am making light of the matter, it is only because the second goal conceded led to a horror show. At one nil down, it felt as though there was everything to play for in the game and the superior passing of Carlisle in the first half would return to bear fruit. At two nil down, it looked much more like a lost cause, but to be fair they gave it a shot and showed some spirit but it was short-lived. The impossibility of the task manifested itself when Jordan Jones received his second yellow for "diving" and at this point, Carlisle's play lost any semblance of pattern or shape. Chasing the game with ten men resulted in a third goal being conceded and unsurprisingly there didn't appear to be any plan for such a scenario. Credit then to Joe Hugill who wrong footed a defender when he took down a cross on the edge of the box before rifling it into the bottom corner of the goal. The best goal of the game but it proved to be of scant consolation as it was still mission impossible for Carlisle.

Substitutions were made with the apparent strategy of someone throwing a handful of coppers into a fountain and making a wish. Against this, the Swindon players, lining up to shoot fish in a barrel, scored a fourth goal and then an ignominious fifth. On the previous Tuesday evening, Notts County players, Carlisle's opponents looked mightily relieved to hear the final whistle as they knew they had been given a hell of a game. Four days later and the Swindon players as the final whistle blew looked as though they had had their party interrupted.

For one of the very few times ever, I left my seat not bothering to respond to any attempts by the players to acknowledge the supporters. Over in the East Stand we did not hear it of course but we were led to believe that the players and Mike Williamson had to face the displeasure of the Paddock as they made their way to the tunnel. It took the form of a chorus of boos with the chant of "Getting sacked in the morning" being replaced with the more direct, "Out! Out!"

In terms of following Carlisle United, I am usually positive. Even when a manager has been in charge whom I don't particularly warm to: Sheridan, Curle or Pressley for instance, I always remain loyal. Give them a chance! Look at the bigger picture! Initially, I had been prepared to listen to Williamson who had a vision and expressed it calmly and coherently, but under pressure, his interview demeanour has degenerated into jargon and psycho-babble. He speaks of the lads

*hurting but always sounds faintly critical of those
"lads." Likewise, his praise for the fans is formulaic
and routine often only appearing after a prompt.
Nowhere does he give the impression that he has
bought into the club. He is passionless. This is Carlisle
United, Mike! It all adds up to a feeling that with the
points gap to safety increasing, Carlisle are in fact
heading for relegation.*

*Eventually, we made our way to the car and the
return journey across Stainmore back to Yorkshire. Too
late now for spotting lapwings and imbuing them with
good luck significance. We are driving in the dark.*

Thursday 6 February – appointment of new head coach.

Events continue to move on apace at Brunton Park. Just
three days after the departure of Mike Williamson,
Mark Hughes has been announced as Carlisle United's
new head coach.

I'm pleased the decision has been taken quickly,
giving Hughes the chance to oversee a couple of training
sessions before Saturday's game at Grimsby. But I'm less
than enamoured with the choice of person. I didn't like
him as a player. I've got plenty of respect for his
considerable playing talent and skill, but I always
thought he was a dirty, niggly sort of player. Nor is his
managerial record particularly impressive. He may have
managed teams in over five hundred Premier League
games, but he's never actually won anything as a
manager – no cups, no promotions, not even in second
or third place. I'm surprised his Premier League
managerial career lasted as long as it did. And his

previous spell as a manager in League 2, at Bradford City, was hardly a resounding success.

Having said all that, John and I will be at Blundell Park on Saturday to cheer on the Blues (mainly because our tickets were purchased before this morning's announcement!). I won't be returning my season ticket which I most definitely would have done if Neil Warnock had been appointed. I sincerely hope that in eighteen games we're celebrating survival and hailing Mark Hughes as a saviour, in much the same way as we hailed Paul Simpson three years ago. My support for the club outweighs my reservations about a single employee. So, I will join all those supporters who have commented online about the need for us all to fully get behind the team and the manager. I just wish I felt a bit more positive about this appointment and what it may herald about the future direction of the club.

Saturday 8 February. Grimsby Town v Carlisle United. Blundell Park. EFL League 2.

As we settled into our seats in the away end at Blundell Park, I put it to John that we could consider ourselves either loyal members of the United faithful, present through thick and thin, or part of a collective delusion shared by the other 550 travelling fans, foolishly believing that things might get better. I'll answer my own question later.

So, this is where the Mark Hughes era began. After an impeccably observed minute's applause for a former Grimsby chairman, it took just five minutes for the first chorus of "Sparky Hughes' blue and white army" to ring out as Carlisle won a corner at the other end of the ground. It took just seconds longer for the Hughes era to get off to the best possible start as Sam Lavell forced home the corner. Joy unconfined!

There was only one change from the starting line-up that caved in to Swindon so spectacularly just a week earlier, Stephen Wearne replacing the suspended Jordan Jones, as the team lined up in a 4-2-3-1 formation. Harry Lewis, having played in goal under Hughes management at Bradford City, remained on the bench. I hardly expected major changes after just two days in the job, but there were signs of minor tweaks. All the players seemed to have been selected in positions in which they were comfortable. No more wide attacking players having to double up as emergency wingbacks. No more players brought in as wing backs being selected in midfield. A real tactical masterstroke from Sparky – picking players in their best position! There seemed to be a bit more urgency and directness about the team's play in the first half. Above all, it felt like the dead hand of Williamson's stultifying tactical straitjacket had been lifted. There was relatively little aimless passing across the back line. Breeze largely went long with his clearances and only threw the ball out to his defenders when they were in plenty of space and not already being pressed. That's not to suggest that we've immediately entered a brave new world of direct, attacking football. Grimsby were a decent side, capable of moving the ball quickly and accurately, knowing each other's moves and runs. It was unfair to expect the same of a Carlisle team that has largely been assembled in the last month by a coach who is no longer in charge.

As the first half wore on Grimsby asserted increasing pressure. It took superb last-ditch tackles by Thomas and Lavell, a brilliant double save by Breeze and an offside flag to preserve Carlisle's lead.

A crucial moment occurred just before half-time. Hugill chased a long ball forward and appeared to be brought down just inside the Grimsby area by their onrushing goalkeeper. A penalty beckoned, but no, the referee awarded Grimsby a free kick and issued Hugill with a yellow card for diving. Given that this was the third card for diving that the team had been issued in less than a game and a half, John wondered aloud whether referees have been issued with an instruction to clamp down on diving. I asked him whether he meant a general instruction for all teams, or a specific one for those supposed cheating bastards from Carlisle. Kick us while we're down, eh!

Carlisle had already had a penalty denied when Stephen Wearne appeared to be bundled to the ground as he chased an overhit cross. I wasn't in a position to comment authoritatively on either incident, as they happened at the far end of the ground, and I haven't seen a replay of either but now is probably the best time to mention that the match referee apparently hails from Cleethorpes. We were probably slightly fortunate to be 1-0 ahead at half time, but it made a welcome change to enjoy the interval in that position.

Carlisle had a chance to double their lead fairly early in the second half. Kadeem Harris cut in from the left and his shot from a narrow angle rebounded off the far post, directly in front of us. Elliot Embleton's powerful shot from the rebound was somehow scrambled off the line. If either of those efforts had gone in, I think we'd probably have gone on to win the game. As it was, I was happy to settle for a last-ditch, backs against the wall battle to secure the three points.

But that proved to be the turning point. Shortly after, Carlisle carelessly conceded possession in the Grimsby half (how often has that happened this season?) and from the subsequent counter-attack Grimsby equalised. As happens so often Carlisle fell away in the final half hour, failing to maintain the urgency and intensity of the first half. A number of supporters are questioning the fitness and conditioning of many of the players, and I have to say that I agree. It's part of the wider question of why so many players are absent on the long-term injured list.

There still remained the hope that we might salvage a draw, without ever seriously threatening to regain the lead. But that hope was dashed in the 81st minute, when a Grimsby player went down in the area, despite an apparent lack of contact. Another yellow card for diving? No, this time the referee pointed to the penalty spot, something he found himself incapable of doing in the first half, and gifted Grimsby their winner. I have seen a replay of this incident, and the referee's decision is ridiculous. It took another excellent double save from Breeze during time added on to keep the scoreline to 2-1. So, we endured yet another afternoon that held out some promise but provided no end result, like so many games this season. I'd hoped for, but not really expected anything from this game, given how recently Hughes had been appointed. The new manager bounce which appeared possible in the first half didn't materialise. To be fair to Hughes, he did, despite the result, come over to applaud the travelling supporters after the final whistle, something that appeared to be beyond Williamson during his ill-fated twenty-five games in charge. It really doesn't take that much effort to get the fans behind you.

A few comments on individuals. Whelan continues to look the best of the recent signings and fell away less noticeably in the second half. Embleton had what I thought was his best game to date in a Carlisle shirt, making more significant contributions than hitherto. That's probably down to such simple factors as settling into his role in the team and getting to know his teammates. Patching remains 'promising', calm in possession but a little one-paced – his pace. And his pace isn't necessarily the same pace as that of everyone else around him. Hugill continues to work hard up front but is still feeding off very meagre scraps.

A final word on the match-day experience. The comfort and catering were in marked contrast to what we experienced at Brunton Park a week earlier!

The saying that a week is a long time in politics is popularly attributed to Harold Wilson during his first spell as Prime Minister in 1964, but I'm not sure about that. My feeling is that the Huddersfield Town supporting premiere most likely adapted it from a passing Carlisle United fan, because in the life of Carlisle United things can happen with a bewildering rapidity in a short space of time, as was proved in the week leading up to this match.

The booing of Mike Williamson at the conclusion of the Swindon game was clearly heard across the Atlantic in Piatak-land. Or at least, it was reported across what is popularly referred to as the Pond. It seems that the Piataks have a low tolerance for booing aimed at any aspect of their British investment. Witness the disgraceful crowd response towards Paul Simpson after the Tranmere home fixture and the club's management response i.e. Simpson was sacked. And booing it was after the Swindon game which cued prompt action American-style with Williamson being dismissed from his post on the following Monday.

With five wins from twenty-five games, this sacking could be filed under "only to be expected," this is what a large number of fans wanted and this is what they got. It was an example of swift and emphatic action which made sense given the unhappiness felt by the fans in response to the fare they were being served. It was mostly a question of tactics and Williamson's stubbornness in persisting in what had been characterised as "tippy-tappy" football, the playing out from the back which had raised the ire of the fans who had only recently been objecting to Simpson's "hoofball."

Williamson had to be sacked. Simple as. However, some might have been tempted to echo Sergeant Wilson's often used question in Dad's Army: "Do you think that's wise?" especially in the light of recent events. As recently as Tuesday 7th January a Fans' Forum held at Brunton Park with the club's hierarchy in attendance had broadcast the clear message that the style of play was the style desired by the ownership and Mike Williamson was definitely the man to coach that style. In other words, he wasn't going anywhere. I'm paraphrasing, of course, but the message had gone out loud and clear and there would be little point in negative shouting; the fans should get behind the team and be positive. The owners had taken a lead in this respect by signing no less than eleven players during the transfer window in addition to Kadeem Harris who had signed a new contract. All of which constitutes excellent support for a manager - unless you are going to sack him of course.

Was this really a case of effective management, or was it something of a panic- stricken response to events which seemed to be running out of control? At least the sacking meant that the club could go out and appoint the person they had got lined up for the job.

Er, no, seemingly not. There was no one stripped and ready for the fray, no one ready for the job of managing the team placed bottom of the football league pyramid with eighteen matches to play to avoid relegation. Names were mentioned and rumours flew, but no, there was no heir apparent, no one in place to accept the poisoned chalice.

Then, with the need for having someone in place for the coming game at Grimsby on Saturday suddenly becoming an imperative, the name of Mark Hughes was announced as the new man in charge. Credit where credit is due, action had been taken, and an appointment of some credibility had been made. Or was it a case of grabbing the last loaf on the shelf? Leaving yourself in the position of looking for a manager when your team is bottom of the league and there are fewer than twenty games left to play looks like something of a debacle. But Mark Hughes, whatever you think about his managerial record, brings with him a mountain of experience and a good deal of credibility. Who else was swimming about in the pool of available managers? In a precarious situation action had been taken, now let it play out. History Will Absolve Me was the title Fidel Castro chose for his autobiography, and I can't help feeling that that the final league places will absolve the decision makers at Carlisle United. Or condemn them.

Travelling to Grimsby has proved to be a dubious pleasure in the past. Two years ago, the Wakefield Blues set a course for the East, for where, in Larkin's words, "Sky and Lincolnshire and water meet." The water that faced us that night was stored in a massive black cloud and as we drew closer it was obvious that it was being jettisoned in huge quantities on to the brave folks heading for the match, and although the game got started, it didn't reach half-time. In farcical conditions play was abandoned and the game was subsequently scheduled for later the following month. That month would be September when once again rain threatened. Thankfully though, this time the game was completed and it is noteworthy because although Carlisle conceded a second-half goal, their two-goal lead was sufficient cushion for an away win. In fact, it wasn't the nerve-shredder the scoreline might suggest. Carlisle controlled the ball and the tempo of the game and the fact that they took three points is testament to their game management in the best sense of the term.

I mention this not to bask in some former glory, although that is always an indulgent pleasure, but to highlight the fact that Grimsby at Blundell Park are always a tricky proposition; fast, strong and dangerous. That evening they were outplayed, but they looked to be in the process of developing a squad firstly to establish a position in Division 2 and then build towards a promotion. It is a process which has been followed by *the likes of Mansfield and Stockport who are both now plying their trade in the third tier. A lesson here for a club which has found itself having to sign twelve players during the January transfer window.*

Even so, the mood amongst the Carlisle fans gathering in the insalubrious bar area below the visitors' stand at Blundell Park seemed to be quietly confident. Quiet that is until the fans took up their places facing the pitch. The word was that Carlisle would be playing with a back four and the expectation was that a little more pragmatism could be expected from the Blues. This proved to be the case and the name of Mark Hughes soon featured in the various chants of the travelling faithful. How Mike Williamson must regret his four-syllable surname.

He might also regret that he rarely fielded a team where every player looked to be playing in their preferred position or playing to a game plan that they fully understood. Despite the pacey threat of Grimsby, the Carlisle back four looked solid. Charlie McArthur and Josh Williams at full back were challenging well for the ball in the air and making some no-nonsense clearances when required. Sam Lavelle and Terrell Thomas produced some highly committed blocks and tackles which was most impressive given that a week earlier Carlisle had conceded the first two goals of five because defenders got in each other's way.

In front of the back four Callum Whelan covered any gaps well and when Carlisle gained possession, he showed the consistent ability to support the man with the ball and use the space he inevitable creates for himself to trigger further moves. Alongside him, Will Patching, trying to play the game at his own pace, produced some tidy, if not eye-catching, passes while Elliot Embleton looked to be gaining greater confidence with each appearance.

Up front, Joe Hugill threatened with his pace and found himself booked for diving when he should have had a penalty. This event took place in the opposite penalty area to where we were standing and I wouldn't like to swear that Hugill was in the box, it was television pictures which later proved that to be the case, but I definitely saw the sprawling keeper make contact with Hugill's foot. Penalty! Penalty! But the referee, who was much closer than I was, didn't see a foul but he was able to discern an intention to cheat on Hugill's part and awarded him a yellow card.

The remainder of Carlisle's attacking threat rested on Kadeem Harris and Stephen Wearne. Of these two, Harris was the more prominent, proving to be a handful for the Grimsby defenders and showing a laudable willingness to track back and work for the team.

I've covered almost all of the starting eleven and written positively about them. I should add that these players produced the best half of football I've seen from Carlisle all season and it was a reminder why we cover the miles we do. I have left out one player though and it is one to whom I owe an apology.

I had questioned whether Gabe Breeze could have left his line to claim the cross which led to the goal at Notts County, but when I watched the tv highlights later I realised that the cross was much deeper than it appeared from the stand at Meadow Lane and what Breeze really needed was a more effective aerial challenge from his defensive colleague, or frankly, for the County striker Alsanna Jatta to be less good.

Secondly, I questioned whether or not Breeze could have got closer to Butterworth's shot for the opening goal for Swindon. Again, viewing on tv with the remarkable power of hindsight, due credit should be paid to the power and accuracy of Butterworth's shot. Time for me to cut and consume a huge wodge of humble pie. Sorry, Gabe.

But back to the action on the pitch where it could be argued that for lengthy periods of the first half, Carlisle were the better side. Certainly, the Blundell Park crowd was largely silent as Carlisle passed the ball on a pitch which a Blues fan close to me described as "not for fannying about on." But is this not a familiar tale unfolding where Carlisle don't see their superiority reflected in the scoreline? Well, yes, except that Carlisle were in front. A dangerous in-swinging corner from the right had found Sam Lavelle remarkably in space in the six-yard box ready to plant a header into the empty goal in the sixth minute! No wonder it was the Carlisle end which was generating all of the noise. No wonder Mark Hughes' name was being loudly acclaimed. No wonder that once again, Carlisle fans began to hope.

Did those fans dare to look forward to bagging three points by the end of the game? I've highlighted the Carlisle performance in the first half but it was by no means outright dominance they had achieved. Grimsby exerted their own pressure and would have equalised but for Breeze's two brilliant point-blank saves after which the ball did end up in the net but much to the pleasure of the Blue Horde behind the goal, the assistant referee was standing with her flag resolutely raised. Offside, I think, but I wasn't absolutely sure. Still, it was an excellent decision, Lino!

In the second half it became obvious that Grimsby were beginning to get the upper hand, and Carlisle would need to hang on, or better still, sneak another goal which they very nearly did when Harris' shot bounced against the foot of the post and rebounded out. Bearing down onto the loose ball with the keeper out of position, Embleton hammered a shot straight into a Grimsby defender. Huge shouts for handball and a penalty which was never going to be given. It's that business of small margins though: Harris' shot a fraction to the left and it would have been a goal, Embleton's shot either side of that defender and bingo, two-nil!

Small margins, small margins and it was not to be for Carlisle. Inevitably Grimsby got their equaliser after some skilful work from their big striker, controlling the ball and turning in the box to put a shot past the wrong-footed Breeze.

Ater that, it was down to the referee to respond to the howled appeal from the Grimsby end for a penalty which he duly granted. No question of a dive now. The previous Saturday, Jordan Jones had received two yellow cards for perceived dives and Joe Hugill had received one in this match but now the theatrical tumbling by the Grimsby forward resulted in what turned out to be the match winning penalty.

Was this another case of small margins, a ref being swayed by the home crowd or just deserts for a powerful second half performance from Grimsby? Whatever, it was hard to take for the travelling supporters now coming to terms with being part of Mark Hughes' Blue and White Army.

And was there hope? Of course there was. Lady Luck was perched seductively alongside those fans,

*winking coquettishly and whispering sweet nothings
about Newport County away in three days' time.*

Tuesday 13 February. Newport County v Carlisle United. Rodney Parade. EFL League 2.

I don't think that this will be a long post as I don't think
I've much to say that hasn't been said already.

I only arrived home from an overnight stay in
hospital about half an hour before kick-off, so an
evening watching Carlisle United in their current
incarnation probably wasn't the ideal form of
recuperation, but what the hell. The game was originally
meant to be played before Christmas, and Adam
travelled down to Cardiff to stay with Ben and go to the
game. A red weather warning put paid to the match and
meant that Adam was stranded in Cardiff for about
three days. This time he watched the first half on his
phone while travelling home from Nottingham and
joined me for most of the second half.

That might sound encouraging given recent
performances, but that only tells half the story. As usual
Carlisle started brightly on the front foot, though we've
become accustomed to that. In this case they dominated
the first half in terms of possession, chances created,
shots on target, just about any metric you choose other
than goals scored. They were the sort of stats that
would have had Mike Wilkinson drooling. We were
finally creating a decent number of chances but still
failing to take them.

The positivity and dominance were even sustained
well into the second half. But as usual it took just one
moment to decide the game. A Carlisle attack broke

down in the Newport half (sound familiar?) and a swift counterattack saw County score in the 76th minute. Carlisle toiled in vain for the remaining twenty minutes of playing time. Opposition teams must realise by now you just have to wait patiently for the inevitable mistake(s) and make sure you take full advantage of it. they must also know that once they've conceded Carlisle rarely force their way back into a game.

Are there any crumbs of comfort? Mark Hughes was always on a hiding to nothing, with minimal preparation time and two tough away games immediately after his appointment. One could argue that any points gained at Grimsby at Newport would be a bonus. Hughes now has one more game in which to affect a great escape than Paul Simpson did three years ago, though the points situation wasn't quite as dire then. One could also hope that now that all the new signings have in effect completed a pre-season spell with the club, they might begin to play with a bit more cohesion. And we now have another striker surnamed Dennis in the squad. But I can't find any other straws at which to clutch.

Saturday 15 February. Carlisle United v Colchester United. Brunton Park. EFL League 2.

This will probably be another relatively short post, though not entirely for the same reasons as last time. On Tuesday I may not have travelled to Newport but was able to watch the match live on Sky Sports +. This time neither travelling nor a live stream was an option.

Following my brief hospital stay earlier in the week, I reluctantly accepted that a 270-mile round trip would not be what the doctor ordered. John was willing to drive (it should have been my turn) but for once, where Carlisle United are concerned, I chose to do the sensible thing and stay at home. I did tell John that he was more than welcome to borrow my season ticket if he could find another mug to go with him. He almost immediately messaged back to say that he already had, but that she preferred to spend the afternoon shopping in Carlisle rather than at the match. Step forward Julie Clarke, John's wife!

All that meant that my match day experience involved checking Jon Colman's online updates every five minutes or so, while watching my local RL team Wakefield Trinity's return to Super League against Leeds Rhinos, which *was* available to stream. While an unchanged Carlisle and Colchester laboured to a half-time stalemate at Brunton Park, Wakefield were streaking into an unexpected 14-0 lead at Headingley, before Leeds pulled a try back.

The story of the second-half at Brunton Park, based on Colman's updates, the brief match highlights and online comments, seems to have been a tale of two goalkeepers. The Colchester keeper made a couple of outstanding saves, while at the other end Gabe Breeze made an absolute worldie to keep the game scoreless. Meanwhile, at Headingley, Wakefield held out for a famous 14-12 victory, despite Leeds scoring a last-minute try. So what are the takeaways from this game? This is not a criticism of Mark Hughes, but the bottom line is that one point in nine since he took charge is not survival form. Neither, as one or two comments online stated, are incremental improvements in performance enough. Right now, we are not talking about some long-term project. The club is currently facing an existential crisis, and minor improvements are meaningless if they don't translate to wins.

I hold onto the following crumb of comfort. There were fifteen games left when Paul Simpson returned to the club three years ago and saved us from relegation. That's exactly the number of games left in this season. Can history repeat itself? If so, a win next Saturday is not just important, it's essential, and it doesn't matter how it happens. I'll end on a more positive note. Late on Sunday morning I found a copy of yesterday's teamsheet/broadsheet through the letterbox. On the front was written, "To Howard, Best wishes from Sparky and the Boys." Thank you, Sparky and the boys, and thank you to John. As I said a week ago, it doesn't take much. I'm beginning to warm to this Mark Hughes feller!

Like flies to wanton boys are we to the gods of football fandom,
They kill us for their sport.

A rough paraphrase from that Bard chap, the one who has blighted so many schooldays for whining schoolboys (and no doubt their female equivalents) creeping unwillingly to school. But, as so often, Shakespeare had his finger on the pulse. We may protest our autonomy and insist that we are creatures of free-will but at every turn we are afflicted by those simple twists of fate or we become playthings for the malign pleasure of the gods.

Take the plan for Howard and I to buy season tickets for instance. Okay, it would involve a long trek to home matches, but the advantage would be that we could get priority for away tickets where we very often have a hundred and twenty-mile advantage over the

Carlisle-based Blue Army. A feast of football in prospect surely! A plan blessed with simplicity but in practise one which has been blighted by adult and family responsibilities. If not that then those pesky gods and their wont for disruption, as Howard's text prior to this game in which he adopted a humble, regretful tone to give his apologies for not being able to attend the game adding the lowest of low-key explanations thus: "I've had an overnighter in Pinderfields hospital after suffering a minor stroke."

Humph! I privately shelved my dark thoughts about lack of commitment on Howard's part and turned my attention to forming a plan B. Howard had decently offered the use of his season ticket so forming the plan should be easy enough especially as I had a seasoned Carlisle United watcher standing in the wings, one who would surely welcome a trip up to Carlisle and back to watch the mouthwatering clash between the Blues and Colchester United.

"No."

"No?"

Nothing comes from nothing, I could have added, but it turned out that not only was my dear wife making a stand against watching any more football, but she was also becoming fed up of random Shakespeare quotes being dished up and served in her direction.

No, though. She'd said "No." To contextualise this I have to mention the 20th February 1982 where in front of 4,797 fans at the Manor ground, despite a Bob Lee goal, Carlisle lost to 2-1 to Oxford United. That would have been only 4,795 fans if I hadn't driven from Hitchin, Herts to Oxford with a young lady who had caught my eye at a Language Development In-Service course for teachers. A dismal round trip drive of three hours for a dismal game in the dead of winter. I certainly knew how to treat a girl in those days. However, she was made of stern stuff and she duly signed up for the long haul which would involve future visits to such glamour spots as Mansfield, Rotherham, Halifax and Scunthorpe. But to be fair, there would also be some high spots including travelling to Stoke to see Carlisle regain their football league status and also to the new Wembley stadium for a wonderful afternoon which was only tarnished by Carlisle's miserable performance against Southampton.

Beyond football, for the sake of clarity, it has to be said that the long haul has involved, at the time of writing, forty-two years of marriage to me which clearly has been an undoubted pleasure, a definitive high spot (Readers will have noticed that an undue optimism is a feature of these pieces.).

Who truly knows how the female mind works though? Now she was saying no. No to standing on a terrace for ninety minutes watching the team occupying the bottom spot of the fourth tier of English football. She would though, be prepared to travel up with me in order to spend the afternoon shopping in Carlisle. Done! She could enjoy the Continental piazza-style elegance of the Town Hall with all of its dug-up surfaces while I took my chances with Mr Sweary on the Paddock Terrace.

Nil each. Sometimes the scoreline does not do justice to the game. Mark Hughes fielded a team who seemed to have a good idea of what the game plan was. Each of the players looked comfortable in their position and they hadn't been saddled with over-complicated demands. Pragmatism ruled and if the ball needed clearing from a defensive position, then so be it. Furthermore, Colchester were set up to keep things tight, but they also had some tricky forwards, and they would break quickly if the opportunity presented itself. In other words, they came to play, and the outcome was that rare thing this season – a good game.

More than that, it was a game marked by flashes of brilliance. Twice, Carlisle looked as though they were going to score but credit to the Colchester keeper Matt Macy who got down sharply to tip Stephen Wearne's shot wide of the post and later produced an even better save to keep Elliot Embleton's curling effort from going in the top corner.

Either of these could have been save of the match/ month/season were it not for a later effort from Gabe Breeze who somehow managed to tip a ball over the bar from point-blank range. Looked certain to score, an open goal yawning, a nailed-on winner, all of the cliches applied and if you're going down that line, you'd have to say that the Carlisle custodian threw himself at the ball while making himself look as big as possible. The Paddock regulars were already invoking the name of Gordon Banks and his save in the 1970 World Cup, but the match wasn't over yet. Colchester created two more chances which were denied, and the final effort of the match came from Callum Whelan whose shot was diverted for a corner by Macey, but before the kick could be taken, the ref blew for full time and a hard-earned point for each team.

The crowd warmly applauded two teams who were "at it." There had been plenty of effort and determination on show and Mark Hughes went up *further in the fans' estimation by responding to the applause with a fist pump. Forming a bond with the fans, how difficult can it be?*

But repeat this: it had been a good game. No goals, but some great attempts thwarted. Two teams competing without the result being a forgone conclusion. Hope kindled, expectation denied and nerves shredded. One more point gained and one more step along the way. I had enjoyed the game and said as much when I met up with Julie by the car. She had bought a new salt and pepper pot and had enjoyed a cup of tea and a piece of brownie in Cakes and Ale. I let a meaningful silence fall in order to let the difference in our two Saturday afternoon experiences be pronounced. She could have said, "My care is loss of care," but she didn't. She leaves it to me to make the snarky Shakespeare quotes.

That should have been the last word on the day, but we stopped off at Scotch Corner on our way home and bumped into Stephen Wearne, easily identifiable in his Peter Tyson-sponsored travelling gear. I made sympathetic noises about not getting three points, but he countered by saying that the team had taken a good deal of satisfaction from the game and that it was only two "worldies" which had prevented them from picking up a win. I didn't respond by saying that it was Gabe Breeze's even bigger worldie which had earned them a point. Instead, I asked him how he was enjoying being at the club and was immediately won over by his enthusiasm and evident relish. Super club, lovely people and fantastic fans was the gist of his response, and I can't summon the words to capture the pride and inner warmth this gave me. For goodness sake, John, you're a grown man and long-time cynic. Why such childish pleasure in meeting this very personable young man who spoke so highly of the club you support?

As I say, I can't find the words but I had decided at that point that Stephen Wearne should be in the starting line-up every week.

Saturday 22 February. Carlisle United v Gillingham. Brunton Park. EFL League 2.

I feel like I've reached a similar point to about the same stage of last season, when I felt that I had little new or of real interest to say on a week-to-week basis, particularly when I hadn't attended games. The really depressing thing is that it's happening all over again, with no sign of any respite.

The bottom line is this. Sam Lavelle scored at Grimsby just five minutes into Mark Hughes' first game in charge. Since then, we've played over six hours of football (allowing for time added on) without scoring a goal. From the match reports I've read since the Grimsby game, we haven't looked much like scoring either. When chances have been created intermittently, the finishing has been pretty woeful. Under Hughes leadership, we've taken two points from a possible twelve, scoring just that solitary goal at Grimsby. That's not enough to give us even a sniff of survival, never mind actually achieving it.

None of this is to criticise Mark Hughes. He's taken on a task that many would have shied away from. He's trying to do his best with the hand he's been dealt, and that's a pretty meagre hand.

I have no truck with supporters who clutch optimistically at minor signs of improvement each time we fail to score. There's only one sign of improvement that matters at the moment, and that's a sequence of wins. There are also those who believe that Hughes must be aware of out-of-contract players that he could bring in. If he is aware of them, he's probably also aware of the reasons why they're out-of-contract.

I've still got another fortnight to wait before I can drive again, and with John otherwise engaged at Leeds Playhouse, I was once again reliant on Jon Colman's in-game posts. As the game wore on and the score remained 0-0, I increasingly got the impression that Jon himself wasn't entirely convinced when he talked about the possibility of Carlisle snatching all three points.

I've got to be honest and say that I'm relieved that I haven't watched a game in which there were no goals, relatively few chances, and no Breeze wonder save to marvel at. One can only hope that some local pride kicks in at Barrow on Thursday evening, and that we see some real passion. At least we'll be able to watch this game on Sky.

Remarkably, home attendances remain resilient, with just under 7,000 at yesterday's game.

To my eternal shame I have never taken my son to a match at Brunton Park. I am a bad parent.

In mitigation I would say that I have taken him to some away games and he can list Mansfield, Rotherham, Halifax, Scunthorpe and, quite oddly given its geographical distance, Orient, as places where he has seen the Blues in action. This list includes games where Carlisle have picked up the full haul of away points: a 2-3 cracker at Mansfield and a one-nil victory at Halifax which staved off for certain the threat of relegation and due thanks are extended to Richie Foran for his late goal. The list of games also includes a couple of abject defeats at Scunthorpe and Orient. My son has seen the pendulum in full swing, he has witnessed the highs and lows and this should be sufficient for a life-long devotion to Carlisle United to take hold.

But no, the bug never really bit. Maybe that's because he has never lived in Carlisle, maybe it's because his interests always lay elsewhere. Despite my entreaties for him to study English Literature, he went off to university to read something called Physics. Now he's holed up in New York earning his living as an Associate Director in an International I.T. Consultancy. Sounds good, eh? But it rules out the possibility of taking up a regular position on the Paddock terraces on cold, wet, Saturday afternoons. Look what he's missing out on!

I mention this now by way of explanation because he is a dutiful son marking Christmas and birthdays with thoughtful presents. Like the tickets he got for us at Leeds Playhouse to see a matinee performance of the Merchant of Venice. That's right, a Saturday afternoon matinee performance meaning that while Carlisle were battling out a nil each draw with Gillingham, I was being entertained by the Bard again and his late 1590s take on religious intolerance and conflict, with his central character, Antonio beginning the play sounding like he possesses a season ticket for the Paddock announcing, "I know not why I am so sad."

Maybe, like me, Antonio resorted to checking out the match stats to see if the data evidence suggested that Carlisle had been denied by ill-fortune or whether there were any discernible trends pointing towards a clear superiority for the home side.

That being the case, the answer would be no, there was no such evidence. Possession was shared almost equally, we had fifteen shots to their fourteen, six of which were on target as opposed to their three and we had six corners to their three. Gillingham made more passes than Carlisle and were three percent more accurate in their passing.

When data analysis became important in my professional life, I proved to be particularly inept, or maybe just disinterested. Tables of figures never really did it for me and the conclusion I drew from the Gillingham match stats was that we should probably move on.

Next match please.

Thursday 27 February. Barrow v Carlisle United. Holker Street. EFL League 2.

At last! A glimmer of hope and some genuine positives to talk about.

I was anticipating this game a bit more keenly than most recent fixtures, for a number of reasons. Most importantly, a failure to win this game would probably see my last lingering hopes of survival disappear. Furthermore, the game was live on Sky Sports Football – not streamed, proper coverage with studio analysis and the rest. And of course this is our local derby. Since regaining Football League status Barrow had drawn one and lost six of the games between the clubs. They had to go back more than six decades to the early sixties for their last victory over Carlisle. So local pride and bragging rights were very much at stake.

Carlisle had sold out their allocation of tickets with 930 present to cheer on the Blues. Given that the overall attendance was just over 4,200, almost 2,300 short of capacity, it's a pity that Barrow didn't see fit to make more tickets available to away fans who would have snapped them up. Perhaps they were worried that the home fans would be outnumbered. Sound familiar?

The away corner at Holker Street has changed since I was there almost two years ago. I say corner because it's an odd situation, where the stand behind the goal is split between home and away fans, with a no-man's land in the middle. There's no stand or terracing behind the other goal. Away fans used to also occupy terracing along part of one side of the ground, some of the worst terracing it's been my misfortune to stand on. That terracing has now been replaced by a small new stand. I call it a stand, though that's probably a touch generous. It looks like something that was bought in a flatpack from IKEA and assembled over a couple of days last summer. There have already been a number of photos posted online by Carlisle fans who had the misfortune to be in that stand, showing just how awful the view was, with numerous metal pillars and beams obscuring sightlines. And I haven't started on the state of the pitch yet!

There was just one change to the starting eleven, with Scott replacing Bevan, and Vela took a place on the bench after a long absence through injury. It's clear that Mark Hughes sees 4-3-3 as the formation for the current situation. For the second game in succession, he displayed a touch of tactical genius by playing two full backs in the full back positions. That may seem obvious, but it's the sort of common sense that appeared to be beyond Mike Williamson.

Barrow started the stronger, dominating possession and creating a couple of chances without seriously troubling Gabe Breeze in goal. But it was Carlisle who scored in the nineteenth minute. Following build-up play on the right, two deft back heels in succession channelled the ball to Matthew Dennis just inside the penalty area. He appeared to stumble slightly as he took his first touch with his back to goal, but he retained his balance sufficiently well to turn and direct his shot inside the right-hand post from near the penalty spot.

The remaining seventy minutes were not pretty. To be honest, even the Brazil team of 1970 would have struggled to play pretty football on that vegetable patch of a pitch. But Carlisle did what they've failed to do on so many occasions this season: they dealt effectively with what was in front of them. They were more careful in retaining possession and dealt more effectively with counter attacks. Breeze was in commanding form in goal, coming to gather crosses and generally dominating his area, a performance that deservedly won him the Sky Man of the Match award. There was robust and sometimes last-ditch tackling, by Lavelle, Thomas and Guy in particular.

As the game entered its closing stages, Carlisle generally did a good job ensuring that the ball was kept in unthreatening areas, that in many cases being the Barrow half. They looked like a team who'd rediscovered the art of game management. There were shouts for a Barrow penalty for handball in the dying seconds and post-match replays suggested that they had strong claims. Maybe it's a sign that our luck is changing when that kind of decision goes in our favour. In any case, it stemmed from a throw-in that was erroneously given in Barrow's favour, so maybe it was just refereeing decisions levelling out.

There were great scenes at the end as the players and management celebrated a desperately needed victory long and hard in front of the fans. Terrel Thomas and Mark Hughes were particularly demonstrative in their reactions. It may have only been a single win, but it seemed like there was a widespread feeling that this might mark a long overdue turning point.

An additional pleasure of the evening was the presence of former Blue Michael Bridges in the Sky Sports studio. He has plenty of TV experience from his time in Australia and it showed. He was disarmingly honest in admitting that he's an ex-Carlisle player and that therefore it was pointless to expect impartiality from him. He looked at the game very much from a Carlisle perspective and made no apologies for doing so. It made a refreshing change from the anodyne impartiality peddled on Match of the Day by the likes of Alan Shearer and Danny Murphy, as they trot out their predictable platitudes. And Bridges was honest about his prejudices in a way that Gary Neville and Jamie Carragher rarely are when commenting on Manchester United and Liverpool.

We had already decided that we would not be making the trip to Barrow for the game originally scheduled for Saturday 1st March and that conviction intensified when the fixture was transferred to the evening of Thursday 27th February at the behest of that nice Mr Murdoch.

Nope. Trailing around the north of England in the wintry dark in pursuit of a football match had no appeal whatsoever, particularly as the match would be televised thanks to the offices of the previously mentioned Mr Murdoch.

Having spotted the chink in my otherwise resolute principles, Howard once again offered me the opportunity to watch the game from the comfort of his sofa, and I was ready to agree except that once again a literary obstacle stood in the way. I had already given my word that I would attend an author event at Horbury's premier independent bookshop. Michael Stewart would be reading from his marvellous new novel, Black Wood Women at Darling Reads bookshop at the very time Carlisle would be taking on Barrow, the interlopers from Lancashire, in what some people refer to as the "Cumbrian Derby."

The lovely managers at Darling Reads can be gratified that I have given a handsome plug to their emporium and likewise, the erudite Mr Stewart can bask in the endorsement I have given his book. So, I hope all three of them can overlook my ill-mannered rush to leave the event. I listened to, and enjoyed, the reading and the question-and-answer session, but as soon as they were finished I made an unseemly dash, barging past some hapless booklovers and crashing through a line of chairs to get my book signed first and complete my exit. I had calculated that, all being well, I could leave the bookshop, reclaim my car and drive, fully observant of the speed limits, across Wakefield to get to Howard's before too much of the match had elapsed.

Done it! Twenty minutes after the kick-off I was knocking on Howard's door and a smiling Mr Falshaw met me saying, "They're warming up."

I did think that was odd. It is customary for both teams to warm up before a game but by twenty minutes in you expect them to be fully warmed up and engaged in the battle before them. When I looked closely at the tv screen though, my misconception became evident. It's to do with defective hearing, isn't it? Carlisle were already in front. Howard had been trying to tell me, "They're one nil up!"

Not only one nil up but ahead on account of a remarkable goal. Replays showed two backheels in a penalty area move and then a finish by Matty Dennis, recently signed on a short-term contract, who hit his shot firmly past ex Carlisle keeper, Farman.

And that, my friends, is how it stayed.

Chapter 9
WADING THROUGH TREACLE

Tuesday 4 March. Carlisle United v Walsall. Brunton Park. EFL League 2.

It's nice to be rediscovering a sense of enjoyment in writing these pieces! Yes, I know it's my own choice, and no-one is making me do anything, but after a season and a half of writing about often abject performances, the joy was sometimes getting a little hard to find. So thanks for that Mark Hughes, and hopefully for much more to come.

I still can't drive until next week, and John had another commitment, so our season tickets remained in storage and Sky Sports + was once again my means of watching the game. The starting eleven saw just one change, with Aaron Hayden replacing Cameron Harper. I can only assume Harper was injured, as he wasn't even named on the bench. Whatever the reason, it proved to be a well-judged decision. This game saw top play bottom, and while Walsall were no longer the runaway leaders of League 2 that they were two or three months ago, the fixture still brought back memories of a woeful night at the Bescot Stadium in October, which had to be one of the worst performances of the ill-fated, but mercifully short-lived, Mike Williamson project. And there was plenty of competition for that accolade.

The early signs weren't good. The teams looked exactly what they were – two sides almost an entire division apart. The grit and cohesion that had propelled the team to victory at Barrow just five days earlier was nowhere to be seen. It was little surprise when Walsall took the lead after just six minutes, a player left criminally unmarked on the far post. Some might argue that Breeze should have done better, but so should the entire defensive line in front of him. Even that setback failed to galvanise Carlisle as Walsall dominated the early stages. But it only takes a moment for things to change, and that moment duly arrived in the nineteenth minute. From the second of two Embleton corners from the left in quick suggestion Hayden rose majestically above everyone else to head powerfully home. We could have done with more goals like that from him this season.

From that point we started to see a different Carlisle, with more purpose and self-belief. You may have noticed that I've rarely referred to match statistics since Metrics Mike departed, but on this occasion the half-time stats did indicate that Carlisle had edged the first half overall, not forgetting the only stat that mattered, a score of 1-1.

The Sky Sports commentator mentioned repeatedly that Walsall tend to come good in the second half, gradually wearing opposition teams down, and it appeared that that might well be the case for the first twenty minutes after the break. Carlisle had Breeze to thank for a couple more excellent saves, and Archie Davies for a goal-stopping challenge. If he'd misjudged it, he would probably have got a red card, but his tackle was timed to perfection. Carlisle had gone toe-to-toe with the best team in the division and emerged with credit, honours shared. The crowd were obviously happy with what they saw, giving the players a good ovation at the final whistle.

It was possible to hear the crowd getting behind the team in the closing stages, though given that there were probably at least a couple of thousand people chanting it wasn't as loud as might be expected if it was properly miked up. Yet the single gobshite in The Paddock, who launched into an expletive-ridden rant at the referee part way through the second half was crystal clear. It was probably John's friend, Mr Sweary.

There is a universal law applicable to football writers that teams who are placed top of their league or thereabouts should be described in the customary manner, therefore I am obliged to say that Carlisle were playing host to "high-flying" Walsall for this fixture. Given Carlisle's position ("lowly" is now the word I am obliged to use) it doesn't do to comment on the visitors from the West Midlands and their current incongruous descriptor. That they were the club from whom we signed Ray Train should allow them free passage and, as current league leaders, they were the sort of side we should be measuring ourselves against.

Readers sensing a certain amount of procrastination at this point would be right. Once again, I am finding it difficult to get to the point and comment in detail about this match for the simple reason that I wasn't there. Nor is the reason for my absence particularly novel as the great beast literature had raised its head again with an invitation to me to give an interview on Chapel fm, an East Leeds Community Radio Station, about my latest book. It is not the purpose of these articles to promote my own work, and to do so would be unseemly and so avoiding such tackiness, we move on.*

The facts are that Carlisle deployed their usual psychological weapon of conceding an early goal, maybe to lull the opposition into complacency, maybe to present themselves with a greater motivational challenge, but seven minutes in and they were behind. They did get an equaliser in the twenty-second minute, courtesy of Aaron Hayden but there was no further score after that.

So, if Carlisle were measuring themselves against such opposition, they could point to the fact that they didn't lose. Or alternatively, they could point out that they had dropped two points at home. It is a glass-half filled scenario and you draw your own conclusions.

If you are of the school of half-full glasses, you might be taking satisfaction from the knowledge that this was a fourth game in an unbeaten run with only one goal conceded and six points gained. Consistency and momentum; the new manager bounce may not have been as pronounced as expected or hoped for, but Mark Hughes appears to be steering the side towards turning a corner. Always within the optimistic fan is the feeling that soon things will click and a resurgent Carlisle will start climbing the table. This could be it: honours shared with a high-flying opposition. Here, pass me that glass carefully as it is half-full.

* How the Northern Light Gets In (Grosvenor House.) Six stories by John Irving Clarke available from all good bookshops.

Saturday 8 March. Harrogate Town v Carlisle United. Wetherby Road. EFL League 2.

Ah well, the "feel marginally better" factor was nice for the few days it lasted. Due to recent health issues, this was the first game in a month that I'd attended in person. Given the health factor, it was probably a good thing that this game required our shortest journey of the season, just forty-five minutes from Wakefield to Harrogate. On the other hand, any Carlisle supporter knows, given United's abysmal record against Harrogate, that a visit to Wetherby Road does not tend to be a joyous occasion. And so it proved.

It all started so well. We made the short journey in glorious weather (for early March), parked at The Woodlands Pub just before two, and enjoyed a pre-match pint outside in the warm sunshine. Most of the warm clothing we' taken wasn't needed, and it was just ten minutes' walk from the pub to the ground. There was a slight hiccup when I mislaid my ticket, but we only missed the first couple of minutes while the ticket office printed a replacement.

I've voiced my less than complimentary views on Harrogate's ground before. It has been expanded slightly since my last visit – one-third of the terracing at the away end now extends about fifteen steps back, rather than the six steps of the rest of the terrace. For such a small ground it's remarkable that it's split up into nine or ten different sections. The attendance for this game was 4,136 (fairly close to capacity) but would have been just over 3,000 without us loyal fools from Carlisle.

What is there to say about the game? With Dennis unavailable, Hughes appeared to have opted for a 5-3-2 formation, with Harper returning to the back line. Personally, I think he'd have been better off sticking to the 4-3-3 formation that had served us reasonably well in the previous few games. With only Harris and Scott up front, the attack lacked any real focal point. The spectator experience was a bit more visceral than usual, due to our proximity to the action. No matter where you are in the ground, you're never far from pitch level! The truth is that Harrogate really weren't very good, and it's difficult to argue that Carlisle were much better. Harrogate played long balls forward most of the time. Carlisle's approach play was slightly more measured, but on the occasions when they did create chances they tended to fall to defenders or midfielders.

As the game reached the latter stages, still scoreless, Hughes reconfigured the attack by sending on Kelly and Hugill. Kelly's height and physical presence, combined with Hugill's pace, gave the Harrogate defence something different to contend with, and might be the way forward for the last few games of the season, though that presumes that Kelly will defy expectation and stay fit.

The winning goal summed up our fortunes against Harrogate. It came in the 95th minute and the highlights showed that the shot was going well wide until it hit Vela and deflected into the net. It was a cruel way to lose. I'm not claiming that we deserved three points, but we did enough to come away something.

Given the exodus that followed the goal, the comments from those who remained, and subsequent online reaction, I think this game probably marked the point at which most Carlisle fans finally gave up hope of survival.

Esteemed commentators on all things relating to Carlisle United within my circle have been known to denigrate Harrogate Town for various reasons. Myself, I retain a soft spot for "the Sulphurites" as we must call them, mainly because theirs is the only league ground on which I have played. In the late seventies, it wasn't a league ground of course, but nevertheless, my college team trotted out onto the hallowed turf of the Wetherby Road ground to face the might of Harrogate Town third eleven in the Sunday morning Claro League.

Unusually, (and believe me, I've tried) I can't claim any personal heroics, goal scoring feats or significant contributions to the game. I can't even remember the score but Colin, my friend and erstwhile teammate, insists that we won. That's as may be, but my abiding memory is that we walked off at half time into the dressing room to find a massive pot of tea on the table. Just like real footballers! The Glory Game indeed. We were living the dream.

The build-up to this game went some way towards cementing my rose-tinted view of Harrogate Town. For early March we were blessed with glorious weather and arriving early we enjoyed a pre-match drink in the car park of the Woodlands pub where Carlisle and Harrogate fans mingled amiably. And were we not buoyed by our current run of form? Four games unbeaten and now we were due to play a team on the fringe of the relegation scrap themselves. This would be the day, surely when the so-called Harrogate Town curse would be lifted.

Let us now remove all such optimism. In a dire game the curse was not banished. Taking our places in the terraced stand behind the goal we witnessed what is best described as a long slog. In anticipation of a bombardment, Carlisle played five at the back to deal with the long balls aimed at the Carlisle defence. Thomas, Lavelle and Hayden were resolute and dominant too when it came to defensive work at corners, but the midfielders struggled to get the ball down and start playing. Callum Guy and Callum Whelan had both been named in the starting line up and the feeling amongst some of the fans was that maybe it should be one or the other as they didn't seem to gel well together. But the sluggish pitch didn't help any fluency, and it was obvious to me that any magic dust I had left after my mercurial performance had long since vanished. Even so, Carlisle did try and get some reasonable service to Harris and Scott up front while Harrogate were unflagging in their huffing and puffing, but well before the end it was evident that they would settle for one point which would leave the relative positions of the two teams unchanged.

No one will thank me for making the observation that when you're down at the bottom things don't go your way. Harrogate saw their prosaic efforts rewarded in the ninety-fifth minute when a player attempted a "try your luck" shot at goal following a corner. The shot was heading wide until it was deflected by the unfortunate Josh Vela into the bottom corner of the United goal.

There was wild rejoicing from the Harrogate fans at this blessing from Fickle Fortune while Carlisle fans could only try and recover from this lowest of low blows. It was a game to be won, and Carlisle had failed to do so in the last minute. The most significant stat is the one that records goals scored. There are no points for aesthetics or artistic merit, Harrogate had got their goal, bagged the three points and it felt significant, ominously significant. That made four points conceded to Harrogate this season and it wasn't difficult to read meaning into that. The curse continues and all we could do was trudge back to the car bemoaning the tinpot stadium with its awful viewing lines, their functional footballing style and their midden of a pitch.

A soft spot for Harrogate? Not any more.

Saturday 15 March. Carlisle United v AFC Wimbledon. Brunton Park. EFL League 2.

The post-mortem/inquest starts here, so this may be a very long entry.

This was a dreadful game. There was nothing on display here that offered any hope, either in the short-term for the remainder of this disastrous season, or for the longer-term future of the club in the National League next season, which is now undoubtedly the fate that awaits Carlisle United. It's pointless analysing the short-term when the very future of the club needs addressing so urgently. I don't want to repeat the points that Jon Colman has already made in The News and Star, but I do want to try to identify what has gone so tragically wrong.

To concede a goal after just two minutes in such a crucial game was criminal, particularly when it was the result of such woeful marking, positioning and concentration. To repeat the misdemeanour so early in the second half was unforgivable. What happened in the other eighty-eight minutes of the game was equally unacceptable. I lost count of the number of Carlisle corners that were either overhit or sailed harmlessly into the arms of the Wimbledon goalkeeper. It was invariably a Wimbledon player who won the second ball or was first to a loose ball. The word "anticipation" seemed to have been erased from the mindset of the Carlisle players. Wimbledon were able to manage the game without duly asserting themselves. They weren't that good, but they were more than good enough.

Too often a Carlisle player was reduced to making a sideways or backward pass. It often wasn't their fault, as a woeful lack of movement further forward gave them no other option. Only Callum Guy seemed to be making an effort to offer his defenders a forward option, and even he found himself having to drop deeper and deeper to do so. On a couple of occasions he ended up making ultimately fruitless forays forward because no teammate provided an option. I have a growing sense that when the team is struggling, they unconsciously revert to a default mode of Williamson-ball, and that's not intended as a compliment.

But what was most depressing was the apparent spinelessness of the performance, the lack of any sense of fight and passion in the players. As the second half wore on and the ball was yet again played ponderously across the back line, I was reduced to shouting in frustration, "we're losing 2-0 for Christ's sake!"

When Mark Hughes made his first substitutions it did produce an immediate dividend. With almost his first touch Callum Whelan delivered a telling pass to Kadeem Harris on the right. Harris took on and beat his defender, got to the byline, and one of the afternoon's few decent crosses was strongly headed home by

Matthew Dennis at the far post. It really was that simple. Yet even that failed to galvanise the team into more determined efforts.

Harris was one of the few players who put in an acceptable shift when out of possession. Too many failed to track back, close down and pressurise Wimbledon players who were in possession or make life difficult for defenders when Carlisle played the ball forward. And no-one seemed to take responsibility for marshalling and organising the players.

Remarkably there were still over 7,000 present to witness this latest debacle, only 500 of whom were supporting Wimbledon. There were probably too many like John and me, determined to get value for money from our season tickets, irrespective of the fare on offer. There are strong rumours that one of the players told a supporter (or supporters) to "fuck off" as he disappeared down the tunnel after the game. Who knows what the provocation may have been, but if true it pretty much sums up a woeful afternoon.

So where do the wider problems lie? I'm going to start with player recruitment because, as I've stated previously, Carlisle's last half-decent transfer window was in January 2023. There have been four disastrous windows since then. The only recruit from the summer 2023 window who still appears for Carlisle on a regular basis is Sam Lavelle. Sam is an interesting one. I wasn't that taken with him initially but was impressed by the way he overcame a shaky start and shrugged off some pretty harsh criticism from some sections of the Carlisle support. To be honest, I think he's a half-decent League 2 centre-half but given that the club have experienced a horrendous time ever since he arrived, he, Guy and

Breeze are probably the only players (now that Jon Mellish has gone) that give the impression that the shirt and the club matter to them. The rest of the summer 2023 intake have either moved on already or are nowhere near the matchday squad.

The January 2024 window was going to be the first dividend of the Piataks new ownership of the club, with funds available to recruit the quality of players who would secure the club's survival in League 1. That didn't happen and only Josh Vela of that cohort started yesterday's game, a rare event for him this season. Armstrong and Harrison have already departed, and Lewis and Kelly only made yesterday's bench. The summer 2024 newcomers fare slightly better. Four of them started yesterday, though only Davies can be said to have made a positive impression, and he's missed a fair chunk of the season with injuries. And finally, to the most recent influx. Remarkably, only one of them started and he's a loanee! Four of them were on the bench, but I think this catalogue of signings over the last two years tells its own sad story and requires no further comment.

The retention hasn't been great either. Joel Senior should not have been released following promotion, and a greater effort should have been made to retain the services of Kris Dennis and Omari Patrick for at least a further season. And I think that the departure of Paul Gerrard from the coaching staff may have had a bigger effect than suspected at the time. Following the signing of Luke Armstrong, a marquee signing by Carlisle's standards, it was ridiculous to allow him to leave on loan just twelve months later. Which leads conveniently to my next point.

There has been considerable tactical inflexibility and ineptitude. The two previous managers must share the blame for this, though not equally. When Paul Simpson returned, he proved superb at getting the best out of the players he inherited to ensure survival. He continued that in the following season, leading what we can now see as an over-achieving squad. But as the League 1 season progressed, he seemed to become increasingly inflexible in both formation and personnel. And I don't think anyone would argue that Billy Barr and Jake Simpson were very successful additions to his coaching staff. I've immense respect and affection for Paul Simpson, for the footballing successes he achieved in his two spells, and for the ways in which he moved the club forward off the pitch. He had a vision for the longer-term future of the club, and I suspect that has at least partly informed the Piataks' plans. If I'm being generous, I'll say that the job of overseeing the club's development both on and off the pitch became too much for one man, and that the playing side suffered. Whatever the case, he does have to take some responsibility for the dire on-field performances we've now endured for almost two seasons.

The Williamson era was an unfortunate aberration that may have done untold damage to the club. It was mercifully short but was still much too long. I quickly tired of watching boring and uninspiring football from a group of players who were patently ill-at-ease with the style of football they were being expected to play. Results didn't seem to matter, as long as the stats were favourable. He should never have been let loose anywhere near Carlisle United.

But he was, and it's now to move on from the "front of house" staff, the players and coaches, to those who have been making decisions away from the pitch.

Having condemned the recruitment at length, it would be remiss of me not to question Greg Abbott's position. I don't know the exact details of his job description, or precisely what his role is in the recruitment process, but it's hard to defend someone whose job title is Head of Recruitment when recruitment has been so awful on his watch.

To dismiss one head coach as a transfer window closes could be seen as unfortunate. To do it twice in a season could be seen as careless, and to be frank it's unforgivable. Twice in a matter of months significant sums have been expended on significant numbers of new recruits by a coach, only for him to be denied the opportunity to work with those recruits, that dubious privilege falling to their successor.

Either the Piataks have made poor strategic decisions, or they've been very badly advised. Some are pointing the finger of blame at CEO Nigel Clibbens and Sporting Director Rob Clarkson. Again, I'm not privy to their precise roles and responsibilities, so I'm not going to judge them guilty without evidence, but there's no doubt that the decision-making process has to improve immediately, as does the quality of the decisions being made. We can all dream of an unlikely miracle over the next ten games resulting in League 2 survival, but the reality is that contingency planning for life in the National League should already have begun, and the quality and success of that planning will determine the future of the club.

Like Jon Colman, I spotted the advertisement on the LED hoardings that proclaimed "Five Mistakes That Changed History" yesterday. Where Jon questioned "Only five?" my question was "this afternoon' or this season?"

Eleven games left to play and a significant points difference to make up. Even the most optimistic of supporters must accept that Carlisle's position looks perilous. There is little consolation to be taken from the view that a team always crashes and burns this late in the season. Which team was that likely to be? Also, the rather conceited view that there will be two teams worse than Carlisle does not stand up to close examination. We've lost to Tranmere twice, lost to Morecambe at home and been turned over by Swindon on our own pitch. Could anyone name these two teams who would save Carlisle?

Certainly not AFC Wimbledon. It was Wimbledon who stuck four goals past us in October without any reply. Now they were contesting a promotion spot. Set against that though, after the setback at Harrogate, Carlisle were heading for four significant games against Wimbledon, Bromley, MK Dons and Doncaster. The first three of these games would be at home with the prospect of nine points to be gained. Was that possible? And who was to say we couldn't get something at Doncaster in the fourth game when we'd given them such a good game at Brunton Park leaving them grateful for their solitary point in a nil each draw. Bring it on! The optimist in me has risen above the murky depths and I'm gulping in fresh air.

Optimism is not well catered for by conceding a goal in the second minute. Nor by conceding another within minutes of the second half starting. On a number of occasions this season the crowd has turned toxic. After only four games and defeat at the hands of Tranmere in August, the crowd vented their anger as the teams left the pitch and if reports are true, some of the abuse aimed at Paul Simpson went beyond disgraceful. Likewise, the defeat to Morecambe at home on Boxing Day led to shouting which lacked seasonal goodwill and then there was the notorious Swindon game (Why always Swindon?) where the chants of "Sacked in the morning" and "Not fit to wear the shirt" were aired. Booing your own team? It doesn't sit well with me no matter what the level of frustration. Unrest was evident in the Paddock after the second goal conceded and another outbreak could have been unleashed but it never really materialised. There was certainly plenty of frustration but also there was an air of weary restraint as though mounting another witch-hunt could not be countenanced. Besides, Mark Hughes would not be the target of any abuse as his stock remains high, at least for the time being.

What undoubtedly eased the situation was Matt Dennis' goal in the sixty-seventh minute. A cross from Kadeem Harris was powerfully headed home by the big striker, setting the scene for a siege on the Wimbledon goal in an attempt to gain an equaliser.

Except that the siege never really materialised. It was time to let slip the dogs of war but the dogs looked unable to raise the effort and Wimbledon were able to see out the game without too much trouble, proving that they are a team with plenty of know how. Streetwise, they weren't going to let a second goal slip. But questions do need to be asked of Carlisle. Is there *any truth in the suggestion that they lack physicality and general fitness? Or, is it that Mark Hughes, the bustling, belligerent player as was, cannot inspire the same qualities in the players he now manages? Has he got his selection and formation right? Shoring up at the back with a four, two, three, one, line up, as he did tonight, leaves you short up front. Er, isn't this why Paul Simpson received a lot of flak?*

Not so long ago I was praising the fighting spirit of the Carlisle players and proclaiming my optimism, but that was after a pleasing result. They lost this one and consequently, the picture looks a lot gloomier. This was the first of four games which was going to garner such rich rewards but the overall number of games to play and the possible points to play for are dwindling.

Saturday 22 March. Carlisle United v Bromley. Brunton Park. EFL League 2.

This was a proper game of football, the kind of game we haven't seen at Brunton Park for too long. We certainly never saw it under the limp stewardship of Mike Williamson. It was a game that had a bit of everything. It had goals, numerous chances, incidents, controversy, fisticuffs and, most importantly, a win. As Jon Colman put it in The News and Star, it was a game that had plenty of "feist".

Much of that feist was generated by the latest return to Brunton Park of man-child Harry McKirdy. Bromley is the latest staging post in the downward trajectory of his football career, where he has been reunited with former Carlisle teammate Byron Webster, of whom more later. But before I lay into McKirdy, let's not forget that just over three years ago he was instrumental in Swindon's 3-0 win at Brunton Park that prompted the departure of Keith Millen and the Director of Football who shall not be named, prompting the return of Paul Simpson. So we do have something for which to thank McKirdy.

The feist also came from the fact that many supporters must have felt that United were drinking in the last-chance saloon, nine points from safety with just nine games left. There had been little in the previous two demoralising defeats to hint at what we saw in this game.

Mark Hughes made two changes to the starting line-up, bringing in Callum Whelan and Steven Wearne, both of them Williamson recruits. Kadeem Harris was the only other Williamson signing to start the game.

Glory be, Carlisle scored as soon as the thirteenth minute, on one of the rare occasions this season where they have scored first. Wearne received the ball just outside the Bromley area and jinked to his right to create space before curling a well-placed shot just inside the right-hand post. Harris should have made it two just minutes later, but his shot cannoned back off the inside of the left-hand post.

When Bromley equalised in the twenty-eighth minute, there was a grim inevitability about the fact that it was McKirdy who applied the coup de grace, after slack defending allowed him to lob Gabe Breeze. But Carlisle groans of despair quickly turned to howls of derision as he was shown a yellow card for his celebratory gestures in front of the Warwick Road End. For a few minutes Carlisle appeared to revert to type, losing their shape and drive, as happens so often after conceding a goal. Whatever happened to resilience? But they rediscovered their mojo sufficiently to earn a decent ovation at half-time.

Carlisle started the second half brightly and were rewarded after just two minutes when they earned a penalty. A goal bound header was blocked by Byron Webster's arm, and we had our first spot-kick since last September. For the second time in the game Harris's kick found the left-hand post and the score remained 1-1. There was a growing sense that the fates might be against us when a Jordan Jones shot rebounded off the crossbar just a few minutes later, and a Harris header was brilliantly saved by the Bromley keeper.

Redemption came just moments later. A low shot from the edge of the area by Callum Whelan took a strong deflection from a Bromley defender and nestled in the bottom of the net. Replays show that the original shot was going wide, but what the hell? The same thing happened against us at Harrogate a fortnight ago. We deserve the odd break in our situation. A couple of minutes after the goal McKirdy was substituted, probably to pre-empt another card and sending off. I have to admit to enjoying a certain grim pleasure watching him disappear down the tunnel with hundreds, if not thousands, of shouts of "Wanker!" ringing in his ears, with accompanying gestures.

From that point onwards it was edge of your seat stuff. Both sides had further chances, and it would have been no surprise if the final score had been about 5-4. There was a flashpoint in the 69th minute when Josh Vela made a "robust" challenge on a Bromley player who reacted aggressively, and fisticuffs ensued. I commented to John that Vela had probably gone a long way to redeeming his reputation with Carlisle fans in that moment. His fourteen months at Brunton Park have hardly been a raging success, but in that moment he demonstrated that he, quite literally, was up for the fight. Later comments on social media confirmed my view.

At this point Byron Webster saw fit to intervene and tell the referee how to do his job. Webster, who Jon Colman described succinctly as "turning as gracefully as a combine harvester" was clearly trying to get Vela sent off and completely ignored the referee's instructions to back off. He also got involved in some ill-advised exchanges with fans in The Paddock. It's not difficult to see why he and McKirdy are such good mates. In the end both players received a yellow card and were probably lucky to do so. Mark Hughes immediately substituted Vela!

To be honest, there was that sense of spirit and fight about the whole team (not before time) and that's what made this performance so encouraging. The defence is still worryingly fragile, but it was great to see players scrapping for possession, and gambling on going past opponents. When the referee finally ended the game, it was noticeable that relatively few headed straight for the exits, the vast majority staying to salute not just a victory, but also the manner in which it was achieved. Win our game in hand on Tuesday, and survival might start looking like a realistic possibility.

There was even incident after the final whistle, as the players were disappearing down the tunnel. Allegedly, Webster was making going down gestures (very mature) and allegedly McKirdy threw a punch at Carlisle coach Jamie Devitt, who allegedly responded by grabbing him by the throat. One comment on Facebook simply said, "I hope he squeezed1"

The attendance remained remarkably stable at just over 6,500, of whom only 200 were away fans. It's hard to credit how the team has maintained such a sizable and loyal support base after two dreadful seasons. Maybe it's partly down to people like idiotic retired teachers who happily make a 270-mile round trip for every home game. Whatever the case, it's great to be part of such special support.

On the way up to Carlisle, John and I had commented on how beautiful the stretch of our journey from Penrith to Bowes is, particularly in the late afternoon-early evening sun. Predictably we returned across Stainmore under heavy skies and driving rain.

"Who are you? Who are you? Chanted professions of ignorance about your opponents is never a good sound, but as far as Bromley were concerned, it was actually a good shout. Bromley, who are you exactly?

Bromley is a London borough bordering Kent, so now you know their location. It's where we played earlier in the season in a dismal November game, where they took the lead after Ben Williams conceded a penalty. They didn't look like scoring another and for all Carlisle's efforts, it didn't look as though they would score either.

It was a televised game of course so a trip to the Kent border was never considered. Not by the Wakefield contingent at any rate. Anyone who did make the trip would have been rewarded with miserable fare offered up on another miserable pitch. How we are spoiled by the surface at Brunton Park.

I should add that Carlisle did get their equaliser in the ninety-second minute when Adu Adjei turned well in the box and placed a shot in the bottom corner of the net.

That was then, but this was now. Bromley who played with Byron Webster at the back and who had somehow achieved a creditable mid-table position were still turning up to be beaten, surely. But nagging thoughts persisted as the previous week we hadn't really laid a glove on Wimbledon, and it was a safe bet that Bromley would not be turning up to play open expansive football. Dismal, miserable, obdurate, choose your own adjective.

I was turning these thoughts over in my mind when Howard dropped a mini bombshell into the conversation. Did I know who was playing for Bromley? No, not really, was the answer as I'd only just found out where Bromley played never mind who played for them. Webster obviously, but that was of little concern as his spell at Carlisle had proved he was a regular dispenser of defensive howlers. Bring it on!

But Howard's bombshell, as bombshells are wont to do, shook me.

"Bromley have signed Harry McKirdy."

The immutable law of the returning ex-player is doubly applicable when the ex-player in question is a pantomime villain and McKirdy has history. Fans know that he is easier to rile than a toddler with a bag of sweets.

Sure enough, McKirdy came in for some jeering from the outset with every piece of lost possession or mis-control gratefully seized upon by the Paddockites. Cameron Harper tackled him well, Kadeem Harris ran past him with the ball and the Paddock loved it, but they would have been better served by watching their own team as Carlisle were playing well. Harris, showing more confidence with every game, was causing problems for the Bromley defenders and when the ball reached the predominately left-footed Wearne on the edge of the box, he neatly jinked back on to his right foot and curled a precise shot into the bottom corner. A touch of class.

Thirteen minutes played, Carlisle one nil up and for the next ten minutes they created a host of chances including when Harris crashed a shot against the foot of the post. But a second goal proved elusive and as is often the case, if you don't take advantage of a period of dominance, later you are likely to pay.

Bromley's equaliser arrived out of nowhere. A simple header over the back four let in, who else but McKirdy, to scamper after the bouncing ball and lob over the advancing Breeze. Slow motion ruled from this point onwards as the ball, in the air for a long time, looked as though it might bounce wide of the goal and produce another opportunity to hurl ridicule on the ex-blue. But no, the ball bounced inside the post and settled inside the goal and the scorer wasted no time in celebrating in front of the Warwick Road End. It was noticeable that the Bromley players did not extend their celebrations with young Harry, they congratulated him and then left him to it. The referee, the experienced Robert Madley was not so keen to overlook this, viewing the reaction as provocative and telling the Bromley man to get back to his own half. It was a simple instruction which McKirdy chose not to follow. Instead, he wheeled away towards the Paddock making further gestures towards the crowd and earned himself the inevitable yellow card.

This was the time to step back from the bating. Some might say he has a screw loose, but the more accurate and perhaps kindly judgement is that such immaturity on his part demonstrates a level of mental instability. McKirdy is not making the best of his talents, he needs positive support. Whether or not the football environment is the best place for such support is another matter.

But back to the football where Carlisle had a game to win. They emerged for the second half intent on re-establishing their dominance and two minutes in, when Webster was judged to have handled a Matt Dennis header, they were awarded a penalty. Hopes were dashed though when once again Harris hit a post with his penalty shot. Joining the party, Jordan Jones also crashed a shot against the frame of the goal and it began to look as though the deserved winning goal would evade Carlisle.

It was Callum Whelan's dogged determination which proved this was not to be the case. In due reward for his tireless efforts, the midfielder fired in a shot which to the delight of the Carlisle crowd was deflected into the corner of the net to spark massive celebrations on the terraces.

With thirty minutes still to play, more chances were created and it should be noted that the best of these fell to the Bromley player, Arthurs who, faced with only Breeze to beat, blazed his shot over the bar. Harper also cleared a shot off the line in a sensational piece of defending which surely kept the points in Carlisle's possession.

The ill-feeling which had simmered throughout the game apparently boiled over at the end with shenanigans in the tunnel in which Messrs McKirdy and Webster played a leading role. It didn't detract from the pleasure of a home win but the thought of how easily they could have lost this game did.

Bromley were eminently beatable, it had been a frenetic and at times exciting game, but in a phrase beloved of my father, Carlisle won but they had made a dog's dinner of doing so.

Tuesday 25 March. Carlisle United v MK Dons. Brunton Park. EFL League 2.

Less than three days after we arrived home from Saturday's game, we were back on the road again, for our latest round of self-torture. This time the sun *did* shine, and the drive along the A66 *was* beautiful, if a bit dazzling at times.

After two of Mike Williamson's signings scored the goals that won Saturday's game, it was the turn of Williamson's former club to visit Brunton Park. MK Dons, Franchise United to many, must be the most unloved club in the EFL. That was reflected in the fact that only 134 of their own supporters made the effort to travel to this game. Given that, an attendance of 6,679 represented a further improvement on Saturday's gate. It was good to see Saturday's spirited performance rewarded with more support, but it seemed to be in defiance of the fact that Carlisle have failed to win two consecutive league games in almost two years.

Josh Vela wasted no time showing he was up for the fight again, receiving a yellow card as early as the third minute. Gone are the days of Graeme Souness, when he would nail the opposition playmaker in the opening minutes, confident in the knowledge that the only punishment would be a free kick. I like Vela's aggression, but he needs to employ it with more discretion.

MK certainly started like a team that used to be coached by Williamson, patiently playing the ball out from the back despite a high Carlisle press. The difference from Carlisle's attempts to play in the same style under Williamson was that they did it quite well. As the ball was played around at the back players further forward actually showed some movement to provide their teammates with some options. They scored after just six minutes, though their goal owed as much to Carlisle's defensive vulnerability as it did to skilful execution on MK's part.

There followed the familiar scenario of Carlisle floundering in the wake of a goal as MK continued to dominate. But for a change United found some resilience. Archie Davies made a superb run down the right, got to the byline, and delivered an excellent cross which Matthew Dennis headed precisely into the right-hand corner of the net. Carlisle dominated the next few minutes before the inevitable frailty in defence re-gifted MK the lead in the 37th minute. However, Carlisle battled on and in time added on were denied a blatant penalty. It mattered not as the ball ran to Kadeem Harris on the right, who crashed home a low cross shot to restore parity. Jordan Jones very nearly gave Carlisle an unlikely half-time lead in the remaining seconds.

It had been an eventful first half, with Carlisle scoring two good goals, but each came after inadequate defending had gifted MK a bad goal. Nonetheless, there was still everything to play for, and there had been encouraging signs of greater resilience.

The second half never really reached the same level. There was plenty of earnest endeavour but not a great deal of real quality. The half was mainly notable for an abysmal refereeing performance. Time and again blatant holding of players off the ball went unpunished, while the most innocuous of tackles were punished with free kicks. The crowd did their best to lift the team, but to no avail. Hughes did replace Vela with Kelly in the 77th minute to increase the attacking options, but generally the substitutions were a case of too little too late. It was the 87th minute before three further substitutions were made, giving little opportunity to influence the shape of the game.

The referee's incompetence continued deep into stoppage time, with Sam Lavelle being wrestled to the ground in the MK penalty area just seconds before the final whistle blew.

This wasn't a bad point to gain, and the performance showed some spirit and determination, reflected in the response of the crowd at the end of the game. But it wasn't enough. A win would have meant that the gap to safety would have been more than halved in just three days. As it was, the gap remained at six points, with games rapidly running out. The season's not over until it's over, but it's hard to hold out much hope anymore.

If doubts had begun to creep in about Carlisle's ability to avoid relegation in their narrow win against Bromley, when they faced Milton Keynes Dons they became much more evident.

The visitors who weren't pulling up many trees in the league themselves settled well into the game and controlled the early stages particularly down their right-hand side where imaginative movement and slick passing showed up the defensive deficiencies of Jordan Jones, and sure enough, they took a sixth-minute lead when a well-constructed move led to a tap-in finish from Tomlinson.

It took Carlisle a further quarter of an hour to gain a foothold in the game allowing Cameron Harper to produce a good cross from the left but there was no-one in a blue shirt in a position to capitalise on it. It was left to Harper's fellow full-back, Archie Davies to produce a telling piece of skill by beating his man and then producing an excellent cross of his own to pick out Matt Dennis in the centre. If Dennis' headed goal against Wimbledon had been an example of Cyrille Regis-esque raw power, here he produced a deft effort superbly placed beyond the keeper's reach into the corner of the net – a beautifully taken goal which had come against the run of play.

The goal was an opportunity for Carlisle to develop some forward momentum in the game and attacks were duly mounted even though Davies was called upon to clear off the line to prevent Carlisle's goal being breached for a second time.

The warning was not heeded though, and on thirty-seven minutes, Davies was now at fault, allowing Gilby to latch on to a through ball and waltz around Breeze to tap home into an empty net. A statement goal from a team who were controlling the ball and moving well, but it was also the sort of goal which a team mounting a serious fight against relegation should be avoiding.

Credit to Carlisle that they were able to get back on terms before the break. Most of the crowd were *appealing for a penalty as play entered into stoppage time, a claim which the referee waved away, but the ball fell to Kadeem Harris who smashed it into the net to settle the issue.*

Two each at the break after an eventful first half.

Against all predictions and expectations, the score remained the same at full-time. Chances had been created by both teams and there had also been some heroic defending, but by the end both teams had to settle for a single point.

Had the game been worth the long trek to Carlisle and back on a Tuesday night? Affirmative, yes, because what is obvious now is that the football under Mark Hughes is of a much more vibrant nature. It is not single tempo, passion is more in evidence and the suggestion that the Carlisle players lack the stomach for a fight has been laid to rest. In a nutshell, the football is now much more exciting.

But doubts persist. This was the third of the vital four games in succession, the third successive home game from which a tally of four points has been claimed out of a possible nine. It does not auger well for the fourth game of the sequence which is an away game at Doncaster Rovers.

Saturday 29 March. Doncaster Rovers v Carlisle United. The Eco-Power Stadium. EFL League 2.

The shortest trip of the season and I couldn't be there! It's that time of year when Birmingham University Dance Society (BUDS) stages its annual production, so Lisa and I were Birmingham-bound to watch eldest daughter Ellie strut her stuff. With hindsight I can't say I'm sorry.

This was the day that my hope finally died. The league table indicates that statistically survival is still possible, but it isn't going to happen. There is neither the quality nor the character in the present squad to retrieve this dreadful situation. My engagement with the game was minimal. I checked my phone just before the second half of the dance show began to see that Doncaster had taken the lead. I checked it again immediately after the finale to see that the game was over and that Doncaster had scored a further two goals. There was nothing more inevitable than that one of the goals was scored by Jordan Gibson, the latest former Blue this season to twist the knife by scoring against his old team.

I've largely avoided the online fans' forums, but when I have dipped into them I've found a lot of perfectly understandable anger. I've no wish to add to that bile. My own overwhelming feeling is one of disbelief that things can have reached this pitch – a second successive relegation despite investment in the club that dwarfs anything that preceded it.

I offered my own post-mortem on the club's decline a fortnight ago, and nothing that's happened since has given me any reason to change my opinion. I've nothing else to say right now. I'm going to start checking out likely National League destinations.

"I'll go with you and I won't whine, and I'll sew your socks and stitch you up when you're wounded, and anything you ask of me I'll do, except for one thing; I won't watch you die – I'll miss that scene if you don't mind."

Etta Place

It was one of those days again. Adult family life interrupted Howard's football watching programme and he quite rightly gave that priority. Julie by now had rejected the role of loyal support and I was left to weigh up the prospect of going to watch a match on my own. Something I've done many times and Oldham, Halifax, York and Mansfield all spring to mind as grounds where I have carried out solo missions to watch Carlisle play. But somehow...

Doncaster is only forty- three miles from where I live. It represents the closest away fixture apart from Harrogate which clocks in at thirty-three miles. So, distance wasn't the deterrent; it was something else which bothered me, some misgiving hanging in the stars and those three previous home games which hadn't offered enough in the way of evidence of a resurgence for Carlisle, there was too little assurance. It was more and more difficult to ignore the writing on the wall and I found myself channelling my inner Etta Place. A bit melodramatic of course to equate myself with the Sundance Kid's girlfriend as marvellously scripted by William Goldman for the Butch Cassidy film, but there you go.

I spent the afternoon in Holmfirth, taking a boxful of books to the Oxfam bookshop where my donation was eagerly received. Then I curried extra favour with the staff by buying a stack of books to replace the ones I'd just brought in. Not content with one bookshop, the independent bookshop, Read was the next port of call where some of the shelves were devoted to the favourite reading of various staff members. Eleanor's shelf caught my attention with recommendations including Charles Frazier's The Trackers which I bought, and other favourites of mine. By sheer coincidence it was Eleanor who served me and we had a chance to compare notes about favourite books and authors. I had a bit of a rave about William Boyd's Any Human Heart and Eleanor agreed but she added that her husband didn't like it at all.

"In that case," I said, "you should divorce him." She laughed, but Julie who had been listening patiently to this exchange looked a bit askance at me. Clearly it was time to win her round with the offer of a cup of tea and a scone. Julie that is, not Eleanor.

We found a bijou café above a bakery, went in, ordered and then sat back and relaxed. Clearly, it was possible to spend a Saturday afternoon in a laid-back manner feeling satisfied with desultory activity. There was even a whiff of self-congratulation involved thanks to the support given to the charity shop. Then I gave in to the compulsion which had been dogging me throughout. I reached into my pocket for my phone.

At the Eco-Power stadium, Doncaster, the home team had beaten Carlisle 3-0. Did ex-Carlisle player Jordan Gibson score one of the goals? You have been reading these articles, haven't you?

Chapter 10
IT'S THE HOPE THAT KILLS

Tuesday 1 April. Chesterfield v Carlisle United. SMH Group Stadium. EFL League 2.

Yes, it was April Fool's Day, and we were the fools for travelling. Having missed the shortest journey of the season on Saturday, only the trip to Harrogate was shorter than this. Despite that, I'm not sure what possessed me to travel to this game, given the league table. Probably something to do with father-son bonding. John was away celebrating his wedding anniversary, but Adam was home from university, bemoaning how much he missed his regular Carlisle United fix, so we decided to go. The one thing we did bond over was our disbelief and despair at what we witnessed.

When the line-ups were announced it seemed quite promising. Georgie Kelly made a rare start, which I thought was probably justified given his recent brief cameos from the bench. A forward line of Kelly, Dennis and Harris looked quite promising. I was less sure about the dropping of Wearne in favour of Fusire. It's not clear whether that change was driven by injury or strategy. The latter probably earned his start as a result of his impact in the dying minutes of the draw against MK Dons. McArthur returned from nowhere to replace the concussed Harper.

That was about as good as it got. We took our seats to discover that Dennis had pulled up during the warm-up, replaced in the starting eleven by Hugill, with Scott promoted to the bench. Chesterfield dominated the opening proceedings, drawing one superb tip-over from Breeze before things really started to go downhill. After about twenty-five minutes Fusire left the pitch for treatment for what transpired to be a major nosebleed. After lengthy treatment had failed to stem the flow, he was replaced by Elliot Embleton.

The less said about Embleton the better. He had been on the pitch a little over ten minutes and had made a minimal contribution when he made a rash challenge, stamping on a Chesterfield player's ankle. A red card ensued, which seemed harsh at the time, but was perfectly justified having seen a replay. Embleton typifies what is wrong with the current group of players. He was brought in by Williamson on a relatively long contract and no doubt good wages by league 2 standards, He has offered little on the pitch and his rash and irresponsible behaviour in this game shows a total lack of responsibility and commitment to the club. I'd shed no tears if he never wears a Carlisle shirt again.

Things still had time to get worse in the first half. In time added on Sam Lavelle went down after a defensive challenge, and after lengthy treatment he too left the pitch to be replaced by Jack Ellis. That meant that McArthur moved into the centre of defence, probably a relief for him after he had repeatedly been turned inside out by Chesterfield's right winger. It was something of a miracle that the score remained 0-0 at half-time.

The second half started with the news that Georgie Kelly had been substituted during the break to be replaced by loanee Bevan. Again, it was unclear whether this was a tactical or a fitness-based substitution. It matters not. Kelly's lacklustre performance in the first half was sufficient evidence that he has been yet another costly mistake.

The expected onslaught from Chesterfield against a depleted Carlisle immediately ensued. They piled forward in numbers and rained in shots on the Carlisle goal. A series of brilliant saves from Breeze, some goal-line clearances, last-ditch tackles and Chesterfield's apparent desire to walk the ball into the net meant that remarkably the score was still 0-0. At one point I turned to Adam and suggested that, in defiance of all the odds, this might be one of those evenings where we emerged with an unlikely, and totally undeserved point. We started to laugh wryly as yet more attacks were repelled and that outcome crept closer minute by minute.

But, of course, it couldn't last. In the 73rd minute Breeze made yet another excellent save but was helpless to do anything about the follow-up shot. At that point Paddy Madden was brought on as a Chesterfield substitute and within minutes he had doubled the lead, heading home a rebound after yet another Breeze save. In doing so he joined Andy Cooke of Bradford. Hallam Hope of Morecambe, Dan Butterworth of Swindon, Omari Patrick of Tranmere, Harry McKirdy of Bromley and Jordan Gibson of Doncaster as ex-Blues to score against their former club this season.

A slack Chesterfield pass in defence let in Joe Hugill to pull a goal back in the 89th minute, and in time added on substitute Ben Barclay had a decent chance to clinch a barely credible draw but headed straight at the keeper. But to be honest a 6-0 scoreline would not have done Carlisle an injustice.

This was a dismal evening. We watched a team without fight, without spirit, and without a great deal of skill apart from Kadeem Harris, slip inexorably closer to relegation to the National League. When the players came over to acknowledge the supporters, they were largely met by a chorus of boos, with the merest smattering of applause. The only players who merited any sort of applause were Breeze and perhaps Harris. Even so, I couldn't understand those fans who aggressively demanded of the applauders to know what they were clapping for. Each to his own. Adam and I chose to join in with neither the applause or the boos, too depressed by the debacle we had just witnessed.

If the Piataks' pockets are deep enough, an almost total clearout of both playing and non-playing staff is required the moment the season ends. I'm not sure how many of the remaining games I'll attend, but when I do go it will be out of residual loyalty to Carlisle United Football Club as an institution, not to the majority of players who are besmirching the reputation of a club that means so much to so many of us.

A genuine can't get out of this one *excuse this time. A wedding anniversary celebration held over three days in Monmouth put paid to any chance of making my first visit to the romantically named SMH Group Stadium, Chesterfield. Glancing at my phone during dinner would also be verboten. So, it was only afterwards that I was able to catch up on the details. Unable to gain any first-hand reports from the game I had to turn to that reliable source of information, the upholder of truth and objectivity – social media – and the details were grisly.*

Carlisle got battered. They reached half-time at nil each but they had lost Elliot Embleton who was red carded on forty minutes. In the second-half, Chesterfield scored twice with the scorers inevitably including the name of Paddy Madden, late of this parish. But according to the posted responses, the Spirites could have had many more. Lurid accounts made it sound like the Alamo with some desperate defending and wonder saves from Breeze.

At two-nil down, Carlisle did manage to score a goal, the traditional consolation goal presumably, when Joe Hugill produced a calm finish to beat Boot in the Chesterfield goal. After that, remarkably, Carlisle got a late chance when Ben Barclay won a header from a corner but directed his effort straight at the keeper. Just imagine what the reaction would have been if the Blues had suffered such an onslaught and yet had emerged with a point. Get out of jail card cliches would have been polished up and flickering flames of hope would have been kindled. Hope? What is it they say about hope?

Still, I had no time for speculation. I had an anniversary waltz to practice.

Saturday 5 April. Carlisle United v Newport County. Brunton Park. EFL League 2.

Let's be realistic. Let's not get carried away. We may be a point closer to survival than we were on Saturday morning, though we've now got one less game to earn that survival. With just five games to go we are still eight points from avoiding relegation and remain odds-on favourites for that fate. But…, but…

Just when I've fully resigned myself to and accepted the reality of a second successive relegation after last Tuesday's abject display at Chesterfield, the team go and produce a performance like this! It's not just that it was a win, it was the nature of the performance that was so enjoyable. On the journey north both John and Adam (the Wakefield Blues were at 75% strength) predicted a narrow win for Carlisle. After last Tuesday I wasn't prepared to commit myself to even a prediction. It was a narrow win, but not in the fashion that either John or Adam had expected. There were three changes to the starting eleven. Aaron Hayden replaced the injured Lavelle, Jack Ellis replaced Charlie McArthur and Stephen Wearne returned in place of Joe Hugill. Carlisle probably edged the opening twenty minutes with the majority of possession and the better chances. But for the next ten minutes things went horribly wrong. Firstly, Archie Davies suffered what looks likely to be a season-ending injury. He was replaced by McArthur, which at least allowed Ellis to resume his more natural position of right-back. But it was through that channel that Newport struck just two or three minutes later when a through ball split the defence, leaving Breeze exposed and unable save the effort that followed. But within moments things got much worse. A speculative shot from well wide on the left soared over Gabe Breeze and into the top right-hand corner. Mark Hughes described it as a worldy, albeit a wind-assisted one. Apparently, the player in question had never scored before, and Hughes added that he would probably never score one like that again.

That didn't really matter to the vast majority of the crowd of nearly 6,000. We were stunned into near-silence, and there was a real sense that we were staring down the barrel. Fortunately, the crowd found its voice in time to celebrate George Kelly's first goal for Carlisle just six minutes later. It had only taken fourteen months since his signing in January 2024. Wearne made a decent run forward before threading a pass to Kelly just inside the area, who proceeded to thread a good shot across the goalkeeper and low into the right-hand corner. It meant that we went into half-time believing there was still life in the game.

After Vela had shot straight at the keeper in the 52nd minute, the crowd really found their voice on the hour when Kelly forced home the equaliser from close range after a scramble in the Newport area. The celebration of his first goal had been relatively muted. This time the reaction was much more effusive. It's time for me to eat humble pie regarding Kelly. He can't be blamed for the injuries he's suffered, and I had been reasonably encouraged by his recent 10–15-minute cameos as a late substitute. But I need no reminding that less than a week ago I had written him off as "yet another costly mistake". I'm delighted that he proved me wrong on Saturday. He led the line with physicality, aggression and tenacity, winning the ball well and also holding it up. And he managed all that despite getting no support from the referee, of whom more later.

With the team and the crowd invigorated, and Matthew Dennis already on as a substitute to increase the attacking options, the momentum of the game had very much swung towards Carlisle. But it took a further double substitution in the 80th minute to finally swing the game. Sparky had obviously decided it was shit or bust time, bringing on Hugill and Bevan, meaning Carlisle now had five strikers on the pitch. Even so, Breeze had to make two superb saves in quick succession to keep the scores equal, before Hugill took a hand.

Firstly, his long throw from the left led to chaos in the Newport area before the ball was eventually cleared. Moments later Carlisle won a free kick in a dangerous position, left of centre and about thirty yards out. As McArthur held the ball, waiting for someone to take responsibility for the set piece, it was Hugill who marched out of the area to line things up. His self-confidence was justified as his shot ricocheted off the left-hand post. The ball was returned into the area from the left and in the ensuing melee Aaron Hayden finally stabbed the ball home to seal an excellent comeback.

It was the first time in almost ten years that Carlisle had overturned a two-goal deficit to win a game. No wonder that players, staff and supporters enjoyed vocal celebrations at the end. The Newport manager approached Mark Hughes after the whistle to take issue over something. Reports from the front of The Paddock suggest that his response was to tell him to "fuck off". Good on you Sparky!

Carlisle now need to overturn another unwanted record. It is ninety-eight games since they last won two league games in succession. It is imperative that they break that sequence next Saturday. The bottom of League 2 has almost turned into a mini league, with a number of teams playing each other. Tranmere were the team we were hoping to catch until recently, but if they beat Accrington, and we can beat both Accrington and Morecambe, then there is a glimmer of hope.

I appreciate that there are a few ifs in that scenario, but you can't expect anyone who has experienced the Jimmy Glass moment to completely give up hope yet.

And so to the referee. I'll be the first to admit that my referee rants tend to come after we've lost a game. Not so this time. This was one of the worst refereeing performances I've seen in a long time and that takes some saying, believe me. It frequently felt as if we were playing against twelve men – no, make that thirteen given the incompetence of the linesman on our side of the ground, who was just as useless as he was when we lost to Harrogate a few weeks ago. Newport received one yellow card, when a player impeded a goalkeeper's clearance. Aaron Hayden received a yellow card for pointing out to the referee that such an offence merited a yellow card. Carlisle's other two yellow cards were for alleged time wasting. This was despite the ages that Newport's goalkeeper took over goal kicks and clearances when they were ahead. It's remarkable how much his distribution speeded up in the last few minutes when they were behind. As if that weren't enough, Kelly was repeatedly held and wrestled to the ground as he attempted to lead the line, without any punishment.

I stand by what I said at the beginning of this post. but while there's the faintest glimmer of hope we'll be there. Obviously, we'll be at the home games, and John and I have tickets for the crucial away games at Morecambe and Accrington. I just hope that our fate isn't decided away to Cheltenham, the one game we can't make.

Heart says, yes. Head says, no. Apply a cold-headed logical analysis to Carlisle's position, and you will reach the conclusion that they are going to be relegated from the fourth tier of English football. Let your heart rule though and they stay up. This is Carlisle, isn't it? Carlisle where miracles happen; Brian Wake scores a hat-trick against Shrewsbury, Richie Foran comes in from the cold to score a survival clincher at Halifax, and an on-loan goalkeeper advances down the pitch for a corner in the ninety-fourth minute. Heart says, yes.

Before this game, although they have turned up in impressive numbers, 5,889, the fans appear to share a sense of foreboding as the effect of the Chesterfield result still lingers. Even so, the players are applauded after their warmup and the applause intensifies for Mark Hughes who has clearly retained his popular standing.

Hughes made three changes to the side which had slumped in midweek: Hayden, Ellis and Wearne were included in place of Lavelle, McArthur and Hugill. So, let the drama unfold.

The drama, such as it was, arrived in the twenty-sixth minute when Newport went ahead and prompted the usual questions in the crowd. Could the marking have been tighter? Could more pressure have been applied? Was Breeze at fault? (video evidence later suggested that he wasn't.) The inquests felt routine but there was insufficient time to complete them as two minutes later, Bobby Kanwa for Newport latched on to a ball which sat up nicely for him outside the box and he hit it beyond Breeze's despairing dive into the top corner. Pundits will tell you that there is a defensive error to be discerned in every goal conceded. Not with this one though, if it wasn't a 'worldie' it was certainly a contender for Goal of the Season.

Recognition of this may have been the reason for the lack of toxicity sweeping down from the stands. Resignation rather than revolt rules. It is a truism of football that when you are struggling at the bottom of the league, opposition teams turn up and score absolute screamers against you.

To the credit of the Carlisle players though, they didn't fold. Callum Whelan was his usual bustling self, Stephen Wearne justified his selection by getting stuck in, supporting the defence and prompting the attack, and it was Wearne who played the pass for Carlisle's important goal before the break, laying the ball off for Georgie Kelly to score his first goal for Carlisle by rolling the ball into the far corner of the net.

Half-time and this game was still alive. On the re-start, United were immediately grateful to Aaron Hayden and his goal saving tackle after Newport had weaved their way through the home defence towards an opening. A third goal at that stage would have been a disaster for Carlisle because they were fighting and forcing a way forward. On the hour mark they received their reward when Kelly again, the man derided so often for being injured, was in the right place to tap home a loose ball in the box after a corner.

Still all to play for. Wearne and substitute Dennis go agonisingly close, Breeze makes an unbelievable double save and Hughes adds substitutes Joe Bevan and Joe Hugill into the mix and finds the right formation for a team which now has four strikers on the pitch. It was now the team from South Wales forced into desperate defending.

Even so, when you reach the eighty-fifth minute, you know that time is running out. A free kick was awarded to Carlisle in a promising position on the left-hand side a few yards outside the box and a moment of indecision occurred in the Carlisle ranks. Archie Davies and Stephen Wearne had both left the pitch and the natural left foot of Harper was also missing. Charlie McArthur looked as though he didn't fancy it. Did Joe Hugill get the call, or did the twenty-one-year-old striker take matters into his own hands? Either way, he trotted out from his position in the box and lined up the free kick which he promptly lashed against the post with the keeper standing rooted. Before the crowd could fully react, Hayden forced the ball in from the rebound to cue pandemonium. A great fightback completed, a win for Carlisle and three goals scored at home. Three sides of the ground were as one: "United! United! United!"

And everywhere, hearts were ruling heads.

Saturday 12 April. Morecambe FC v Carlisle United. The Mazuma Mobile Stadium. EFL League 2.

I'm breaking with habit and starting this post before the game has actually taken place. The reason for that is that I'm feeling an unhealthy anticipation about tomorrow's game. I say unhealthy because both the league table and my head tell me that Carlisle's chances of avoiding relegation remain minimal, despite last week's win. But the nature of that win means that there's a tiny spark of hope that remains unextinguished. IF we win tomorrow and IF Accrington lose to Tranmere, then it's game on again, with Carlisle still to travel to Accrington. Whatever the outcome, it's going to be one hell of an atmosphere tomorrow. The away allocation of 1600 tickets has sold out, and I wouldn't be surprised to discover that some United fans have infiltrated the home sections, which I can't imagine will have sold out. We could probably have sold twice as many away tickets. Add the small matters of local rivalry, and the perilous situation of both clubs, and it's obvious that the Mazuma Mobile Stadium will be no place for the faint-hearted tomorrow. How appropriate that I'm wearing an ECG heart monitor this weekend. I just hope that it's one of those games I'll look back on in the future and proudly proclaim "I was there."

Two days on and that little spark of hope is still alight and actually burning a little more brightly. Carlisle did what they needed to do and results elsewhere probably worked out in our favour.

I shared my worrying sense of anticipation with John when I picked him up, readily admitting that I was setting myself up for crushing disappointment. The Mazuma Mobile Stadium was a new destination for both of us. I was still a child the last time I visited Morecambe, to see the illuminations, more than half a century ago. We found free street parking about five minutes from the ground and initial impressions of the ground as we approached were good – neat, tidy and modern. Once we entered the ground, we realised we had approached and were seated in the most impressive part of the ground. The main stand is sizeable and all-seated. There is covered terracing at each end, though not particularly deep, and a narrow terrace along the far side with no more than three or four steps. No wonder the camera gantry is positioned on that side of the ground. A capacity of 6,476 tells you what you need to know about the scale of things. Oh, and parts of the pitch were in a woeful condition.

As I predicted on Friday, the atmosphere in the away section was vibrant. The official figure for away fans was 1,725, entirely filling one of the end terraces and occupying a decent section of the adjoining seats in the main stand, constituting more than a third of the crowd. Given that the overall attendance of 4,901 was over 1500 short of capacity it's a pity more Carlisle fans weren't given the opportunity to see the game in person. To put things in perspective, Bradford City, who were top of League 2 going into yesterday's games, bigged themselves up for taking 1200 to their away fixture. We were bottom and we took nearly half as many again!

Given such impressive numbers and the volume generated in the build-up to kick-off, there was always the possibility that the action on the pitch would fail to match the atmosphere off it, particularly with so much at stake. The bottom two teams were facing off against each other, with the two teams immediately above them doing the same a little further south. So perhaps it was no surprise that the first real attempt on goal didn't come for twenty minutes.

That didn't stop us from keeping up the volume in the stands. I love it when you're part of an away support that is making so much noise that you've no way of knowing whether the home fans are responding.

Carlisle should have had a penalty as early as the 10th minute when Sean Fusire was sent crashing to the ground in the Morecambe area under what looked like an extremely dubious challenge, but nothing was given. I suspect the referee bottled it, nervous about giving a potentially big advantage to the away team so early in such an important game. For the second week in a row, we found ourselves battling against thirteen men with another infuriatingly inconsistent referee, and a linesman on our side of the pitch who didn't seem to realise that he had a flag in his hand and that he was entitled to use it. I feel entirely justified in my criticism of match officials in the last two games. We've won both games anyway, so it's not exactly sour grapes or looking for excuses.

Carlisle were adapting well to both the state of the pitch and the situation, playing football that wasn't particularly attractive but was effective. Reward came in the 27th minute when a long, deep cross from Jack Ellis was headed home by George Kelly. Having scored three times in two games, Kelly needs just one more goal to become this season's joint leading scorer!

Elsewhere things were not working out in our favour as Accrington raced into a 3-0 half-time lead against Tranmere. But it was good to enjoy the rare pleasure of a half-time lead, even though Hallam Hope had an excellent chance to extend the ex-player scoring jinx just before the interval. That threat was removed during the break, with Hope one of four players withdrawn by Morecambe manager Derek Adams in an attempt to galvanise his team.

Fortunately, it didn't have the desired effect. In the 60th minute a Carlisle corner was cleared but only as far as Jack Ellis. His ball into the box was superbly controlled and driven home by Terrell Thomas, still up after the corner, and we now had a bit of breathing space. It's fair to say that Thomas celebrated his first goal for the club as wildly as we were celebrating in the stands.

Carlisle proceeded to see out the rest of the game in a manner they used to manage regularly in the promotion season when Paul Huntington was marshalling the defence, but which has proved to be almost entirely beyond them this season. Gabe Breeze had to make one excellent save to push a curling shot beyond the post, but Carlisle were unlucky not to extend the lead in the closing moments, when a second goal from Kelly was disallowed for an alleged handball by Bevan in the build-up. We were then treated to the exquisite pleasure of watching home fans streaming towards the exits before the final whistle.

When that whistle went, we were able to celebrate an absolutely crucial and essential win against our most immediate rivals. It was also the first time in over two years and ninety-nine games (thank god it didn't creep into three figures) that we could celebrate successive league wins. Even better, John and I were present to witness both wins in person.

As we left, I paid a quick visit to the gents before the journey back across the Pennines. When I rejoined John just outside the ground, he reported that there'd been considerable excitement amongst departing Carlisle fans. A quick check of my phone revealed that Tranmere had achieved the unlikely feat of overcoming their three-goal deficit to draw 3-3 at Accrington. That meant that we'd gained two points on each team, meaning that they both remain tantalizingly catchable. There were three remarkable features about Tranmere's comeback. Firstly, the three goals came in the 78th, 87th and 101st minutes. Secondly, all three were scored by former Carlisle players in Omari Patrick and Kris Dennis. Thirdly, they were all absolute belters.

So, in classic Jon Colman phrase, what can we learn from this victory?

Well, Hughes was right not to tinker too much with a winning team. A fit again Cameron Harper replaced the injured Archie Davies in defence, allowing Ellis to continue at right back. Captain Sam Lavelle was also fit to return, but Hughes was right to retain the central defensive partnership of Hayden and Thomas who had performed so well against Newport. Hayden proceeded to have his second excellent game in succession (as rare as two successive wins) and Thomas was massive in defence as well as scoring the second goal.

George Kelly is emerging as the totemic figure of this mini revival. For the second game in succession, he scored and led the line superbly, this time supported by the added physical presence of Matthew Dennis up front, to give the forward line real physical presence and threat. Even when he doesn't win the ball, he makes it very difficult for defenders to control the ball. On Saturday he won seven heading battles, more than the Morecambe starting attackers combined. He is playing like a man desperate to make up for lost time.

There was an encouraging pragmatism about this performance. On a dreadful playing surface the players kept things simple, adapting to the situation and conditions well, probably better than Morecambe. For example, Callum Whelan readily accepted that this was a day to spend much of his time sitting in front of the defence, manning the trenches and foregoing his more usual playmaker role for much of the game. Jack Ellis had an immense game at right back. In the previous game he looked a better player the moment he switched to that flank, and he maintained and improved those levels here. His positioning was excellent, he won tackles firmly and clearly, he made good aerial challenges, and there's the small matter of providing the assist for both goals. He was my man of the match, without a shadow of doubt.

And so we move on to Friday and Port Vale at home. There couldn't be a much tougher test, with Vale top of the league and on an excellent run of form. For the third game in a row, we face a match that could break or make our season. With the two recent wins fresh in the memory, and a cheap ticket promotion, there should be a bumper crowd at Brunton Park.

In the meantime, it's nice to start feeling proud again of my team, rather than ashamed, and privileged to be part of such magnificent support. I stated at the beginning of this post that I hoped it would be a game about which I could be proud to say "I was there" and indeed it was. It was one of those afternoons that makes it all worthwhile.

Once or twice, I went to Morecambe as part of the annual treat for the church choir. Eventually, the event was replaced with a nosh-up in the Go Sun in Tait Street. Thereby proving that singing to the glory of God every Sunday was not without its perks.

I mention this because even at that tender age, I realised that as a seaside resort Morecambe was lacking in a lot of respects. Not a patch on Silloth eh? I didn't ever expect to be going to see a key football fixture involving Carlisle United and Morecambe. My first away trips were to Blackburn Rovers and Newcastle United. Both were epic FA Cup encounters, both resulted in wins for the Blues. But Morecambe versus

Carlisle as a battle for Fourth Tier survival? How have things come to this?

There could be no room for sentiment here and no talk of plucky opponents. This had to be a cold-blooded, efficient despatching of inferior opposition and I said that in the full knowledge that at the kick off, Morecambe stood above Carlisle in the league. As, in fact, did every other team. I repeat, how have things come to this?

Once again, Carlisle sold out their full allocation of tickets, all 1,725 of them, but the Mazumo Stadium was an unprepossessing sight and to feel as though the fans had got their money's worth, they would have to witness a clinical victory. Not that that would be so easy, as it was another day in what Phil Collins once ironically described as paradise. Another bottom of the league encounter where balls were regularly pumped into the corner and chased across a stodgy pitch. Another day of a ref failing to penalise blatant pushing and foul play. In the early stages, falling on a through ball, Breeze collected a cowardly kick on the head. He was awarded a free kick but no card was brandished which begged the question - what was the offence which led to the free kick? A coming together of the keeper's head and the forward's boot. A case of "not enough in it for me"? This is arrant nonsense. Refs could eliminate this sort of foul play by firm decision making. Or growing a pair.

Later Sean Fusire made a strong run down the right and into the box where he was eventually manhandled to the ground. He was in the box and he was pulled down. Now it was down to the ref. Was he going to award an early penalty to the bottom team in the league playing away from home? Was Hell going to freeze over any time soon?

I'm not one to accuse referees of being cheats, why should they be? But I do think too many of them bottle big decisions in the hope of "managing" the game well and keeping things quiet. As a result, the game is debased and the pushers and the foulers hold sway. Sean Fusire's skill was cancelled out and a message was given to all players about the "arts" of defending they could expect to get away with. Personally, I want a little more for my money than that.

To the game though, where the deadlock was broken in the twenty-seventh minute when a magnificent long cross from Jack Ellis was headed home by Georgie Kelly. We were right behind the line of the header, able to appreciate its accuracy and the fact that it was goalbound from the moment it left Kelly's head. The Morecambe defenders might be asking themselves a few questions though.

It was Jack Ellis again in the second half who produced another great cross and this time it was Terell Thomas who produced a perfect touch to bring the ball down and then slot it past the advancing keeper. Cool, calm and collected, just what you need from your centre-half in the opposition's box.

In the meantime, Hallam hope had failed to exercise the inalienable right of former players to score against previous employers after badly miscuing his only chance of the game.

The game ended with a win for Carlisle which is how I felt things should be, but the afternoon's fare had been strangely unfulfilling, just like those trips for the choir all those years ago and indeed for the Chinese chips in the Go Sun.

Friday 18 April. Carlisle United v Port Vale. Brunton Park. EFL League 2.

This is a game that deserves writing about while the memories and emotions are still fresh and raw.

This was a game for the ages, a game that transcended the routine grind of supporting a football club. It was so special that I'm considering whether it merits inclusion in the list of "Top Ten Matches" in my Carlisle memoir. It was that good an afternoon.

Inevitably, there was an enormous amount at stake. For the third game in a row Carlisle faced a game that had the potential to end the club's season and virtually condemn us to relegation. The difference between today and last Saturday was that we weren't playing our closest relegation rival, we were playing the current League 2 leaders, fresh from a 5-0 thrashing of Bromley, their fifth win in six games.

It being Good Friday, our journey from Wakefield to Carlisle was far from straightforward. How inconsiderate of people who aren't retired, or who don't enjoy school holidays, to choose Easter weekend to travel for a short break, when there's a vital football match to be attended. Various delays and detours meant that Adam saw parts of North Yorkshire and Cumbria he'd never seen before, and that we might struggle to make kick-off time. In the end we arrived by about 2.30 only for it to appear that our regular car park was full. But when the attendant saw who was in the car, he removed the sign blocking the entrance and ushered us in. Loyalty has its rewards.

By the time we'd disembarked and walked along Warwick Road, there was no time to linger in the fan zone, particularly as there were actually queues at the Paddock turnstiles, so we hastened to take our place in the 12,000 plus crowd. Not bad for a team in the League 2 relegation zone. We were in time to see the end of the pre-match warm-up and then give the team a rousing reception as they emerged for the pre-match formalities.

Mark Hughes had wisely chosen an unchanged starting line-up with just one change on the bench. After a couple of uncertain moments from Aaron Hayden in the opening minutes Carlisle soon settled into the game and began to establish some shape. After an opening twenty minutes which saw little in the way of chances for either team, Carlisle began to assert some dominance. Controlled in defence and increasingly threatening in attack, it was the sort of period that has you saying, "we need a goal from this period of dominance." Fortunately, that's exactly what happened in the 36th minute. Following a corner, Fusire recycled the ball to George Kelly who never looked likely to miss. His low cross shot nestled into the bottom left-hand corner of the net.

Carlisle were dominant at this stage of the game, and further reward came just seven minutes later. This time Kelly turned provider. He made ground down the left before delivering a dangerous cross into the area. Fusire was again involved, his shot striking the right-hand post, rebounding to Matty Dennis, who scored from close range. The team received a deserved ovation as they left the pitch at half-time.

Port Vale were clearly rattled. Two substitutions at half-time made that clear. Adam voiced the hope that Carlisle would start the second half as positively as they had ended the first, on the front foot. They certainly did that. Within ten seconds they had won a corner, and just four minutes later they scored a third goal. A free kick in an attacking position was partially cleared towards the left touchline where Callum Whelan controlled it before delivering a high and hopeful lob back into the area, Aaron Hayden rising high above the defence to power home a superb header.

A 3-0 lead after fifty minutes in an absolute must-win game against the top team in the division. We were in dreamland. Brunton Park was bouncing!

Of course it was never going to be as simple as that. When have Carlisle United ever opted to do things the easy way? In the 62nd minute Vale finally pulled a goal back and eight minutes later they had a second. The euphoria that had coursed around the ground just twenty minutes earlier had largely dissipated. There was potential controversy moments before the second goal. Carlisle had strong penalty claims for both handball and a foul ignored by the referee before Vale broke forward and scored. Had a Carlisle penalty been awarded and converted at that point the score would have been 4-1 and the game as good as won. Fortunately, those moments did not prove to be pivotal to the final result.

Although almost eleven thousand hearts were in mouths for the next twenty minutes, Carlisle generally did a decent job of managing the game and situation. Fusire and Dennis were substituted in the 84th minute, Dennis earning a petty but needless yellow card for the length of time it took him to leave the pitch. When the fourth official indicated five minutes of added time, it felt like job almost done.

If only. In the 92nd minute the referee awarded a penalty to Port Vale for a high boot from Terrel Thomas. There was no denying the high boot, but it was arguable that Thomas had been fouled himself just seconds before. It looked as if all the hard work of the previous ninety minutes, and the late battle to avoid relegation were going to come tumbling down in an instant. But there was one last twist to come. The penalty was well-hit, fairly low and just inside the right-hand post, but Gabe Breeze dived to his left to make a brilliant save, pushing the ball round the post for a corner. The ground erupted, as did the Carlisle bench. In the mad moments that followed the referee showed Mark Hughes a yellow card, and Matthew Dennis a second one, apparently for throwing a protein shake onto the pitch in celebration. That means that he'll be suspended for Monday's trip to Accrington.

Someone asked on Facebook what Dennis received his red card for. I'm with the respondent who suggested that the referee was pissed off that Vale had squandered the penalty that he'd awarded them and vented his frustration on the Carlisle bench. Even after the penalty save had been made and the subsequent corner cleared, he still allowed an inordinate amount of further added time. It seemed as if he was determined to prolong the game until Vale eventually scored. Fortunately, that wasn't to be. The whistle finally blew, the great escape was still a possibility, and we could celebrate victory, albeit in a slightly relieved manner. I was impressed that amidst the celebrations The Paddock and Main Stand still made sure they booed the match officials as they walked off. Darren Moore, the Port Vale manager, admitted in his post-match comments that his team had tried to play the occasion rather than the opposition. That's a tribute to the part the crowd played in the game.

I always believed that Carlisle would win this game. That's not based on any logic or rational analysis. It's simply because I couldn't bear to contemplate any other possible outcome. Even when the penalty was awarded and I felt a horrible pit in my stomach, there was a little part of me believing that Gabe Breeze might be about to become the hero of the hour. And so it proved.

Accrington Stanley also won, which means that Tranmere Rovers are now the team most immediately in our sights, though obviously we can pin back Accrington when we visit them on Monday for what is yet another absolutely massive game. Most important of all, we have that indefinable thing called momentum, something that seemed impossible just nineteen days ago, after the fiasco at Chesterfield. You can sense it in the players, the staff and the fans. The support was magnificent, both in number and volume. The ticket promotion pretty much ensured a decent attendance, but I never imagined a crowd of over 12,000, the biggest gate since the League 2 playoff semi-final, when the away dugout was occupied by one Mark Hughes. Whenever the away fans made their presence known, they were almost immediately drowned out by over 10,000 Cumbrian voices. Even on the two occasions when Port Vale scored, the response from three sides of the ground was instantaneous. Credit to the 1500 Vale fans who made the journey to support their table-toppers. That's nearly as good as our away support!

What Sparky seems to have done is to identify a core of players who are prepared to run through the proverbial brick wall for him, for their teammates and for the supporters. That includes those who spend most of the game on the bench before playing a role in the latter stages, and even those substitutes who don't make it onto the pitch at all. Some of the biggest celebrations on the bench came from Ben Barclay, who was an unused sub. And the contribution of George Kelly cannot be underestimated. Just three games ago I wrote him off as a costly mistake. How wrong I was. Once again he led the line magnificently, scoring the first goal and setting up the second. He controlled long balls superbly, brought teammates into the game, and didn't allow the Vale defence a moment's respite.

Carlisle are still odds-on for relegation at 1-6, but those odds are shortening with every game. I think a lot of us thought our fate would have been sealed by now, but each win has brought growing belief and confidence, amongst both the team and us supporters. We can travel to Accrington on Monday with real expectation of another good result, rather than vague hopes. It may all come crashing down, but at the moment it's a wonderful roller-coaster ride.

Whatever our eventual fate, this was a glorious afternoon. A must-win game; a massive crowd in magnificent voice and affecting the performance of the opposition; the luxury of a three goal lead; Georgie Kelly's magnificence up front; the resilience in the face of a strong comeback; and the crowning glory of Gabe Breeze's penalty save at the death. This was a game that will live long in the memory.

This was more like it. Mathematical certainties had not yet been reached and Port Vale were in town looking

*for a win to boost their promotion prospects. They
would want to come and play and this would suit
Carlisle who had so often come unstuck against
opponents who were content to clog up the midfield
and hold what they started with i.e. they would be
satisfied with a point and if they got more than that,
then that would be a bonus. But against opposition who
wanted to play, Carlisle could show a few flourishes
themselves.*

*Yes, this could be good and if the Goddess of Hope
smiled in our direction, then all the better. This line of
thought then led me to thinking about who exactly was
the Goddess of Hope, was she in fact someone I had
just invented?*

*As the first half got underway, it was quite difficult
to determine quite what the mindset of the opposition
was as they certainly didn't look like title contenders.
Nor did they look as though they were up for a dour
scrap. Carlisle were on top, simple as. They were
generally controlling play and breaking forward with
the confidence to try some shots. Admittedly, these
shots went over the bar, but it would just be a case of
adjusting the sights.*

*When Port Vale didn't clear a corner, the Blues found
that they didn't have to shoot from range. Sean Fusire
took possession of the loose ball and made it to the
by-line where he pulled back the ball for Georgie Kelly
to score from close range. Kelly's fourth goal in three
games and Sick Note had become the Goal Machine!*

*Within ten minutes, Kelly also became the Goal
Provider when he took the ball down the left and slid it
into the box only to see Sean Fusire's effort rebound
from the post. I have to admit that I was unsighted at*

this point and I thought the chance had gone and we had been thwarted by the woodwork once again. But no, the spectators around me suddenly erupted and being quick on the case, I joined in the goal celebrations, finding out later that Matty Dennis had pounced on the rebound and scored.

United had a two-goal lead against fancied opposition and Keily and Dennis, supported by Fusire, were forming a formidable strike force. Oh, that they had been available all season as this was the stuff that dreams are made of and it was a pity really that the half came to an end. It would be difficult to maintain this momentum and Carlisle would have to show that they were able to manage this two-goal lead.

It was inevitable that Port Vale would be looking to stir themselves from the lower gear performance and they would need a purposeful start to the second half. The one scenario I hadn't anticipated was for Carlisle to score a third goal but that is exactly what happened when another Carlisle corner broke down. But not entirely as the ball broke loose to Callum Whelan who lobbed the bouncing ball back into the penalty area but he had put too much into it surely. At that height, the defenders would have enough time to form themselves and see off the threat, or else the keeper would come and claim the ball. Neither of these things happened and as the defenders appeared to dither, Aaron Hayden produced a prodigious leap and a powerful header to bullet the ball into the back of the net.

Three-nil up with over half an hour still to play. Surely not, surely not! Don't think the unthinkable from this point. It should have been all over from this point, but this is football and it is also Carlisle United.

Just over the hour mark, Port Vale did pull one back through Garrity who got a touch on a loose ball to send it past Breeze and eight minutes later they got a second. This time, Breeze had made a brilliant save from Hart but the Vale player recovered first to force the ball home and suddenly the visiting Vale fans roused from their torpor into full voice. For the first time that afternoon they could see something in this for their team and their players were picking up on their newfound energy. Elsewhere in the ground nerves were like dangling wind chimes in a gale.

Still ten minutes to play plus whatever was deemed appropriate for time added on, and the thrust and the energy was all one-way. As if to validate this feeling, the referee Mr Martin Woods awarded a penalty to Port Vale. Again, from where I was, I didn't get a clear view of the incident, nor can I comment on how far justice had been served, but what I would say is that with a table-topping team suddenly in the ascendancy in front of 1,500 baying fans, it was an easier penalty to award rather than turn down.

A sour comment? Maybe, but there was little else to do at that moment but consider the slings and arrows of outrageous fortune which can be dealt out in League Two football. That and reach out for Elpis, for it is she, the Greek goddess of Hope, the fickle friend of all football fans. A fanciful diversion, I know, but shortly I was expecting to be contemplating losing a three-goal lead and the prospect of an invigorated Port Vale team mounting a charge for a fourth goal. Unless...

Unless the penalty taker took a perfectly well-placed penalty towards the bottom corner of the net but failed to employ any disguise into his effort. Unless Breeze guessed the right way and pulled off a fantastic save. Which is exactly what happened. Like Rossy at Newcastle and Caigy at Wembley, Gabe (not Breezy, surely) became a hero.

It was the signal for some on-pitch and on-terrace bedlam. The fans celebrated with enough energy to expunge all of the misery of the last two seasons, while the players looked to be taking over the running of the game. Someone had to because Mr Woods appeared to have lost control. Dennis had been booked for a slow departure on being substituted and now he chose to throw a drink bottle on the pitch as part of his penalty saved celebrations thus earning himself a second yellow and therefore red card. Meanwhile several other interruptions, animated discussions and wild gesturing took place. What was going on? No-one seemed to know but eventually some semblance of the game resumed until Mr Woods had had enough and he blew his whistle.

An absolutely cracking game and a richly deserved win for Carlisle but still the relegation picture remained unresolved.

So, it would be a trip to Accrington in three day's-time with the earnest wish that Elpis would be travelling with us.

Monday 21 April. Accrington Stanley v Carlisle United. The Crown Ground (currently known as The Wham Stadium). EFL League 2.

This was an anti-climactic afternoon in so many respects. It would have been foolish to expect an occasion that matched the epic encounter with Port Vale just three days earlier, but I didn't expect the comedown to be quite as pronounced as this.

The journey from Wakefield to Accrington was reasonably short and straightforward, despite steady rain and more Bank Holiday traffic. When we arrived, parking was almost ideal. We were directed to a school playing field less than two minutes' walk from the ground, with no charge, just a polite request for a small donation. As we approached the ground we were directed to where we needed to be by helpful and friendly staff. But I'm afraid that's where the compliments end.

The Crown Ground is something of a sorry apology for a Football League ground. It says much that our seats in Row F of the seated away section meant that we found ourselves on the back row of the stand, and no side of the ground extended significantly further back from the pitch. The rest of the away support was accommodated on an uncovered terrace behind one of the goals, which looked like it could have found room for quite a few more than were admitted.

Despite the importance of the game, the crowd was just 3,380, of which very nearly a third were away fans. That was more than two thousand short of capacity. With a more generous allocation of away tickets, the game could have been close to a sell-out. That would have incurred extra stewarding costs for Accrington, but they would have been more than offset by the increased ticket revenue. The attendance was barely a quarter of the gate at Brunton Park three days earlier.

For such an important game there was a surprising lack of atmosphere. There were plenty of chants early on, and there's no way just over 1,000 supporters can make the sort of noise that was made by almost 11,000 three days earlier, but there wasn't the same sense of the supporters getting behind the team as one.

Hughes understandably made just one enforced change to the starting team, with Joe Hugill replacing the suspended Matthew Dennis in attack. I was reasonably happy with that, believing Hugill's pace and willingness to chase lost causes might trouble the Accrington defence. I was less happy with the inclusion of the disgraced Elliot Embleton on the bench, having completed his suspension for his irresponsible sending-off at Chesterfield.

It soon became evident that Accrington's defenders were being allowed to get away with murder when it came to holding, pulling and pushing. I'm not pretending that Georgie Kelly doesn't put it about a bit himself, but the fouling of him and Hugill was so blatant that it beggared belief. Hugill lacks the physical presence of Dennis, and ultimately disappointed. He badly fluffed the one decent opportunity he had. Stephen Wearne, a diminutive figure, also failed to impose himself physically, often finding himself challenging for high balls against much taller players. Both players worked hard, but to little effect.

There was little flowing football on display from either team. Accrington kept going for a long ball over the top, and Carlisle also favoured the long ball, an approach that became counter-productive once it was obvious that Kelly and Hugill were receiving no protection from the referee. The long ball game meant that Harris was getting relatively little opportunity to run at the Accrington defence. It was something of a relief when the referee blew his whistle the moment the scoreboard clock reached forty-five minutes.

Carlisle did manage to string together a couple of flowing moves in the second half and almost took the lead from one of them in the 55th minute. Hugill played in Kelly whose shot rebounded off the post, Wearne's follow-up effort being blocked by a defender. Who knows what a difference a Carlisle goal at that point might have made? As it was, it was Accrington who took the lead after 68 minutes, with just about their only real attempt on goal.

At this point we were staring down the barrel. A late goal from Tranmere at Barrow and our relegation would be confirmed. Hughes rang the changes with his substitutions, the most significant being to bring on Barclay in defence, moving Aaron Hayden forward as a makeshift striker. All this was to no avail until the second of six minutes of added time. Callum Whelan drove into the Accrington area and left a defender on his backside before shooting across former United keeper Mike Kelly into the far corner.

Carlisle strove desperately for a winner but received no help for the referee, who glanced at the scoreboard and blew the final whistle five seconds before the minimum six extra minutes had elapsed. He added no time for the celebration of the Carlisle goal, and no time for the feigning of injury by an Accrington defender which also led to a yellow card for Hayden. The official fully merited the chant of "You're not fit to referee" as the game ended.

So, an underwhelming afternoon. A win would have taken us within touching distance of both Accrington and Tranmere. As it is, Accrington are effectively safe, and we need to make up four points on Tranmere in the final two games. If we do that, our goal difference will be better than theirs. It's long odds, but I'm not totally without hope. Cheltenham on Saturday is a journey too far, but I'll be happy to travel to Brunton Park for the final game of the season with even an outside chance of survival,

Things were becoming a little clearer, although ominously so. Beat Accrington on their patch, turn over Cheltenham in a second successive away game and then beat Salford City at Brunton Park and then Carlisle might stay up.

A tall order as Accrington had been picking up points with their obdurate style, Cheltenham were never an easy proposition on their own ground and Salford wouldn't yet be entertaining thoughts of sea and sand because they were still chasing a play-off place. Hopes of staying up now were strictly for optimists who could cling to the recent memory of the miraculous game against Port Vale.

Games elsewhere had not gone their way and yet, once again, Carlisle sold out on their away ticket allocation and their fans, 1,050 in total, were placed on a desolate standing terrace behind one goal or else seated in a rickety stand which ran alongside the pitch opposite the tunnel. Both sets of Carlisle fans made a brave noise which was a testament to one undisputed feature of the season that their support for their team had been outstanding. We love you Carlisle, we do and Carlisle till I die. A stubborn denial of what most likely lay in store. This was a must-win match which they didn't win. As the scrappy game progressed Carlisle created the better chances. An early shout for a penalty for Joe Hugill was turned down as of course it had to be. As discussed previously, early penalties are not awarded to the away side. Players, well away from playing distance of the ball, grappling with each other was a common sight, as was the blatant pushing of players as they went to head the ball. Referees could stamp this out straight away. Penalise all of these offences and remain consistent. Shirt holding is a bookable offence, so brandish some cards. Get rid of all this nonsense and let the football flourish.

The rare bright flashes of football in this game involved Kelly taking the ball down well and crashing his shot against the post. Later, on a rare occasion when Accrington left themselves exposed after an attack, Carlisle broke forward and the ball was transferred swiftly the whole length of the pitch as a result of some exquisite one-touch passing. Sadly, it did not result in a goal but several of the Accrington players looked panic-stricken at the ease with which they had been ripped apart by penetrative, sparkling football.

That Accrington went one-nil up was a sickener. A cross into the box not dealt with and a faint touch was sufficient to see the ball nestle in the net beyond Breeze. The Wham Stadium (I kid you not) came alive and it was no longer a place for optimistic Carlisle fans. That writing on the wall was becoming bigger and bolder. In fact, it was now in block letters and the mood collapsed amongst those fans in blue. This was it.

Then in one more dramatic twist of fate's knife, Callum Whelan collected a forward ball and drove into the opposition box. It looked as though he had taken it

DOWN, DOWN, DEEPER AND DOWN

too far leaving a left foot shot from an unlikely angle as his only option. However, he chopped the ball back on to his right foot, putting the covering defender on his backside in the process, and drove the ball with his right foot into the far inside netting. It was a gem of a goal, a pearl in amongst the afternoon's claggy silt, and it was also a statement from Whelan. Look! I will give my all for this team and that is an example of what I can do.

But it was still only one point instead of the necessary three. The short walk from the stadium to the adjoining car park was sufficiently long to let the fact sink in that now Carlisle definitely needed to win their two remaining matches and they also need results elsewhere to go their way. A Bank Holiday Monday in April and Carlisle's fate is sealed (almost certainly.)

Saturday 26 April. Cheltenham Town v Carlisle United. Whaddon Road (or, alternatively, the much sexier EV Charger Points Stadium). EFL League 2.

I'm one game shy of four seasons of writing about Carlisle games, and this is probably the most difficult piece I've had to compose. Less than two years ago I was describing the joys of promotion to League 1 via a play-off final at Wembley. I now have to find the words to explain Carlisle United's second successive relegation, this time out of the EFL and into The National League. I know it's only football and that no-one has died or suffered serious injury, but that doesn't stop it hurting like hell.

Before I embark on any analysis of what has gone wrong, I need to deal with the narrative of Saturday's events.

The long round trip to Cheltenham was never seriously on the cards, and John made sure of that by arranging the launch of his new collection of short stories for Saturday afternoon. He claimed that was because he thought Carlisle would have nothing to play for by this stage of the season. I suspect it was because he'd done the calculations and worked out that it would be his turn to drive! Whatever the reason, Saturday afternoon found us both at the Barnabas Rooms in Walton, just outside Wakefield, as football events unfolded in Gloucestershire and The Wirral.

The scenario was stark. After three wins in succession had sparked irrational hopes of an improbable escape from relegation, Easter Monday's draw at Accrington left the club staring down the barrel. A win for Tranmere, or the failure of Carlisle to better Tranmere's result would condemn us to relegation, again. I just hoped desperately that we could head into the final game of the season with survival still a possibility, however slim.

The early news was not good, Tranmere taking the lead against Crewe in the 22nd minute. Some hope was revived when Matthew Dennis, back from suspension, gave Carlisle the lead in the 29th minute. The lead was short lived, as Cheltenham were gifted a penalty just four minutes later. I've watched the replay, and Gabe Breeze clearly gets a hand to the ball before the Cheltenham striker goes to ground dramatically over his arm. I'm not suggesting that poor refereeing is the reason for Carlisle's relegation. The problems run much deeper than that. But the standard of refereeing over the last few games, even when we've won games, has been absolutely diabolical.

Things got worse on the stroke of half-time, when Terrel Thomas apparently failed to deal with a long ball forward, and Cheltenham scored a second. It couldn't be much worse at the interval, with Tranmere winning and Carlisle losing.

That's how things remained for much of the second half, by which time I was back at home but still following Jon Colman's updates on The News and Star website. When a bandaged George Kelly equalised in the 73rd minute, some hope was revived. A late winner, coupled with an equaliser for Crewe would take us into the final game still alive. I should have known better. The coup de grace was particularly cruel. Tranmere's second and survival clinching goal was scored by Kris Dennis, Carlisle's twenty-goal plus leading scorer just two seasons ago. By this stage a Cheltenham winner in time added on was largely academic, just more salt in the wound.

When the final whistle went, it was down to the 850 plus travelling fans to mark Carlisle's second relegation from the Football League in just over twenty years. While some supporters loyally chorused "I'm Carlisle 'til I die" others vented their frustration and disappointment on the players. I can understand both reactions.

How has it come to this? Just under eighteen months ago I was at Brunton Park for the League 1 game against Charlton Athletic which marked the beginning of the Piatak family's ownership of the club. We might have been struggling in the League, but we had a recent stunning victory at Bolton to celebrate, and the prospect of quality new signings in the next transfer window. Following an unlikely promotion engineered by Paul Simpson, the club had new owners who placed Carlisle on a financial footing way beyond anything experienced in the past.

Yet what has followed is two successive relegations, taking the club to one of its lowest ebbs. Plenty of supporters have already taken to Facebook with their own analysis of what has gone wrong and what needs to be done now, so I'll try to keep my own comments relatively short.

I was a massive fan of Paul Simpson but having signed a player of the calibre of Luke Armstrong, his failure to bring the best out of him counts heavily against him. When you make a marquee signing, you have to adapt your tactics to the new player, but his shortcomings were nothing compared to those of Mike Williamson. I will never forgive that man for what he did to my football team. He imposed a style of play on a squad that was patently unsuited to and uncomfortable with it. As the defeats racked up, he repeatedly took refuge in statistics like possession and expected goals while ignoring the league table reality that was staring him in the face. I'm entirely with those fans who say he's the worst manager/coach the club has ever had. The only difference is that I've had nearly sixty years of managers to reflect on, more than most I suspect. I've never found Carlisle a less attractive team to watch than when Williamson was in charge.

Both Simpson and Williamson were sacked at the end of transfer windows, having spent significant funds on recruiting new players, who were then inherited by a new manager/coach who had to make the best of players he had not chosen. Whether the blame for such bad decision-making lies with the owners or those that advise them, the timing was abysmal, twice.

The Piataks' ownership has seen things transformed off the pitch. The match day experience is a million miles away from most of my time as a United fan, whether it be the fan zones, the giant video screen, or the hospitality packages. Events on the pitch have been correspondingly awful, so how can that be corrected?

I wasn't particularly impressed when Mark Hughes took charge, given his previous managerial record. I know he hasn't kept us up, but I think he's done a decent job. He simplified the team's tactics. He identified those players who were up for the fight. He reconnected with the fans, perhaps not difficult after Williamson's vapid efforts. So maybe he could be the best man to take the club forward, if he's willing, given his working knowledge of the players.

As for the players, do everything to retain Kelly, Dennis, Harris, Whelan and Breeze. Probably Callum Guy too. A fit and functioning Guy is an asset to any team. There are others who might have a role to play, but I can't think of any who are essential to building a promotion campaign next season. If anyone thinks they're too good for non-league football, then help them on their way. They're obviously not too good, as the last few months have proved.

It's probably too early to get a proper perspective on what has happened. The bloodletting has already started, with the departure of Sporting Director Rob Clarkson after less than six months in post. It's not clear yet whether he jumped or was pushed but rarely can so much have been paid for so little return. I'm not privy to the internal workings of the club, but I'm not aware of a single positive contribution he made to Carlisle United. At least one other departure should follow.

Enough for now. John and I will be there on Saturday, to eke the final value out of our season tickets and to witness our final game as a League club (hopefully for the time being only). It will be very interesting to see the size of the crowd, the attitude of the crowd, and how the players respond to the situation.

Very early in the season I had looked at the fixture list very closely before planning a launch for my book, How the Northern Light Gets In (Grosvenor House) Six stories set in Carlisle and wider Cumbrian locations, currently available from all good bookshops which I may have mentioned before, I forget. Anyway, I looked at the date Saturday 26th April when the FA Cup semifinals were due to be played and shrewdly decided that this would not involve Carlisle United. Nor did I think that a game against Cheltenham away on the penultimate Saturday would have any serious implications for Blues followers, so I chose this as the date for my book launch.

At the event there were some fellow Carlisle United fans present including some of the Wakefield travelling army, as I've just named them, and the message reached me that Carlisle had scored to go one up. A fact I made smiling reference to later as I addressed the book-hungry horde in the audience, only to be met with ashen faces from those in the know. Cheltenham had scored two goals to take a lead. They went on to win the game 3-2. Obviously, this result for Carlisle did not better

Tranmere's. Nails could now be hammered into the coffin of Carlisle United's fight against relegation.

A grim day but not one that was unexpected. The only remaining bright spot being the availability of a cracking good book of short stories. Did I mention about all good bookshops?

Chapter 11
THE FAT LADY HAS SUNG

Saturday 3 May. Carlisle United v Salford City. Brunton Park. EFL League 2.

This was a strange afternoon in some respects. Ben in Cardiff and Adam in Nottingham understandably saw no reason to travel for this game, and as John drove us north, I did question why we were making the familiar 270-mile round trip to watch a game that had absolutely no bearing on the future of Carlisle United. I suppose it was a combination of a morbid curiosity to witness our last game as an EFL club, for the time being at least, and a pathetic desire to eke the last few pounds of value out of our season tickets, purchased last August in the expectation of a rapid return to League 1, with the Piataks' money behind us.

Anyway, despite the nightmare that has unfolded in the last ten months, I'm glad we went. The weather was bright and sunny, in defiance of the prevailing mood, and our journey was less hampered by Bank Holiday traffic than on Good Friday, despite the occasional delay. Simon Hackney had posted that he would be attending the game, and I was hopeful that we might meet up, before it transpired that he was enjoying private hospitality courtesy of the Piataks.

The Riverside car park appeared a bit less busy than usual, given the time we arrived, and we anticipated a reduced gate, though we were subsequently to be proved wrong. We had no problem finding crush barrier space in The Paddock, and meeting up with John's sister Cathrine, whose son Thomas will be a goalkeeping member of next season's playing squad.

There were no selection surprises, with Mark Hughes selecting the same eleven who have started most recent matches, and just a couple of changes on the bench. Carlisle might have had nothing to play for, but plenty was at stake for Salford. A win for them would guarantee a place in the promotion play-offs. I hadn't realised until yesterday that their director of football is currently Ryan Giggs, presumably part of his post-court-case rehabilitation, courtesy of his former Old Trafford mates who constitute the ownership group at Salford.

Carlisle very nearly opened proceedings in just the second minute when Sean Fusire shot narrowly over, but it took a superb save from Gabe Breeze, diving low at his right-hand post, to deny Cole Stockton in the twelfth minute. The game was transformed just five minutes later. Firstly a well-judged Kelly pass down the right allowed Fusire to approach the by-line, and his well-judged pull back was met perfectly near the penalty spot by Stephen Wearne to side foot home the first goal of the afternoon. There followed possibly the most muted goal celebration of the season.

Just a minute later, it got better. Jack Ellis made excellent progress down the right, and his delivery was met comfortably at the far post by Matthew Dennis, who bundled the ball home to double the lead. Salford's play-off ambitions were in tatters, and I was wondering why we've been relegated when scoring goals is apparently so easy. Of course it wasn't that simple. In the 37th minute Cole Stockton was unmarked to head home from a Salford free-kick and reduce the deficit. In doing so he perpetuated this season's curse of the returning ex-player. I'll have to check the stats, but there must be almost an entire eleven of ex-players who have scored against United this season.

Nonetheless, we reached the interval in the lead, which is not something it's been possible to say too often this season. And things perked up further during half-time when someone won the golden goal challenge, worth over £1200 pounds.

The second half was largely academic. Salford pulled back another goal in the 62nd minute, the second time in the game that Breeze had been beaten at his near post. His shot-stopping has been brilliant since his promotion to first-choice goalkeeper, but his positioning is certainly an area for improvement. Despite a couple of goalscoring opportunities for Whelan and Kelly in the later stages, the main interest became whether United could deny Salford a winner and a place in the play-offs. We succeeded in doing that, which provided a certain wry satisfaction of its own.

As Carlisle played out their remaining minutes as an EFL club, two things were remarkable in the closing stages. The first was the attendance which numbered 8,128. Only 724 of those were away fans, which means that the attendance of home fans was higher than the season's average total attendance, despite the fact that we already knew we were relegated. The second was the attitude of the crowd in the closing stages of the game. For the last ten minutes or so, chants of "Mark Hughes' blue and white army" rang out from three sides of the ground. That indicates two things to me. Firstly, the supporters are still very much behind the club, despite two appalling seasons. Secondly, most of the supporters see Mark Hughes as the man to take us forward and restore our fortunes in the National League.

I still retain some doubts about Hughes, which I voiced when he was first appointed, but I am much more kindly disposed towards him now, particularly after his personal message wishing me well! He has done a great job of identifying and motivating the players capable of taking the club forward in the National League. More remarkably, he has got the vast majority of the club's supporters behind him and has enabled them to reach the end of two dreadful seasons with some hope for the future.

There's still much to be said about what needs doing in the immediate future to ensure an immediate rebound. But that's for another post, as the post-season shenanigans at the club work out. For now, I'm glad to say that we marked our departure from the EFL with dignity and in significant numbers.

That it should come to this.

That phrase is associated with Shakespeare's anguished Danish prince, reflecting on his father's murder by his uncle no less, and then his mother's subsequent shacking up with the murderer. It's an expression of extreme dismay, resignation over the undesirable state of affairs.

But if Hamlet thought he had it bad, he should try watching his team win a glorious promotion at Wembley and sink to two successive relegations. He should witness the hubris entailed in claiming to own the North and then watch two badly timed manager sackings, complete about turns regarding preferred playing styles and a January recruitment campaign aimed at persuading quality players to sign for a club rooted to the foot of the league.

And to intensify the sense of tragedy he should watch 7,404 fans turn up to watch an already relegated team without rancour or publicly stated recrimination, to continue to support their team as the team makes its way to the fifth tier of English football – the National League.

O that this too solid flesh would melt.

Wednesday 14 May – post-season update.

In the eleven days since the season ended, there has been no end of speculation about the club on online forums, much of it uninformed and most of it unnecessary. There's been speculation about what is or isn't happening at the club, about what should or shouldn't be happening, when it should or shouldn't happen, and why it should or shouldn't happen. What do people realistically expect?

Yes, there needs to be detailed and thorough planning for life in the National League, and to ensure an early return to the EFL. But that means sound, considered choices, not hurried decision making to appease impatient supporters. The club cannot afford to make further mistakes of the magnitude of the Mike Williamson and Rob Clarkson appointments.

Obviously the most important decision revolves around whether Mark Hughes will lead the team into next season. If that's not the case, his successor needs to be given sufficient time to recruit new players and hit the ground running at the start of the new season.

So far, the only decision has been to dispose of Sporting Director Rob "Mr Invisible" Clarkson. His replacement is Marc Tierney, formerly Director of Football at Altrincham, though his role has been redefined as Head of Football Operations. I know nothing about him, but trust that he has to be an improvement on Mr Clarkson. Other changes may or may not follow. If and when they do, and the retained and released list is published, will be the time for serious and detailed comment, not now.

Friday 16 May.

The retained and released list is published, and we move a step closer to drawing down the final curtain on this woeful season. All that remains is for an announcement to be made about the Head Coach position and whether anyone else will be following Rob Clarkson out of the club.

There were no major shocks or surprises in the published list. I'm pleased that the club has activated a clause in Jack Ellis's contact to extend his time at Carlisle. It's also encouraging that Matthew Dennis and Kadeem Harris have been offered new deals. The size of the offers that have been made will probably determine whether they choose to stay. I'd be more than happy with a front three of Kelly, Dennis and Harris to kick off our National League campaign. And if Luke Armstrong is still at Carlisle, as his contract suggests he should be, he could be rejuvenated if he has a coach/

manager who knows how and where to play him to bring the best out of him.

Personally, I'm very sorry to see Callum Guy leave. He never let the club down, and a fully fit Guy always improved the side. His graft in midfield was just as important a part of the promotion campaign as Moxon's guile and Dennis's goals. His departure, along with those of Charter and Barclay, means that Ellis is the only remaining member of the promotion squad, just two years on.

Taylor Charters, a penalty shoot-out hero at Wembley, never quite kicked on as might have been expected, and Ben Barclay never really established himself as a regular starter over his three years at the club. McGeouch and Vela were players who promised much but ultimately delivered very little, for a variety of reasons. Paul Dummett might have helped us survive if he'd stayed fit but will forever be a symbol of the hapless Williamson regime.

I had my doubts about Sam Lavelle when he first featured in the League 1 season. To be fair, he won me, and probably many other supporters, over with his whole-hearted commitment and general attitude. But ultimately his two seasons at the club both ended in relegation, and this season he has been part of a central defence that has been woefully vulnerable. His fellow centre-backs Thomas and Hayden remain contracted to the club, but central defence is the part of the team that needs addressing most urgently.

There are at least a couple of contracted players who I'd be happy to see moved on and it'll be interesting to see if there are further departures during the close season. But far more significant will be the new arrivals.

I think the club owe the supporters a good transfer window!

Monday 19 May.

Two further announcements from the club today effectively draw the final line under this season to be forgotten. This afternoon we were told that Greg Abbott has left his position as Head of Recruitment. Given that the club's record of poor recruitment now covers the last four transfer windows, it's difficult to mount any case for his defence. I'm surprised he lasted so long.

Earlier this evening came the widely anticipated news that Mark Hughes will be remaining as Head Coach. I voiced my reservations about Sparky when he was first appointed, but he's done a lot to win me over since then. I think he quickly identified those players who were up for the fight and regularly formed the match day squad. He came up with the radical idea of playing people in their best position. He restored some fight to the team, and he quickly reestablished a rapport with the supporters. Despite the club failing to avoid relegation, I think some stability is needed now. Hughes already knows what the issues are and he no doubt knows which of the contracted players he'll be happy to move on which gives him a head start over any new arrival.

I sense his decision to stay is widely welcomed by supporters. Good luck Sparky!

www.ingramcontent.com/pod-product-compliance
Lightning Source LLC
Chambersburg PA
CBHW022114080426
42734CB00006B/121